COLLECTIBLE GLASSWARE from the 40's 50's 60's...

Third Edition
an illustrated value guide
by Gene Florence

COLLECTOR BOOKS
A Division of Schroeder Publishing Co., Inc.

ABOUT THE AUTHOR

Gene Florence, born in Lexington in 1944, graduated from the University of Kentucky where he held a double major in mathematics and English. He taught nine years in Kentucky at the junior high and high school levels before his glass collecting "hobby" became his full-time job.

Mr. Florence has been interested in "collecting" since childhood, beginning with baseball cards and progressing through comic books, coins, bottles and finally, glassware. He first became interested in Depression glassware after purchasing an entire set of Sharon dinnerware for $5.00 at a garage sale.

He has written several books on glassware: *The Collector's Encyclopedia of Depression Glass* in its twelfth edition; *Kitchen Glassware of the Depression Years*, in its fifth edition; *Elegant Glassware of the Depression Era*, in its sixth edition; *The Collector's Encyclopedia of Akro Agate* in its third printing; *The Collector's Encyclopedia of Occupied Japan, Volumes I, II, III, IV and V*; *Very Rare Glassware of the Depression Years, Volumes I, II, III and IV*; and the *Pocket Guide to Depression Glass*, now in its ninth edition. He also authored six editions of a baseball book that is now out of print.

His Grannie Bear Antique Shop in Lexington, KY, closed in 1993 due to the sudden death of his mother, "Grannie Bear," who oversaw that store. Mr. Florence continues to sell glassware, however, via mail order and at Depression Glass shows throughout the country. Recently, much of his time is spent in Florida where writing is easier without the phone ringing every five minutes — and fishing is just out the office door!

If you know of unlisted or unusual pieces of glassware in the patterns shown in this book, you may write him at Box 22186, Lexington, KY 40522, or at Box 64, Astatula, FL 34705. If you expect a reply, you must enclose a SASE (self-addressed, stamped envelope) — and be patient. His writing, research and travel often cause a backlog of the hundreds of letters he receives weekly. He appreciates your interest and spends many hours answering letters when time and circumstances permit. Remember that SASE! He does not open mail. Most letters without SASE are never seen by him!

On The Cover: Moroccan Amethyst 3 tier tidbit, $30.00. Forest Green iced tea, $12.00. Boopie Royal Ruby cocktail, $10.00. Bubble amber creamer, $15.00.

Cover Design: Beth Summers
Book Design: Beth Ray

The current values in this book should be used only as a guide. They are not intended to set prices, which vary from one section of the country to another. Auction prices as well as dealer prices vary greatly and are affected by condition as well as demand. Neither the Author nor the Publisher assumes responsibility for any losses that might be incurred as a result of consulting this guide.

Additional copies of this book may be ordered from:

COLLECTOR BOOKS
P.O. Box 3009
Paducah, Kentucky 42002-3009

or

GENE FLORENCE
P.O. Box 22186   or   P.O. Box 64
Lexington, KY 40522   Astatula, FL 34705

@$19.95. Add $2.00 for postage and handling.

Copyright: Gene Florence, 1996.

ACKNOWLEDGMENTS

Thanks to all readers, collectors and dealers who kept me informed with new information on patterns for this book and *The Collector's Encyclopedia of Depression Glass*! All have helped me add an additional thirty-two pages of patterns and information to this third edition of the *Collectible Glassware from the 40's, 50's, 60's...* in only two years!

Thanks, particularly, to Cathy, my wife, who, over twenty-four years of writing, is still my chief editor and critic. She tries to make my sentences tell you what I meant to say as I process my 8.25 words a minute. Some surgery has slowed her down, but her pencil is as sharp as ever. (She keeps me entertained by mailing my UPS overnight letters in US Post Office Express Next Day Air boxes, a two day trip rather than the one needed.) It has been easier writing this book since Cathy has been here in Florida to help rather than in Kentucky as usual. It's also been cheaper than "overnighting" pages and phoning book proofs!

"Grannie Bear," Mom, who died suddenly last year, was especially missed when it came time to get ready for the photography sessions for this book. It had always been her task keeping glass that I purchased between sessions divided into different photography categories: Elegant, Depression, 1950's and Kitchenware. She enjoyed doing that and helping in pricing. As it was, Cathy and I had two weeks of sorting, painfully overshadowed by memories of Grannie Bear at every turn.

Thanks, too, to Cathy's Mom, Sibyl, who helped sort and repack glass for days and to Charles and Dan Tucker who built shelves so I could have a place to store glassware between photography sessions. Charles, Sibyl and Marc kept everything under control at home while we traveled. Marc has even taken over some book shipments along with his college courses. Chad is now married; but he's faithfully been around to load and unload photography glass. It has taken all hands on deck (and then some) to keep these books current and available to you on a regular basis.

Glass, catalogue and pricing information were furnished by collectors and dealers from all over the country. Among these caring people are the following: from Illinois, Dick and Pat Spencer, and Floyd Craft; from Tennessee, Jimmy Gilbreath and Bob James; from Missouri, Gary and Sue Clark, and Evelyn Rhoades; from Texas, John and Maria Tebbetts; from Ohio, Dan Tucker and Lorrie Kitchen, Fred Bickenheuser, Sam and Becky Collings, and Ralph Leslie; from Oklahoma, Charles and Peggy McIntosh; from New Jersey, Rene Fry; from Washington, Carrie Domitz; from Kansas, Thomas Smith Jr.; from Alabama, Kathryn Forest; from Kentucky, Gwen Key. Additional information came from numerous readers across the U.S.A., Canada, England, Puerto Rico, and New Zealand! Please know I am beholden! Even information given that I can't yet use is still much appreciated — and filed.

Photographs for the book were taken by Richard Walker of New York, and Charley Lynch of Kentucky, both of whom provided numerous photographs during one six day session and another five day session that about undid our crew from Collector Books. Glass arranging, unpacking, sorting, carting and repacking was accomplished by Dick and Pat Spencer, Jane White, Zibby Walker, Sherry Kraus, Lisa Stroup, Cathy Florence and the guys from the shipping department at Collector Books. Everyone dropping by at these sessions wondered if we were ever going to finish. Glassware brought in by collector friends filled an extra room with boxes of glass! I had a hard time coordinating all these photographs in the time available. With two photographers working four different photography stations, we made it and almost on time! Believe me, everyone was busy that entire week. The New York photographer said he climbed his ladder *slowly* in order to rest between shots.

Thanks for all the measurements and the photographs confirming new discoveries that you readers have sent! It takes photographs to confirm new pieces. If you have trouble photographing glass, take it outside in natural light, place the glass on a neutral surface and forget the camera has a flash attachment. A cloudy bright day works best. If you wish them returned, please enclose a **self addressed stamped envelope** that is large enough to send back your pictures.

Thanks to Beth Ray in the Editorial Department at Collector Books who turned my computer disks (when they finally got there) into actual pages of a book. There are benefits to not knowing how to use Quark or Pagemaker. It is all I can do to keep up with new software updates that come out between books without learning publishing skills! If I've failed to mention by name someone who contributed, please forgive me and know that collectors everywhere are appreciative of your efforts.

FOREWORD

By this third edition, I assume that most glass collectors know the story of how this 50's book came to be. If not, briefly, there was no room for additional patterns in *The Collector's Encyclopedia of Depression Glass* without going over the page limitations that we sustain to try to keep the price of the book down. I had information on newer glassware that I felt would be useful to collectors. This *Collectible Glassware of the 40's, 50's, 60's...* book has gone through modifications from the initial concept; but basically, the book covers glassware made after the Depression era that is now being bought by glass collectors. Patterns post 1940 were removed from *The Collector's Encyclopedia of Depression Glass* except for a few that overlapped both time periods. This allowed me to explore newer glass being gathered and to expand *The Collector's Encyclopedia of Depression Glass.*

Initially, it took five years to put the 50's book together, but it has been received so well that some Depression Glass Clubs and show promoters are calling and asking what I think about rewriting contracts to make allowances for glassware made in this era. Twenty-five years ago when I first started writing about glass, Depression Glass was found regularly at garage, estate and rummage sales. Now, glassware made later, (i.e., in 40's and 50's) is being found. Time changes all things — including collecting habits. Before this book, there was little information available for collectors on glassware from this period.

Both mass produced and handmade glassware from this 50's era are included here since both types are being collected. A few handmade glassware patterns included were begun near the end of 1930, but their principal production thrust was during the 1940's, 1950's or later.

Anniversary and Fire-King patterns have always been thought of as Depression Glass, but neither were introduced until after 1940. I have spent considerable time compiling available information on Fire-King lines. I have included examples of most Fire-King patterns that were mass marketed through the early 1960's. There are other Fire-King patterns made after this period that I will possibly include in later editions.

Fenton had few dinnerware lines introduced before 1940. I have included some of their lines made since then.

I am continuing to add company catalogue pages of various patterns when available. Thanks for all the letters affirming that you like that idea even when it uses up other pattern space. With actual catalogue pages, many pieces are precisely identified for those collectors who want to know exactly what each piece is.

I have added nine new patterns (especially Fostoria) that have been requested; let me know what additional patterns you would like to see included in the next edition. I am only scratching the surface of this vast time period, but it is a start! If you have collections from this era that you would be willing to lend for photography purposes or copies of glass company advertisements listing pieces which you received with your sets, let me hear from you about those.

Collectors' requests and accumulating proclivities will establish the direction the book will take in the future. It will probably take a few more editions to make this book's format standard. I hope you find the learning enjoyable! Keep writing me of your discoveries! I will pass them along to other collectors.

PRICING
ALL PRICES IN THIS BOOK ARE RETAIL PRICES FOR MINT CONDITION GLASSWARE. THIS BOOK IS INTENDED TO BE ONLY A GUIDE TO PRICES SINCE THERE ARE SOME REGIONAL PRICE DIFFERENCES WHICH CANNOT REASONABLY BE DEALT WITH HEREIN.

You may expect dealers to pay from 40%-50% less than the prices quoted. Glass that is in less than mint condition, i.e., chipped, cracked, scratched or poorly molded, will bring only a small percentage of the price of glass that is in mint condition. Since this book covers glassware made from 1940 onward, you may expect that dealers and collectors will be less tolerant of wear marks or imperfections than in glass made earlier.

Prices are now fairly standardized due to national advertising of glassware and dealers who market it at numerous glass shows held coast to coast. Still, there are **some regional differences in prices** due partly to glass being more readily available in some areas than in others. Many companies charged more initially for wares shipped to the West Coast, and companies distributed certain pieces in some areas that they did not in others. This happens today, also. It's called "test marketing."

Prices tend to increase dramatically on rare items. In general, they increase due to **demand** from additional collectors entering the field and from people becoming more aware of the worth of Depression and 1950's glass.

One of the most important aspects of this book is the attempt to illustrate as well as realistically price those items that are in demand. My desire is to give you the most accurate guide to collectible glass patterns available.

MEASUREMENTS
All measurements are taken from company catalogues or by actually measuring each piece if no catalogue lists are available. Capacities of tumblers, stemware and pitchers are always measured to the very top edge until nothing more can be added. Heights are measured perpendicular to the bottom of the piece, not up a slanted side. In company catalogues plate measurements were usually rounded to the nearest inch or half inch, across the widest point; this creates problems, today, when we require exactness!

CONTENTS

ANNIVERSARY JEANNETTE GLASS COMPANY, 1947-49; late 1960's - mid 1970's

Colors: pink, crystal, and iridescent.

The increase in sales of both 50's glassware and this book has been phenomenal! The book has now been enlarged (from the first edition written only four years ago) to include eighty pages of additional patterns and information.

When first published, some dealers questioned the inclusion of Anniversary because it had traditionally been considered to be Depression glass. I said for twenty-four years that even though some patterns have been collected as Depression Glass, they truly are not. Anniversary, though previously collected by Depression Glass collectors, was never made during that time.

Pink Anniversary was only included in Jeannette catalogues from 1947 until 1949; but crystal and iridescent could be bought in boxed sets in "dish barn" outlets as late as 1975. You will find crystal decorated with both silver (platinum) and gold. Decorated items presently do not sell for any more than regular pieces. Indeed, trimmed pieces are often more difficult to sell unless you have an entire set. Certainly, they are rarer and harder to find; but in this glass, trims are considered to be a detriment rather than an advantage.

Iridescent Anniversary is often displayed at flea markets and antique malls; but this later color is still being banned from most Depression era glass shows since it is considered to be too recently manufactured. Considering that crystal Anniversary was made as late as the 1970's, this makes an interesting contradiction! However, iridescent is collectible and even "asked for" at shows. Be aware that iridescent is sometimes priced as if it were Carnival glass by "amateur" dealers. Iridescent Anniversary actually has obtained the same status as collecting pink.

I accidentally omitted iridescent candlesticks from the price listing in the first book; so I have shown one this time to make up for getting all those letters pointing out my error. Also shown for the first time is the Shell Pink cake plate in Anniversary. Note that the pattern only shows from the bottom view! That groove around the top edge is the rest for the aluminum lid. This groove is also on the crystal cake plate. There are several styles of aluminum lids found on the cake plate. No, I have no idea if there is a "correct" one. Glass companies did not make metal lids, but sold the bottoms to someone who made the tops by special order. Maybe they even let bids to supply the lids!

Crystal Anniversary remains harder to find than pink or iridescent, as many collectors of crystal have found out; but it is not as eagerly sought by collectors. This is a great crystal pattern to use, since the price is reasonable compared to many other patterns of this era. The pattern itself is bold enough to not get lost on the table.

The pink butter dish, pin-up vase, candy dish, wine glass and sandwich plate are difficult to find. The price of the wine and pin-up vase remain reasonable considering how few of them are displayed at shows. That pin-up vase is similar to the style of old limousine vases that some collectors are now seeking. (Fresh flowers were placed in early cars to make them more pleasant for passengers.)

The bottom to the butter is harder to find than the top. This holds true for other patterns that have heavy lids and flattened or thinner bottoms. Note the bottom is almost "plate-like."

The Jeannette catalog from 1947 lists the open, three-legged candy as a comport and not a compote. They mean the same thing, but Jeannette chose the word comport when they made Anniversary. Terminology has simply changed over time. Today, we usually think of a compote as a single footed dish.

	Crystal	Pink	Iridescent
Bowl, 4⅞", berry	3.50	7.00	4.00
Bowl, 7⅜", soup	7.50	16.00	6.50
Bowl, 9", fruit	10.00	22.00	12.00
Butter dish bottom	12.50	26.00	
Butter dish top	13.50	26.80	
Butter dish and cover	26.00	52.50	
Candy jar and cover	22.00	42.00	
*Cake plate, 12½"	7.00	16.00	
Cake plate w/metal cover, round	15.00		
Cake plate, 12⅜" **square	20.00		
Candlestick, 4⅞" pr.	16.00		22.00
Comport, open, 3 legged	5.00	12.00	5.00
Comport, ruffled, 3 legged	6.00		
Creamer, footed	4.50	10.00	6.00

*Shell Pink   150.00
**Cake plate has just been discovered.

	Crystal	Pink	Iridescent
Cup	4.50	8.00	4.00
Pickle dish, 9"	5.00	12.00	7.00
Plate, 6¼", sherbet	1.75	3.00	2.00
Plate, 9", dinner	5.00	12.00	6.00
Plate, 12½", sandwich server	6.50	13.00	8.00
Relish dish, 8"	5.00	12.00	6.50
Saucer	1.00	2.00	1.00
Sherbet, ftd.	3.50	8.00	
Sugar	4.50	8.50	5.00
Sugar cover	6.00	10.00	3.00
Tid-bit, berry & fruit bowls w/metal hndl.	13.00		
Vase, 6½"	13.00	27.50	
Vase, wall pin-up	15.00	27.50	
Wine glass, 2½ oz.	8.00	16.00	

Please refer to Foreword for pricing information

"BEADED EDGE" (PATTERN #22 MILK GLASS) WESTMORELAND GLASS COMPANY, late 1930's-1950's

"Beaded Edge" is a collector's name for Westmoreland's Pattern #22 milk glass. Note that the catalogue sheet shown on page 13 shows a red edge which Westmoreland called a "rich coral red." According to them, "this pattern is also hand decorated in a full dinner or luncheon service in a series of eight matching fruit designs, and it is also made without decoration."

This is one of the patterns that I enjoy trying to find pieces with different decorations. Like Petalware in the Depression era, you never know exactly what piece or decoration will be on that next table at a show or in the next booth at an antique mall! I have tried some vertical shelf photographs in this book, so you can (hopefully) see the pieces better. On page 9 are examples of flowers and the lone bird I have been able to capture. I have spotted a few others in my travels, but I could have bought several live birds for the prices being asked! The fruits, flowers and birds seem to come in sets of eight designs.

On page 10 are "Strawberries" and assorted purple fruits including "Plums," "Raspberries," and "Grapes." I tried to obtain varied pieces in each of these fruit patterns. The creamer and covered sugar shown with grapes are the same ones shown on page 11 with cherries. Rotating these to the other side reveals the other fruit which was a time saving decorating idea for Westmoreland. The sugar and creamer shown actually belong to another Westmoreland line (Pattern #108) and not "Beaded Edge"; but the fruit decorations make it a great item to go with the fruit decorated "Beaded Edge." If you collect either one of these fruit patterns, I suggest you find a set of these Pattern #108 instead of the normally found footed ones, shown in the catalogue on page 14. Note that these patterns were numbers and not the names that collectors are so fond of using. This is true of many companies' glassware lines.

The 12" platter, 15" torte plate and three-part relish remain the key pieces to find in any of the decorated lines. I was excited to find the 15" torte plate with the Apple design shown on page 12. The opposite side of that plate surprised me and is pictured at the bottom of page 12. The embossed zodiac symbols photographed better than I could have imagined!

In addition, I have included a couple of other catalogue listings on pages 14 and 15. Westmoreland pieces shown on page 15 that are not "Beaded Edge" are not priced in this book. Many times glass catalogues pictured more than one pattern on a page.

	Plain	Red Edge	Decorated
Creamer, ftd.	11.00	13.00	17.50
Creamer, ftd. w/lid #108	18.00	25.00	30.00
Cup	5.00	7.00	13.00
Nappy, 5"	4.50	6.50	16.00
Nappy, 6", crimped, oval	7.00	10.00	20.00
Plate, 6", bread and butter	5.00	7.00	10.00
Plate, 7", salad	7.00	10.00	13.00
Plate, 8½", luncheon	7.00	10.00	13.00
Plate, 10½", dinner	12.00	17.50	30.00
Plate, 15", torte	20.00	35.00	50.00
Platter, 12", oval w/tab hndls.	18.50	32.50	75.00
Relish, 3 part	22.50		
Salt and pepper, pr.	22.00	27.50	40.00
Saucer	2.00	3.00	5.00
Sherbet, ftd.	6.50	10.00	16.00
Sugar, ftd.	12.50	15.00	17.50
Sugar, ftd. w/lid #108	18.00	25.00	30.00
Tumbler, 8 oz., ftd.	8.00	12.00	18.00

Please refer to Foreword for pricing information

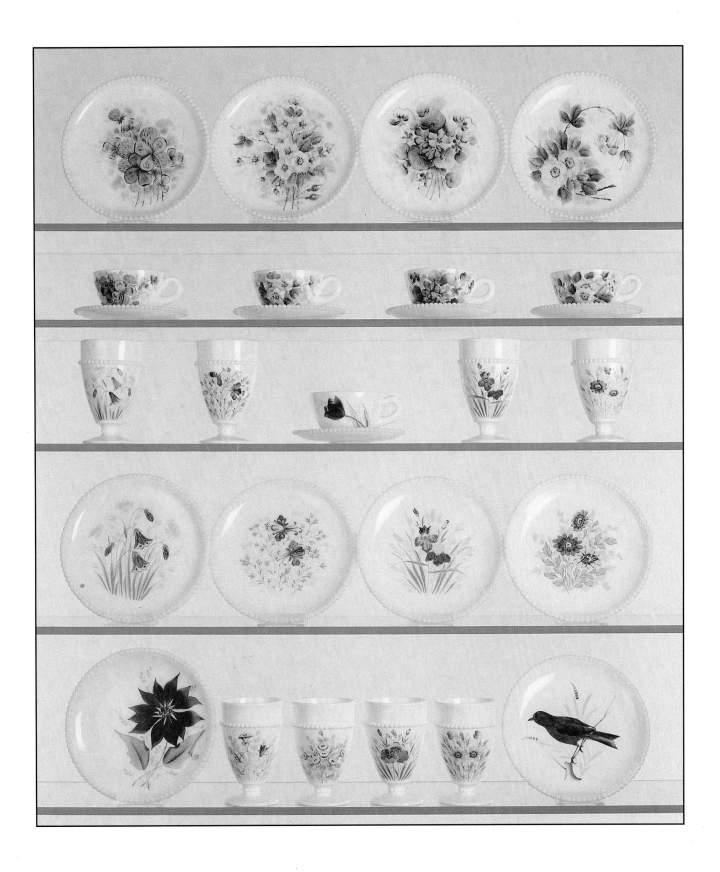

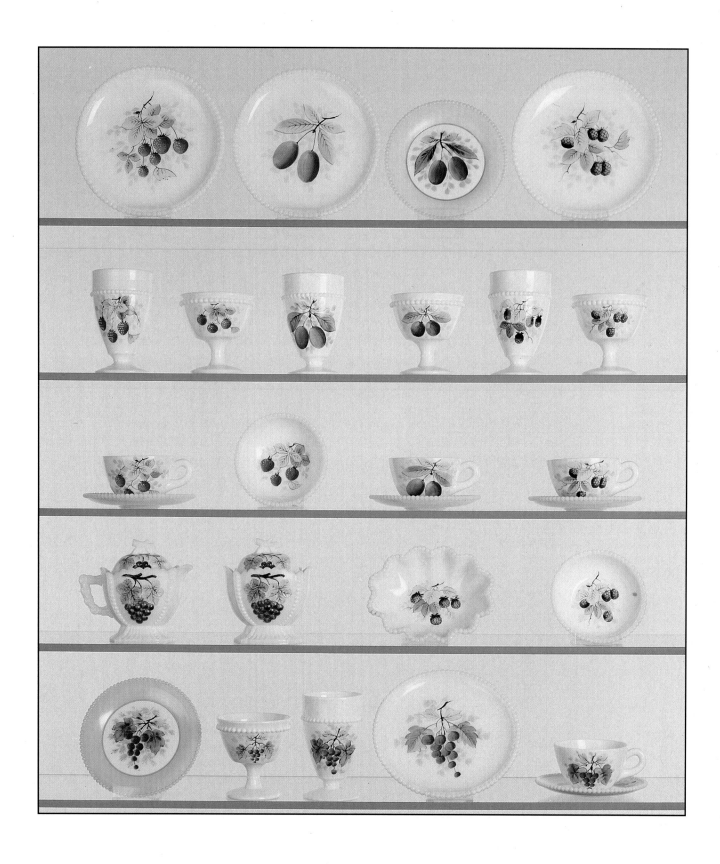

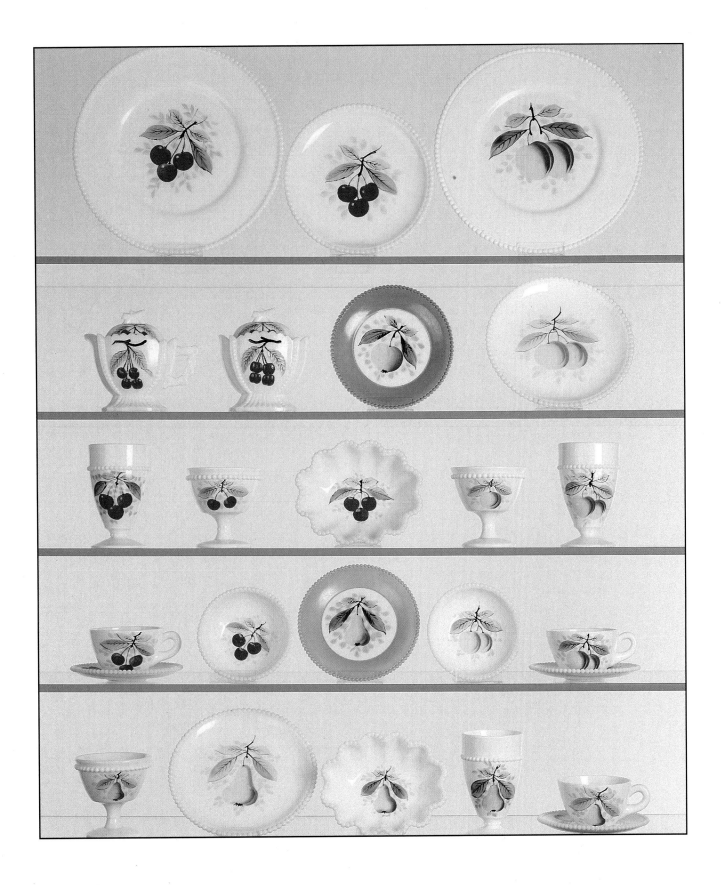

"BEADED EDGE"

America's Finest Handmade Milk Glass

The Lazy Susan breakfast, so cheerful and so companionable, is an occasion where the mood of leisure and the friendly atmosphere of informality are complemented by the sparkle and intimate loveliness of Westmoreland authentic handmade early American Milk Glass reproductions.

Illustrated in natural color is the handmade Beaded-edge pattern with the narrow row of beads hand decorated in rich coral red. This pattern is also hand decorated in a full dinner or luncheon service in a series of eight matching fruit designs, and it is made without decoration.

WESTMORELAND GLASS COMPANY

GRAPEVILLE, PENNSYLVANIA

"BEADED EDGE"

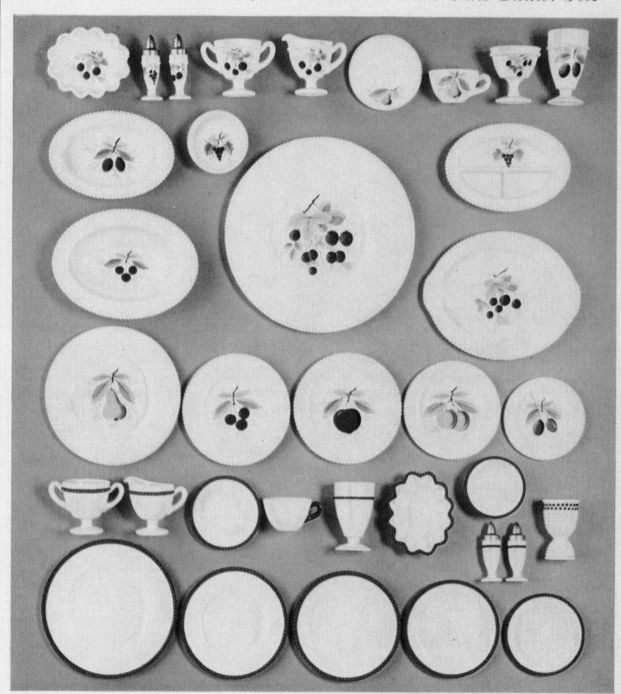

Westmoreland Handmade, Hand Painted Milk Glass Dinner Sets

Top Row: No. 22/6"/64-2. Oval crimped Nappy, "Beaded Edge." Note: all items are available in a set of eight different hand painted fruit decorations: Grape, Cherry, Pear, Plum, Apple, Blackberry, Strawberry and Peach, or in any fruit decoration specified above.
No. 22/64-2. Salt and Pepper.
No. 22/64-2. Cream and Sugar.
No. 22/64-2. Cup and Saucer.
No. 22/64-2. Sherbet, low foot.
No. 22/64-2. Tumbler, footed.

Second Row: No. 22/64-2. Celery Dish, oval.
No. 22/5"/64-2. Nappy, round.
No. 22/15"/64-2. Plate, torte.
No. 22/3part/64-2. Plate, relish, 3-part.

Third Row: 22/64-2. Dish, vegetable.
No. 22/12"/64-2. Platter, oval.

Fourth Row: 22/10½"/64-2. Plate, dinner.
No. 22/8½"/64-2. Plate, luncheon.
No. 22/1/8½"/64-2. Plate, luncheon, coupe shape.
No. 22/1/7"/64-2. Plate, salad, coupe shape.
No. 22/6"/64-2. Plate, bread and butter.

Fifth Row: No. 22/A-28. Cream and Sugar, coral red "Beaded Edge" pattern.
No. 22/A-28. Cup and Saucer.
No. 22/A-28. Tumbler, footed.
No. 22/6"/A-28. Nappy, oval, crimped.
No. 22/5"/A-28. Nappy, round.

No. 22/A-28. Salt and Pepper.

No. 77. Egg Cup, "American Hobnail" with coral red decoration.

Bottom Row: No. 22/10½"/A-28. Plate, dinner.
No. 22/8½"/A-28. Plate, luncheon.
No. 22/1/8½"/A-28. Plate, luncheon, coupe shape.
No. 22/1/7"/A-28. Plate, salad, coupe shape.
No. 22/6"/A-28. Plate, bread and butter.

(The "Red-Beaded Edge" pattern is also available in torte plate, platter, relish, vegetable dish and celery.)

Handmade, Hand Painted Fruit, Bird and Floral Plates

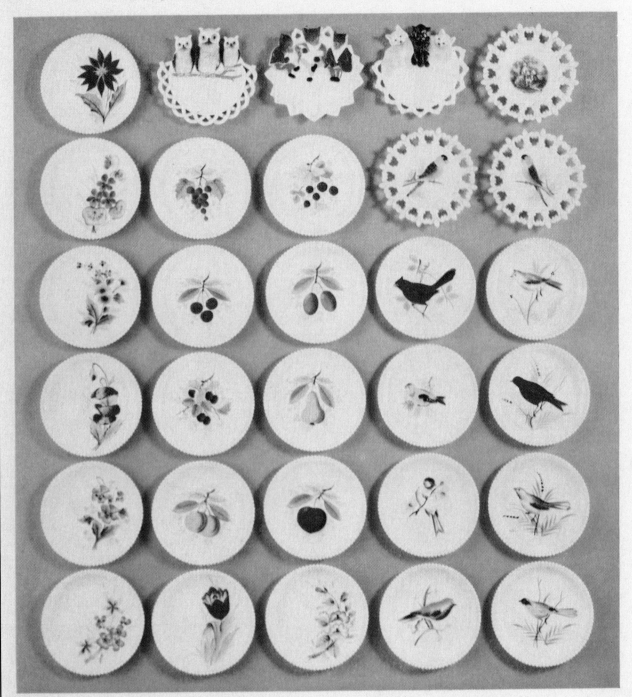

Any of the hand painted Floral, Bird, and Fruit designs shown above on "Beaded-Edge" dessert plates are available on No. 22/15" torte plate shown on opposite page. A set of eight salad plates and footed tumblers, and a 15" torte plate make an attractive luncheon or bridge set.

Top Row: No. 22/1/7"/4. Coupe shape, dessert or salad plate, with Poinsettia decoration. One of eight hand painted floral designs as illustrated below: Violet, Yellow Daisy, Poppy, Pansy, Apple Blossom, Tulip and Morning Glory.

No. 6/7"/4. Plate, "Three Owls" decoration.

No. 24/7"/7. Plate, "Three Bears" decoration.

No. 5/7"/1. Plate, "Three Kittens" decoration.

No. 4/7"/WFD. Plate, "Fleur-de-lis," hand applied decal, French, Watteau Scene.

Second Row, second item: No. 22/1/7"/64-2. Coupe Shape dessert or salad Plate, with Grape decoration. One of eight hand painted fruit designs as illustrated at right and below: Strawberry, Cherry, Plum, Blackberry, Pear, Peach and Apple.

No. 4/7"/76 B-R. Fleur-de-lis Plate with hand painted Parakeet (facing right).

No. 4/7"/76 B-L. Fleur-de-lis Plate with hand painted Parakeet (facing left).

Third Row, fourth item: No. 22/1/7"/70. Coupe Shape dessert or salad Plate, with Cardinal decoration. One of eight hand painted bird designs as illustrated at right and below: Titmouse, Goldfinch, Scarlet Tanager, Chickadee, Mocking Bird, Bluebird and Yellow Warbler.

4

"BUBBLE," "BULLSEYE," PROVINCIAL ANCHOR HOCKING GLASS COMPANY, 1940-1965

Colors: pink, Sapphire blue, Forest Green, Royal Ruby, crystal and any known Hocking color.

"Bubble" is the one pattern that is easily recognized by neophyte collectors! The simple, circular design blends well with many of today's decorating schemes. The copious supply of blue cups, saucers and dinner plates makes this pattern seem readily available and effortlessly obtained. Assembling an entire set is a different matter! Although basic pieces are abundant in blue, other items are in shorter supply. Creamers have always been scarce, but the 9" flanged bowl has virtually disappeared from the collecting arena. You will look long and hard for grill plates and 4" berry bowls without inner rim damage. Grill plates are usually divided into three sections, and were used in many of the diners of those days. They kept the food separated and allowed smaller portions to fill the plate.

The original labels on the crystal Bubble on the top of page 18 read "Heat Proof." A 1942 ad guaranteed this "Fire-King" tableware to be "heat-proof," indeed a "tableware that can be used in the oven, on the table, in the refrigerator." Presumably since this ad is dated 1942, they are referring to the light blue color. This added dimension is unique to "Fire-King" since most Depression glass patterns will not hold up to sudden changes in temperature. Forest Green or Royal Ruby "Bubble" does not proclaim these heat-proof qualities, however; so be forewarned!

I received a light green colored plate from New Zealand. It was very similar to our Bubble, but was of other manufacture. Maybe the English made a look-alike pattern for "Bubble" as they did for Fostoria's American!

Forest Green (dark) and Royal Ruby (red) dinner plates have both become difficult to find without scratches and knife marks on the surface. Observe the two green plates on the middle row of page 17. The first plate measures 1/8" larger than the normally found dinner plate. The center of this plate is smaller and there are four rows of bubbles outside the center, whereas the normally found dinner has three rings of bubbles. I point this out because there are purists who will not accept the smaller centered plate in their collection. One collector said that the smaller center plates were not even made by Hocking. A dealer told me she had some with labels, but they were never forth coming. You have to decide which style you like. The smaller center plates are harder to find.

It's hard to believe that in the late 1970's a Georgia dealer found a warehouse filled with Royal Ruby dinner plates and tidbit trays; and today, both are difficult to find! At his original price of $3.00 each for dinner plates, it took the collecting world several years to recover from such a quantity. Many collectors use the red and green "Bubble" for their Christmas tables.

That green water goblet in the bottom row was oft times used for advertising endeavors. Usually, the only collectors buying these pieces are intrigued by a representation of their home town or organization. Also, the first green "Bubble" sugar shown there has been iridized, not a common treatment for this ware. The amber creamer and cup pictured are not commonly found, but I have yet to meet a collector of amber "Bubble!" Perhaps the cover shot will stimulate interest in this rare color.

Pink is hard to find except for the 8⅜" bowl that still sells in the $6.00 to $7.00 range. The inside depths of these bowls vary.

That 8⅜" berry bowl can be found in almost any color that Anchor Hocking made (including all the opaque and iridescent colors common to Hocking). Milk White was only listed in the 1959-60 catalogue, but they must have been prolific in those two years since so many of them still exist today. You do not have to write telling me which colors you find. Any color is possible! Price all other colors as crystal; however, there are few collectors buying other colors.

According to one Anchor Hocking catalogue, Bubble stemware was accurately called "Early American" line. Both of these stemware lines were manufactured after production of blue Bubble had ceased; so, there are no blue stems to be found. Sorry!

The other stemware line that was sold along with Bubble, shown on the bottom of page 20, has been called "Boopie" by collectors. The Royal Ruby "Boopie" is still priced about the same as the "Bubble" stemware, but the Forest Green "Boopie" is selling for less than the Forest Green "Bubble" stemware shown on page 21. The catalogue lists an iced tea in "Boopie" with a capacity of 15 oz.; but all we have actually been able to put in one is 14 oz!

	Crystal	Forest Green	Light Blue	Royal Ruby		Crystal	Forest Green	Light Blue	Royal Ruby
Bowl, 4", berry	4.00		15.00		***Stem, 4 oz., juice	4.50	10.00		10.00
Bowl, 4½", fruit	4.50	7.00	11.00	8.00	Stem, 4½ oz., cocktail	4.00	12.50		12.50
Bowl, 5¼", cereal	5.00	12.00	12.50		Stem, 5½ oz., juice	5.00	12.50		12.50
Bowl, 7¾", flat soup	6.50		15.00		***Stem, 6 oz., sherbet	3.00	6.00		7.00
Bowl, 8⅜", large berry					Stem, 6 oz., sherbet	3.50	9.00		9.00
(Pink-$7.00)	6.50	14.00	16.50	17.00	***Stem, 9 oz., goblet	7.00	10.00		12.50
Bowl, 9", flanged			325.00		Stem, 9½ oz., goblet	6.00	13.00		13.00
Candlesticks, pr.	16.00	35.00			***Stem, 14 oz., iced tea	7.00	14.00		
Creamer	6.00	12.00	35.00		Sugar	6.00	12.00	18.00	
*Cup	3.50	6.00	5.00	7.00	Tidbit, 2 tier				35.00
Lamp, 3 Styles	40.00				Tumbler, 6 oz., juice	3.50			8.00
Pitcher, 64 oz., ice lip	60.00			55.00	Tumbler, 8 oz., 3¼",				
Plate, 6¾", bread and					old fashioned	6.00			16.00
butter	2.00	4.00	3.00		Tumbler, 9 oz., water	5.00			9.00
Plate, 9⅜", grill			20.00		Tumbler, 12 oz., 4½",				
Plate, 9⅜", dinner	6.00	20.00	7.00	20.00	iced tea	12.00			12.50
Platter, 12", oval	9.00		16.00		Tumbler, 16 oz., 5⅞",				
**Saucer	1.00	5.00	1.50	5.00	lemonade	14.00			16.00
***Stem, 3½ oz., cocktail	4.00	10.00		10.00					

*Pink - $100.00   **Pink - $40.00   ***Boopie

Please refer to Foreword for pricing information

"BUBBLE"

Royal Ruby Anchorglass

R1074

R1078

		PACKING
R1074—4½"	Dessert	6 doz. — 30 lbs.
R1078—8"	Large Bowl	1 doz. — 18 lbs.

PROVINCIAL DINNERWARE

R1650 — R1628

R1664

R1641

R1650—	Cup	3 doz. — 12 lbs.
R1628—	Saucer	3 doz. — 13 lbs.
R1664—4½"	Dessert	3 doz. — 12 lbs.
R1641—9¼"	Dinner Plate	3 doz. — 43 lbs.

PREPACKED SETS

R1600/60

R1600/59—16 Pce. Luncheon Set
Each Set in Ptd. Parchment Box—
4 Sets in Shipping Carton — 39 lbs.
COMPOSITION:
Four R1650 Cups
Four R1628 Saucers
Four R1664 Desserts
Four R1641 Plates

R1600/60—20 Pce. Luncheon Set
Each Set in Ptd. Parchment Carton — 12 lbs.
COMPOSITION:
Four R1650 Cups
Four R1628 Saucers
Four R1664 Desserts
Four R1641 Plates
Four R1612 Tumblers

Ruby Tumblers to Match are shown on Page 35.

"BUBBLE"

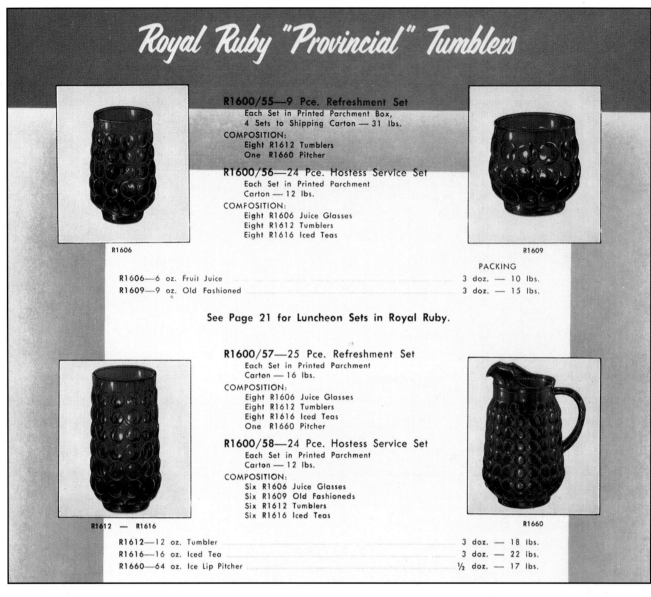

Royal Ruby "Provincial" Tumblers

R1600/55—9 Pce. Refreshment Set
Each Set in Printed Parchment Box,
4 Sets to Shipping Carton — 31 lbs.
COMPOSITION:
    Eight R1612 Tumblers
    One R1660 Pitcher

R1600/56—24 Pce. Hostess Service Set
Each Set in Printed Parchment
Carton — 12 lbs.
COMFOSITION:
    Eight R1606 Juice Glasses
    Eight R1612 Tumblers
    Eight R1616 Iced Teas

R1606

R1609

PACKING

R1606—6 oz. Fruit Juice	3 doz.	10 lbs.
R1609—9 oz. Old Fashioned	3 doz.	15 lbs.

See Page 21 for Luncheon Sets in Royal Ruby.

R1600/57—25 Pce. Refreshment Set
Each Set in Printed Parchment
Carton — 16 lbs.
COMPOSITION:
    Eight R1606 Juice Glasses
    Eight R1612 Tumblers
    Eight R1616 Iced Teas
    One R1660 Pitcher

R1600/58—24 Pce. Hostess Service Set
Each Set in Printed Parchment
Carton — 12 lbs.
COMPOSITION:
    Six R1606 Juice Glasses
    Six R1609 Old Fashioneds
    Six R1612 Tumblers
    Six R1616 Iced Teas

R1612 — R1616

R1660

R1612—12 oz. Tumbler	3 doz.	18 lbs.
R1616—16 oz. Iced Tea	3 doz.	22 lbs.
R1660—64 oz. Ice Lip Pitcher	½ doz.	17 lbs.

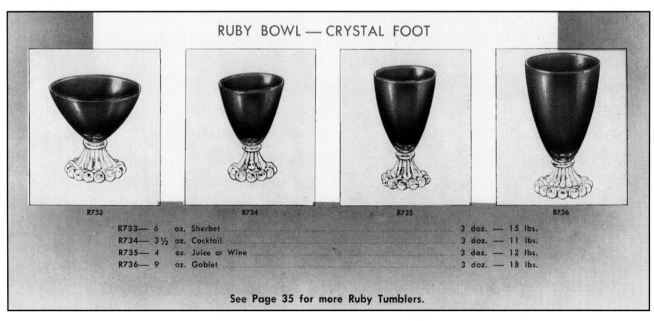

RUBY BOWL — CRYSTAL FOOT

R733   R734   R735   R736

R733— 6	oz. Sherbet	3 doz. —	15 lbs.
R734— 3½	oz. Cocktail	3 doz. —	11 lbs.
R735— 4	oz. Juice or Wine	3 doz. —	12 lbs.
R736— 9	oz. Goblet	3 doz. —	18 lbs.

See Page 35 for more Ruby Tumblers.

FOREST GREEN Anchorglass®
Dinnerware

E1600/46—22 PCE. LUNCHEON SET
Each Set in Gift Ctn., 4 Sets to Shipping Ctn.—50 lbs.
COMPOSITION:

Four E1650 Cups	Four E336 Goblets
Four E1628 Saucers	One E1653 Sugar
Four E1665 Cereals	One E1654 Creamer
Four E1641 Dinner Plates	

E1600/45—18 PCE. LUNCHEON SET
Each Set in Gift Ctn., 4 Sets to Shipping Ctn.—42 lbs.
COMPOSITION:
Four E1650 Cups   Four E1641-9¼″ Plates
Four E1628 Saucers   One E1653 Sugar
Four E1665 Cereals   One E1654 Creamer

E1600/47—30 PCE. LUNCHEON SET
Each Set in Shipping Ctn.—22 lbs.
COMPOSITION:
Four E1650 Cups   Four E336 Goblets
Four E1628 Saucers   Four E333 Sherbets
Four E1665 Cereals   One E1653 Sugar
Four E1630-6⅜″ Plates   One E1654 Creamer
Four E1641-9¼″ Plates

FOREST GREEN AND CRYSTAL STEMWARE

E336—9½ OZ. GOBLET
Pkd. 3 doz.—17 lbs.

E335—5½ OZ. F. JUICE
Pkd. 3 doz.—10 lbs.

E334—4½ OZ. COCKTAIL
Pkd. 3 doz.—9 lbs.

E333—6 OZ. SHERBET
Pkd. 3 doz.—16 lbs.

E1650—8 OZ. CUP
Pkd. 6 doz.—22 lbs.

E1628—5¾″ SAUCER
Pkd. 6 doz.—24 lbs.

E1665—5¼″ CEREAL
Pkd. 6 doz.—35 lbs.

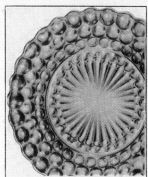

E1630—6⅝″ PIE OR SALAD PLATE
Pkd. 6 doz.—38 lbs.

E1641—9¼″ DINNER PLATE
Pkd. 3 doz.—38 lbs.

E1653—FOOTED SUGAR
Pkd. 3 doz.—18 lbs.

E1654—FOOTED CREAMER
Pkd. 3 doz.—18 lbs.

BUTTERCUP, ETCHING #340, FOSTORIA GLASS COMPANY 1941-1960

Color: crystal

I introduced Buttercup in the last edition of *Elegant Glassware of the Depression Era*. Since the production dates fall entirely within the years that encompass this book, I am moving it here. I had received numerous requests to include this Fostoria pattern, so here it is! It seems that people who had Buttercup as their crystal are beginning to split it up within the family, and there is no where to turn to find this glassware other than glass shows. Antique glassware dealers provide one of the few choices left to obtain discontinued glassware.

Vases are hard to find in Fostoria crystal patterns. The smaller vase pictured on the left of the photo is the 6" footed #6021. An ice tea tumbler is between it and the larger is the 7½" footed #4143. The little pieces in front are an individual ash tray and a cigarette holder. That cigarette holder might make a better toothpick holder. Stemware and salad and luncheon plates were still in catalogue listings in 1960.

	Crystal		Crystal
Ash tray, #2364, 2⅝", individual	20.00	Plate, #2337, 8½"	17.50
Bottle, #2083, salad dressing	200.00	Plate, #2337, 9½"	40.00
Bowl, #2364, 6", baked apple	16.00	Plate, #2364, 6¾", mayonnaise	7.50
Bowl, #2364, 9", salad	50.00	Plate, #2364, 7¼" x 4½", crescent salad	40.00
Bowl, #2364, 10½", salad	55.00	Plate, #2364, 11¼", cracker	30.00
Bowl, #2364, 11", salad	55.00	Plate, #2364, 11", sandwich	35.00
Bowl, #2364, 12", flared	60.00	Plate, #2364, 14", torte	45.00
Bowl, #2364, 12", lily pond	55.00	Plate, #2364, 16", torte	85.00
Bowl, #2364, 13", fruit	65.00	Relish, #2364, 6½" x 5", 2 part	22.50
Bowl, #2594, 10", 2 hdld.	55.00	Relish, #2364, 10" x 7¼", 3 part	30.00
Candlestick, #2324, 4"	15.00	Saucer, #2350	5.00
Candlestick, #2324, 6"	27.50	Shaker, #2364, 2⅝"	32.50
Candlestick, #2594, 5½"	25.00	Stem, #6030, 3¾", 4 oz., oyster cocktail	18.00
Candlestick, #2594, 8", trindle	35.00	Stem, #6030, 3⅞", 1 oz., cordial	40.00
Candlestick, #6023, 5½", duo	32.50	Stem, #6030, 4⅜", 6 oz., low sherbet	17.50
Candy w/cover, #2364, 3¾" diameter	90.00	Stem, #6030, 5¼", 3½ oz., cocktail	22.50
Celery, #2350, 11"	27.50	Stem, #6030, 5⅝", 6 oz., high sherbet	20.00
Cheese stand, #2364, 5¾" x 2⅞"	20.00	Stem, #6030, 6", 3½ oz., claret-wine	32.50
Cigarette holder, #2364, 2" high	35.00	Stem, #6030, 6⅜", 10 oz., low goblet	22.50
Coaster	15.00	Stem, #6030, 7⅞", 10 oz., water goblet	27.50
Comport, # 2364, 8"	35.00	Sugar, #2350½, 3⅛", ftd	13.00
Comport, #6030, 5"	30.00	Syrup, #2586, sani-cut	225.00
Creamer, #2350½, 3¼", ftd	14.00	Tray, #2364, 11¼", center handled	32.50
Cup, #2350½, ftd.	15.00	Tumbler, #6030, 4⅝", 5 oz., ftd. juice	20.00
Mayonnaise, #2364, 5"	25.00	Tumbler, #6030, 6", 12 oz., ftd. ice tea	27.50
Pickle, #2350, 8"	25.00	Vase, 6", ftd., #4143	80.00
Pitcher, #6011, 8⅞", 53 oz.	250.00	Vase, 6", ftd., #6021	65.00
Plate, #2337, 6"	7.00	Vase, 7½", ftd., #4143	115.00
Plate, #2337, 7½"	12.00	Vase, 10", #2614	120.00

CABOCHON A.H.HEISEY & COMPANY, 1950-1957

Colors: Amber, crystal and Dawn.

This 1950's Heisey pattern has received some notice (outside the world of Heisey collectors) after its introduction in this book. I recently had a call from a collector in Oklahoma who had fallen in love with it after seeing it in the book. "It's the most beautiful pattern I've ever seen!", she exclaimed.

Although there are a few pieces found in the desirable Amber and Dawn, Cabochon is mostly found in crystal. Prices now are reasonable for this pattern that was manufactured in the last years before the closing of the Heisey plant in 1957. This listing is taken from a 1953 catalogue.

Notice the 6¼" Dawn candy dish in the top row. This candy is rarely seen. Just recently, I found a crystal one like this except it had an Orchid etch. You will find other pieces of Cabochon that are cut or etched, but Orchid and Rose etchings are the designs that most intrigue collectors.

	Crystal
Bon bon, 6¼", hndl.,	
(sides sloped w/squared hndl.) #1951	24.00
Bottle, oil, w/#101 stopper #1951	28.00
Bowl, 4½", dessert #1951	4.00
Bowl, 5", dessert #1951	5.00
Bowl, 7", cereal #1951	6.00
Bowl, 13", floral or salad #1951	18.00
Bowl, 13", gardenia	
(low w/edge cupped irregularly) #1951	18.00
Butter dish, ¼ lb. #1951	25.00
Cake salver, ftd. #1951	62.50
Candle holder, 2 lite, ground bottom, pr. #1951	150.00
Candlette, 1 lite (like bowl), pr. #1951	35.00
Candy, 6¼", w/lid (bowl w/lid) #1951	35.00
Cheese, 5¾", ftd., compote for cracker plate	17.50
Cream #1951	9.00
Creamer, cereal, 12 oz. #1951	27.50
Cup #1951	6.00
Jelly, 6", hndl., (sides and hndl. rounded) #1951	24.00
Mayonnaise, 3 pc. (plate, bowl, ladle) #1951	27.50
Mint, 5¾", ftd., (sides slanted) #1951	22.50
Pickle tray, 8½" #1951	20.00
Plate, 8", salad #1951	6.00
Plate, 13", center hndl. #1951	40.00
Plate, 14", cracker w/center ring #1951	18.00
Plate, 14", party (edge cupped irregularly) #1951	18.00
Plate, 14", sandwich #1951	18.00
Relish, 9", three part, oblong #1951	22.00
Relish, 9", three part, square #1951	20.00
Salt and pepper, square, w/#60 silver	
plated tops, pr. #1951	13.00
Saucer #1951	1.50
Sherbet, 6 oz. #1951 (pressed)	4.00

	Crystal
Sherbet, 6 oz. #6092 (blown)	4.00
Stemware, 1 oz., cordial #6091	20.00
Stemware, 3 oz., oyster cocktail #6091	4.00
Stemware, 3 oz., wine #6091	8.00
Stemware, 4 oz., cocktail #6091	4.00
Stemware, 5½ oz., sherbet #6091	4.00
Stemware, 10 oz., goblet #6091	8.00
Sugar, w/cover #1951	14.00
Tidbit, 7½" (bowl w/sloped outsides) #1951	12.50
Tray, 9", for cream and sugar #1951	40.00
Tumbler, 5 oz. #1951 (pressed)	7.00
Tumbler, 5 oz., juice, flat bottomed #6092 (blown)	7.00
Tumbler, 5 oz., juice, ftd. #6091	7.00
Tumbler, 10 oz., beverage #6092 (blown)	8.00
Tumbler, 10 oz., tumbler #6092 (blown)	8.00
Tumbler, 12 oz. #1951 (pressed)	12.50
Tumbler, 12 oz., ice tea #6092 (blown)	12.50
Tumbler, 12 oz., ice tea, ftd. #6091	8.00
Tumbler, 14 oz., soda #6092 (blown)	11.00
Vase, 3½", flared #1951	18.00

CAMELIA PLATE ETCHING #344, FOSTORIA GLASS COMPANY 1952-1976

Color: crystal.

Camelia was a contemporary pattern of Heisey's Rose, Cambridge's Rose Point and Tiffin's Cherokee Rose. Fostoria's Camelia pattern outlasted all the other companies' rose patterns, but it has never reached the collecting status of those of Heisey or Cambridge. There are a multitude of serving pieces that can be found in Camelia unlike many other patterns of this time, where only stemware is seemingly available.

All pieces in the listing below that have no line number listed are found on #2630 blank, better known as Century. You may find additional pieces to this pattern. Let me know what you discover.

Basket, 10¼" x 6½", wicker hdld.	77.50	Plate, 9½", small dinner	27.50
Bowl, 4½", hdld.	15.00	Plate, 10", hdld., cake	30.00
Bowl, 5", fruit	16.00	Plate, 10¼", dinner	40.00
Bowl, 6", cereal	25.00	Plate, 10½", snack, small center	30.00
Bowl, 6¼", snack, ftd.	18.00	Plate, 14", torte	40.00
Bowl, 7¼", bonbon, 3 ftd.	25.00	Plate, 16", torte	70.00
Bowl, 7⅛", 3 ftd., triangular	18.00	Platter, 12"	47.50
Bowl, 8", flared	30.00	Preserve, w/cover, 6"	55.00
Bowl, 8½", salad	30.00	Relish, 7⅜", 2 part	18.00
Bowl, 9", lily pond	35.00	Relish, 11⅛", 3 part	32.50
Bowl, 9½", hdld., serving bowl	42.50	Salt and pepper, 3⅛", pr.	40.00
Bowl, 9½", oval, serving bowl	45.00	Salver, 12¼", ftd. (like cake stand)	67.50
Bowl, 10", oval, hdld.	40.00	Saucer	4.00
Bowl, 10½", salad	47.50	Stem, #6036, 3¼", 1 oz., cordial	40.00
Bowl, 10¾", ftd., flared	50.00	Stem, #6036, 3¾", 4 oz., oyster cocktail	17.50
Bowl, 11, ftd., rolled edge	50.00	Stem, #6036, 4⅛", 3½ oz., cocktail	22.00
Bowl, 11¼", lily pond	42.50	Stem, #6036, 4⅛", 6 oz., low sherbet	10.00
Bowl, 12", flared	52.50	Stem, #6036, 4¾", 3¼ oz., claret-wine	30.00
Butter, w/cover, ¼ lb.	40.00	Stem, #6036, 4¾", 6 oz., high sherbet	15.00
Candlestick, 4½"	20.00	Stem, #6036, 5⅞", 5½ oz., parfait	25.00
Candlestick, 7", double	35.00	Stem, #6036, 6⅞", 9½ oz., water	25.00
Candlestick, 7¾", triple	45.00	Sugar, 4", ftd.	14.00
Candy, w/cover, 7"	55.00	Sugar, individual	10.00
Comport, 2¾", cheese	20.00	Tid bit, 8⅛", 3 ftd., upturned edge	30.00
Comport, 4⅜"	25.00	Tid bit, 10¼", 2 tier, metal hdld.	45.00
Cracker plate, 10¾"	30.00	Tray, 4¼", for ind. salt/pepper	17.50
Creamer, 4¼"	15.00	Tray, 7⅛", for ind. sugar/creamer	20.00
Creamer, individual	11.00	Tray, 9½", hdld., muffin	32.50
Cup, 6 oz., ftd.	15.00	Tray, 9⅛", hdld., utility	30.00
Ice Bucket	75.00	Tray, 11½", center hdld.	38.00
Mayonnaise, 3 pc.	35.00	Tumbler, #6036, 4⅝", 5 oz., ftd. juice	20.00
Mayonnaise, 4 pc., div. w/2 ladles	40.00	Tumbler, #6306, 6⅛", 12 oz., ftd. ice tea	30.00
Mustard, w/spoon, cover	32.50	Vase, 5", #4121	60.00
Oil, w/stopper, 5 oz.	50.00	Vase, 6", bud	25.00
Pickle, 8¾"	25.00	Vase, 6", ftd., #4143	65.00
Pitcher, 6⅛", 16 oz.	67.50	Vase, 6", ftd., #6021	45.00
Pitcher, 7⅛", 48 oz.	125.00	Vase, 7½", hdld.	77.50
Plate, 6½", bread/butter	7.00	Vase, 8", flip, #2660	75.00
Plate, 7½", crescent salad	45.00	Vase, 8"., ftd., #5092	65.00
Plate, 7½", salad	10.00	Vase, 8½", oval	75.00
Plate, 8", party, w/indent for cup	27.50	Vase, 10", ftd., #2470	95.00
Plate, 8½", luncheon	15.00	Vase, 10½", ftd., #2657	95.00

Please refer to Foreword for pricing information

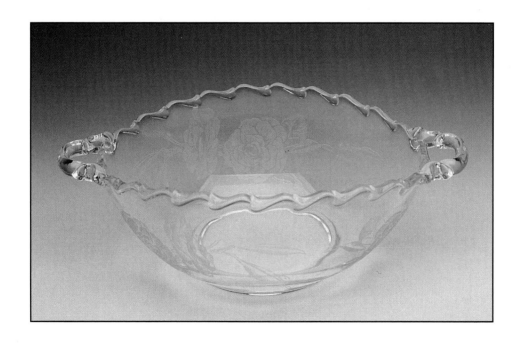

CAPRI "SEASHELL," "SWIRL COLONIAL," "COLONIAL," "ALPINE"
HAZEL WARE, DIVISION OF CONTINENTAL CAN, 1960's

Color: Azure blue.

I am now certain that "Capri" originally referred to the blue color of this ware rather than a pattern name per se. In this book I have tried to organize the various Capri patterns so that collectors have some form of reference while discussing this pattern with other collectors. Pictured at the top of page 29 is Colony on the right and "Colony Swirl" on the left. The Colony name comes from actual labels while the "Swirl" is my added name for the same pattern but with a distinct twist in it. Notice that the bases of both patterns are square or rectangular. Until someone finds a piece of the swirled with a pattern name, it will remain "Colony Swirl." That sounds great except I do have a **crystal** Colony shaped bowl sent me by Donna Hall that has the label "Simplicity." An amber tumbler has also been discovered with a Colony label attached. Perhaps the colored ware was named Colony but the crystal was dubbed Simplicity. "Colony Swirl" seems rarer than Colony, but time will determine that. Pricing for both styles are the same for now.

The bottom photo on page 29 shows pentagonal flat tumblers, hexagonal stems and octagonal dinnerware items. Only labels with Capri have been found on these pieces so far. Being a former mathematics teacher, shape names are the only way to describe these now. Neither the crystal stem nor the avocado green tumbler were found with labels; so their name remains a mystery.

The top of page 30 shows the pattern known as "Seashell." The ash trays all fit the same moulds as Moroccan Amethyst; so they are obviously Capri. The tumblers in the back left seem to be the same mould as Moroccan swirl, but they have different blue color than Capri. The coaster and candlestick are only Capri possibilities until somebody finds a piece with a label. The square ash tray in the back is an advertisement for IHOP.

On the bottom of page 30 are some more problem children in this pattern. On the right are pieces, I have been calling "Tulip," but a crystal piece with similar characteristics is called "Daisy" (shown by the box on the bottom of page 31). The crystal may be made by someone else. It is only similar! On the left is the pattern I have called "Hobnails" to differentiate it from "Dots." Note the small Hobs as is seen in some of our Depression era patterns. The creamer and sugars shown here have round bases and seem to fit with the handle style of the "Hobnail" cups. The interesting thing here is the swirled creamer similar to the squared "Colony Swirl" pattern. Hopefully, some company catalogue information will make an appearance and deal with all this speculation!

On the top of Page 31 is the pattern I have called "Dots." Some collectors are calling it "Drip-Drop." The box pictured at the bottom of the page had 24 of these tumblers in three sizes. It says "Skol Swedish style glasses," but the box says "Hazel-Atlas" and not Hazel Ware as you might expect. The tumblers had only Capri labels attached. Since it also says American made, I wonder if they were to be exported. The "Dots" Capri pattern seems to be abundant in my Florida area!

Price other colors half or less than the Capri color, and good luck finding someone to buy them! Keep those cards and letters coming about this fascinating pattern!

	Blue		Blue		Blue
Ash tray, 3¼", triangular	6.00	Creamer, round	8.00	Sugar w/lid, round	12.50
Ash tray, 3¼", round	6.00	Cup, octagonal	6.00	Tid bit, 3 tier (round 9⅞" plate,	
Ash tray, 3½", square, embossed		Cup, round, "Hobnails"	6.00	7⅛" plate, 6" saucer)	22.50
flower	12.00	Cup, round, swirled	6.00	Tumbler, 2¾", 4 oz., "Colony Swirl"	7.00
Ash tray, 5", round	7.50	Cup, round, Tulip	7.00	Tumbler, 3", 4 oz., fruit "Dots"	7.00
Ash tray, 6⅞", triangular	12.00	Plate, 5¾", bread and butter,		Tumbler, 3", 5 oz., pentagonal bottom	7.00
Bowl, 4¾", octagonal	7.50	octagonal	5.00	Tumbler, 3 1/16", Colony or	
Bowl, 4¾", swirled	8.00	Plate, 7", salad, round, "Colony Swirl"	7.00	"Colony Swirl"	8.00
Bowl, 4⅞", round, "Dots"	7.00	Plate, 7⅛", round, salad, "Colony		Tumbler, 3⅛", 5 oz., pentagonal	8.00
Bowl, 5⅜", salad, round, "Hobnails"	7.50	Swirl"	7.00	Tumbler, 3¼", 8 oz., old fashioned,	
Bowl, 5⅝, "Colony Swirl"	8.50	Plate, 7¼", salad, "Hobnails"	7.50	"Dots"	7.50
Bowl, 5¾", square, deep, Colony	10.00	Plate, 7¼", salad, octagonal	7.50	Tumbler, 3⅝", 3 oz., "Dots"	7.00
Bowl, 6", round, Tulip	12.00	Plate, 8", square	9.00	Tumbler, 4", "Dots"	7.00
Bowl, 6", round, "Dots"	9.00	Plate, 8", square, w/square cup rest	8.00	Tumbler, 4¼", 9 oz., "Colony Swirl"	7.50
Bowl, 6", round, sq. bottom, Colony	8.00	Plate, 8⅞", square	10.00	Tumbler, 4¼", 9 oz., water, pentagonal	
Bowl, 6 1/16", round, "Colony Swirl"	8.00	Plate, 8⅞", square, w/round cup rest	9.00	bottom	7.50
Bowl, 7¾", oval, Colony	16.00	Plate, 9½", round, snack w/cup rest,		Tumbler, 5", 12 oz., "Colony Swirl"	9.00
Bowl, 7¾", rectangular, Colony	16.00	Tulip	9.50	Tumbler, 5", 12 oz., tea, pentagonal	
Bowl, 8¾", swirled	18.00	Plate, 9¾", dinner, octagonal	10.00	bottom	9.00
Bowl, 9⅛" x 3" high	22.00	Plate, 9⅞", dinner, round, "Hobnails"	10.00	Tumbler, 5¼", "Dots"	7.50
Bowl, 9½" x 2⅞" high	20.00	Plate, 10", snack, fan shaped w/cup rest	8.50	Tumbler, 5½", 12 oz., tea, swirl	9.00
Bowl, 9½" oval 1½" high	9.00	Saucer, 5½" square	2.00	Tumbler, 6", 10 oz., "Dots"	10.00
Bowl, 10¾", salad, Colony	25.00	Saucer, 6", round, "Hobnails"	2.00	Vase, 8", "Dots"	25.00
Candy jar, w/cover, ftd.	30.00	Saucer, octagonal	2.00	Vase, 8½", ruffled	35.00
Chip and dip, 2 swirled bowls		Stem, 4½", sherbet	7.50		
(8¾" and 4¾" on metal rack)	30.00	Stem, 5½", water	10.00		

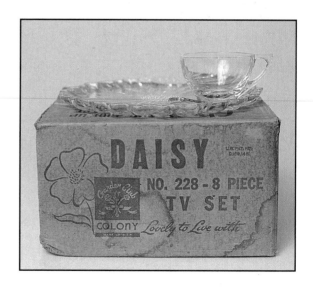

CAPRI

Footed Bowl

Mayonnaise Set

Ash Tray

CASCADE
By CAMBRIDGE

Like a stream of pure light tumbling rhythmically into sun-splashed pools, Cascade brings you one of the most fascinating, brilliant *new* crystal designs to be seen in years. It is hand-made *modern* crystal in a variety of pieces . . . substantial, practical . . . ideal for formal or informal occasions.

You will fall in love with Cascade for yourself and willingly share its beauty in gifts to others. Be sure to see this fine American crystal now . . . at good stores, priced moderately.

THE CAMBRIDGE GLASS COMPANY • CAMBRIDGE, OHIO

CASCADE, 4000 LINE CAMBRIDGE GLASS COMPANY, 1950'S

Colors: Crystal, Emerald Green, Mandarin Gold and Milk White.

Cascade is one of the later made patterns of Cambridge that is just now being noticed by collectors. Two styles of stems are shown on the water goblets at the bottom of page 36. One is turned upside down from the other. I do not know which is the harder to find.

Notice that several Cascade items had more than one purpose. The 8" ash tray serves not only in that capacity, but as the punch bowl base when it is turned upside down. Then, too, it rests on top of the 21" plate to make a buffet set. The versatility of the plate is shown as it becomes the punch bowl liner in the punch set. It was an economical way to save the cost of making expensive moulds at a time when Cambridge was about to go out of business.

	Crystal	Green	Yellow		Crystal	Green	Yellow
Ash tray, 4½"	6.00			Plate, 6½", bread & butter	5.50		
Ash tray, 6"	10.00			Plate, 8½", salad	7.50		
Ash tray, 8"	20.00			Plate, 8", 2 hdld., ftd. bonbon	12.50		
Bowl, 4½", fruit	7.00			Plate, 11½", 4 ftd.	17.50		
Bowl, 6½", relish	13.00			Plate, 14", 4 ftd. torte	22.50		
Bowl, 6½", relish, 2 pt.	13.00			Plate, 21"	50.00		
Bowl, 6", 4 ftd. bonbon	11.00			Punch base (same as 8" ash tray)	20.00		
Bowl, 7", 2 hdld., ftd., bonbon	13.00			Punch bowl liner, 21"	50.00		
Bowl, 10", 3 pt., celery	18.00			Punch bowl, 15"	120.00		
Bowl, 10", 4 ftd., flared	22.00			Punch cup	7.50		
Bowl, 10½", 4 ftd., shallow	25.00			Saucer	2.50		
Bowl, 12", 4 ftd., oval	27.50			Shaker, pr.	18.00		
Bowl, 12½", 4 ftd., flared	30.00			Stem, cocktail	11.00		
Bowl, 13", 4 ftd., shallow	30.00			Stem, sherbet	10.00		
Buffet set (21" plate w/8" ash tray)	70.00			Stem, water goblet	14.00		
Candlestick, 5"	15.00	27.50	27.50	Sugar	8.00	18.00	18.00
Candlestick, 6", 2 lite	22.50			Tumbler, 5 oz., flat	10.00		
Candy box, w/cover	35.00	60.00	60.00	Tumbler, 5 oz., ftd.	10.00		
Cigarette box w/cover	22.50			Tumbler, 12 oz., ftd.	13.00		
Comport, 5½"	17.50			Tumbler, 12 oz., flat	12.00		
Creamer	8.50	18.00	18.00	*Vase 9½"	30.00	65.00	65.00
Cup	8.00			Vase, 9½", oval	35.00		
Ice tub, tab hdld.	32.50						
Mayonnaise spoon	7.50			*Milk White $40.00			
Mayonnaise, w/liner	17.50	50.00	50.00				

CASCADE

Reflecting your good taste . . .

your choice of

fine handmade Fostoria crystal

to grace your own table

or for a gift to be remembered

Century BY **Fostoria** MADE IN U.S.A.

FOSTORIA GLASS COMPANY · MOUNDSVILLE · WEST VIRGINIA

ALL FOSTORIA IS HANDMADE IN AMERICA, AVAILABLE IN OPEN STOCK.

CENTURY LINE #2630, FOSTORIA GLASS COMPANY

Color: crystal.

I am trying to eliminate duplications in my books; so I am warning you that from now on, Century will not be included in my *Elegant Glassware of the Depression Era*! I used that warning on patterns in my *Collector's Encyclopedia of Depression Glass* when I split it into two time periods and still some collectors wrote wondering why some of the patterns disappeared. Remember, Century was the line used for many of Fostoria's later etched patterns, just as Fairfax was used for many of the earlier patterns.

Prices for stemware and serving pieces in Century continue to increase. Wines, water goblets and footed iced teas have all increased due to demand more than scarcity. Nationally, prices are beginning to stabilize. However, prices for Elegant glassware in general are more reasonable in the western states than are the prices for Depression glassware. Dealers are now having a difficult time stocking basic patterns in Depression ware, and serving pieces are fetching whatever the market will bear. It's very possible that scarcity will occur twenty years hence in the 40's, 50's and 60's glassware.

Catalogue listings for plates are different from the actual measurements by up to one-half inch. I have tried to include actual measurements for Fostoria patterns in this book. I understand that this has been an extreme problem for people ordering through the mail.

There are two sizes of dinner plates (as happens in most of Fostoria's patterns). The larger plate (usually listed as a service plate) is the harder to find. They were priced higher originally, and many people did without the larger plates. One problem with this pattern is glass abrasions and scuffs. Since all the pieces are very plain in the center section, scratches show more than with patterns having center designs.

The ice bucket has button tabs for attaching a metal handle. One is pictured in the top photograph. The 8½" oval vase is shaped like the ice bucket but without the "tabs." A few damaged ice buckets (sans handles) have been sold as vases. Pay attention to the glass you buy!

A 7" candy is shown in the top photo. The 6" preserve is not as deep and is shorter; do not confuse these.

	Crystal		Crystal
Ash tray, 2¾"	10.00	Pitcher, 7⅛", 48 oz.	97.50
Basket, 10¼" x 6½", wicker hndl.	70.00	Plate, 6½", bread/butter	6.00
Bowl, 4½", hndl.	12.00	Plate, 7½", salad	8.00
Bowl, 5", fruit	14.00	Plate, 7½", crescent salad	35.00
Bowl, 6", cereal	22.50	Plate, 8", party, w/indent for cup	25.00
Bowl, 6¼", snack, ftd.	14.00	Plate, 8½", luncheon	12.50
Bowl, 7⅛", 3 ftd., triangular	15.00	Plate, 9½", small dinner	25.00
Bowl, 7¼", bonbon, 3 ftd.	20.00	Plate, 10", hndl., cake	22.00
Bowl, 8", flared	25.00	Plate, 10½", dinner	32.00
Bowl, 8½", salad	25.00	Plate, 14", torte	30.00
Bowl, 9", lily pond	30.00	Platter, 12"	47.50
Bowl, 9½", hndl., serving bowl	35.00	Preserve, w/cover, 6"	35.00
Bowl, 9½", oval, serving bowl	32.50	Relish, 7⅜", 2 part	15.00
Bowl, 10", oval, hndl.	32.50	Relish, 11⅛", 3 part	25.00
Bowl, 10½", salad	30.00	Salt and pepper, 2⅜", (individual), pr.	15.00
Bowl, 10¾", ftd., flared	35.00	Salt and pepper, 3⅛", pr.	20.00
Bowl, 11, ftd., rolled edge	40.00	Salver, 12¼", ftd. (like cake stand)	50.00
Bowl, 11¼", lily pond	32.50	Saucer	3.50
Bowl, 12", flared	35.00	Stem, 3½ oz., cocktail, 4⅛"	20.00
Butter, w/cover, ¼ lb.	35.00	Stem, 3½ oz., wine, 4½"	30.00
Candy, w/cover, 7"	35.00	Stem, 4½ oz., oyster cocktail, 3¾"	20.00
Candlestick, 4½"	17.50	Stem, 5½" oz., sherbet, 4½"	12.00
Candlestick, 7", double	30.00	Stem, 10 oz., goblet, 5¾"	22.50
Candlestick, 7¾", triple	40.00	Sugar, 4", ftd.	9.00
Comport, 2¾", cheese	15.00	Sugar, individual	9.00
Comport, 4⅜"	20.00	Tid bit, 8⅛", 3 ftd., upturned edge	18.00
Cracker plate, 10¾"	30.00	Tid bit, 10¼", 2 tier, metal hndl.	25.00
Creamer, 4¼"	9.00	Tray, 4¼", for ind. salt/pepper	14.00
Creamer, individual	9.00	Tray, 7⅛", for ind. sugar/creamer	14.00
Cup, 6 oz., ftd.	15.00	Tray, 9⅛", hndl., utility	25.00
Ice Bucket	65.00	Tray, 9½", hndl., muffin	30.00
Mayonnaise, 3 pc.	30.00	Tray, 11½", center hndl.	30.00
Mayonnaise, 4 pc., div. w/2 ladles	35.00	Tumbler, 5 oz., ftd., juice, 4¾"	22.50
Mustard, w/spoon, cover	27.50	Tumbler, 12 oz., ftd., tea, 5⅞"	27.50
Oil, w/stopper, 5 oz.	45.00	Vase, 6", bud	18.00
Pickle, 8¾"	15.00	Vase, 7½", hndl.	70.00
Pitcher, 6⅛", 16 oz.	50.00	Vase, 8½", oval	67.50

Please refer to Foreword for pricing information

CHINTZ PLATE ETCHING #338, FOSTORIA GLASS COMPANY

Color: crystal.

Fostoria's Chintz was added to this 50's book because it fit the time parameters better than those of the *Elegant Glassware of the Depression Era*. As with the Century pattern, I will now be dropping Chintz from the Elegant and putting it only in this one.

New listings for Chintz include the 9½" oval vegetable bowl, 9¼" footed bowl and a cigarette box. That elusive oval vegetable bowl is pictured on its side in the top photograph. I found the 17½" plate (in the background of the same photo) at a tent sale outside an antique shop near Pittsburgh. I mention that because I had stopped going to that shop, since it had proved to be a waste of time looking for glassware there. I found several other bargains from the dealers having their own show outside the shop. I almost passed the mini-show, but I was glad I had not! Sometimes it pays to revisit a shop you've "written off!"

Currently, Chintz stemware continues to be bountiful as is the case for many patterns in this period. Evidently, people acquired stemware whether they bought the serving pieces or not. Serving pieces are elusive as anyone collecting this pattern will tell you. Watch for cream soups, dinner bells, finger bowls, salad dressing bottles, syrups and any of the vases. All these pieces are considered to be uncommon in this pattern!

Contrary to many of the Fostoria patterns, only one size dinner plate exists in Chintz. You will have to settle for a 9½" plate. Scuffed and worn plates are a nemesis; choose your wares carefully. Prices below are for mint condition plates and not ones with so called "light" scratching!

The drip cut syrup with metal lid was listed as Sani-cut in sales brochures. Evidently, this was not a "to-die-for" item since they are so scarce today.

Those oval bowls in the bottom photograph were called sauce dishes by Fostoria. The oval sauce boat liner came with both, but a brochure listed it as a tray instead of liner. Many pieces of Chintz are found on the #2496 blank (known as Baroque). For novice collectors, a prominent fleur-de-lis is the giveaway design for the Baroque blank.

	Crystal		Crystal
Bell, dinner	120.00	Plate, #2496, 9½", dinner	50.00
Bowl, #869, 4½", finger	55.00	Plate, #2496, 10½", hndl., cake	42.50
Bowl, #2496, 4⅝", tri-cornered	22.50	Plate, #2496, 11", cracker	40.00
Bowl, #2496, cream soup	75.00	Plate, #2496, 14", upturned edge	50.00
Bowl, #2496, 5", fruit	30.00	Plate, #2496, 16", torte, plain edge	115.00
Bowl, #2496, 5", hndl.	25.00	Plate, 17½", upturned edge	135.00
Bowl, #2496, 7⅝", bon bon	32.50	Platter, #2496, 12"	95.00
Bowl, #2496, 8½", hndl.	55.00	Relish, #2496, 6", 2 part, square	33.00
Bowl, #2496, 9¼" ftd.	300.00	Relish, #2496, 10" x 7½", 3 part	40.00
Bowl, #2496, 9½", oval vegetable	195.00	Relish, #2419, 5 part	40.00
Bowl, #2496, 9½", vegetable	70.00	Salad dressing bottle, #2083, 6½"	325.00
Bowl, #2484, 10", hndl.	60.00	Salt and pepper, #2496, 2¾", flat, pr.	90.00
Bowl, #2496, 10½", hndl.	65.00	Sauce boat, #2496, oval	75.00
Bowl, #2496, 11½", flared	60.00	Sauce boat, #2496, oval, divided	75.00
Bowl, #6023, ftd.	40.00	Sauce boat liner, #2496, oblong, 8"	30.00
Candlestick, #2496, 3½", double	30.00	Saucer, #2496	5.00
Candlestick, #2496, 4"	18.00	Stem, #6026, 1 oz., cordial, 3⅞"	47.50
Candlestick, #2496, 5½"	30.00	Stem, #6026, 4 oz., cocktail, 5"	26.00
Candlestick, #2496, 6", triple	42.50	Stem, #6026, 4 oz., oyster cocktail, 3⅜"	27.50
Candlestick, #6023, double	37.50	Stem, #6026, 4½ oz., claret-wine, 5⅜"	40.00
Candy, w/cover, #2496, 3 part	135.00	Stem, #6026, 6 oz., low sherbet, 4⅜"	20.00
Celery, #2496, 11"	35.00	Stem, #6026, 6 oz., saucer champagne, 5½"	22.00
Comport, #2496, 3¼", cheese	25.00	Stem, #6026, 9 oz., water goblet, 7⅝"	33.00
Comport, #2496, 4¾"	32.50	Sugar, #2496, 3½", ftd.	16.00
Comport, #2496, 5½"	37.50	Sugar, #2496½, individual	21.00
Creamer, #2496, 3¾", ftd.	17.50	Syrup, #2586, Sani-cut	375.00
Creamer, #2496½, individual	22.50	Tidbit, #2496, 8¼", 3 ftd., upturned edge	26.00
Cup, #2496, ftd.	21.00	Tray, #2496½, 6½", for ind. sugar/creamer	22.00
Ice bucket, #2496	135.00	Tray, #2375, 11", center hndl.	40.00
Jelly, w/cover, #2496, 7½"	85.00	Tumbler, #6026, 5 oz., juice, ftd.	27.50
Mayonnaise, #2496½, 3 piece	57.50	Tumbler, #6026, 9 oz., water or low goblet	27.50
Oil, w/stopper, #2496, 3½ oz.	100.00	Tumbler, #6026, 13 oz., tea, ftd.	32.50
Pickle, #2496, 8"	32.00	Vase, #4108, 5"	85.00
Pitcher, #5000, 48 oz., ftd.	360.00	Vase, #4128, 5"	85.00
Plate, #2496, 6", bread/butter	10.00	Vase, #4143, 6", ftd.	100.00
Plate, #2496, 7½", salad	15.00	Vase, #4143, 7½", ftd.	135.00
Plate, #2496, 8½", luncheon	21.00		

"CHRISTMAS CANDY" NO. 624 INDIANA GLASS COMPANY, 1950'S

Colors: Terrace Green (teal) and crystal.

"Christmas Candy" is another of Indiana's numbered lines (#624), and almost all the colored pieces I have bought over the years have come from my trips into Indiana. "Christmas Candy" may have been only regionally distributed. Dunkirk, the home of Indiana Glass, is not far from Indianapolis where I used to attend several Depression Glass shows each year. After mentioning that in the previous book, I ran into a batch of the Terrace Green in Florida! Crystal is seen nationally, but not so the green; or so I thought.

Teal, or Terrace Green as it was named by the company, is the color everyone wants. Unfortunately, there is very little of this color found today. Usually, "Christmas Candy" is found in sets rather than a piece here and there. Any glassware made in the 1950's is often found in sets — having been carefully stored in someone's attic, garage or basement.

One good thing about buying glassware in Florida, is the "snow birds" who yearly bring glass to sell from all over the country. Retirees also bring their glassware south with them, and as they move about or leave for a better world, much of that glass comes into the marketplace!

That 9½" round vegetable bowl continues to be the only one known. It created quite a stir among "Christmas Candy" collectors, since it had been a long time since a new piece of this pattern had been found! You might expect that the newly discovered vegetable bowl would be found in Indiana and be brought to the Indianapolis Depression Glass show!

The bowl atop the tidbit measures 5¾". Crystal "Christmas Candy" has few collectors, but it is a pattern that can still be found at reasonable prices. Some of the pieces of teal are no longer "reasonably priced" as you can see below. (Of course, pricing is relative. Ten years from now, we may think these were very reasonable prices for these scarce items!)

I will repeat from the first book the information found on a boxed set. On a 15-piece set was the following: "15 pc. Luncheon set (Terrace Green) To F W Newburger & Co. New Albany Ind Dept M 1346; From Pitman Dretzer Dunkirk Ind 4-3-52." This was valuable dated information because this color was attributed to much earlier production in other published information.

	Crystal	Teal		Crystal	Teal
Bowl, 5¾"	4.50		Plate, 8¼", luncheon	7.00	17.50
Bowl, 7⅜", soup	7.00	35.00	Plate, 9⅝", dinner	11.00	32.50
Bowl, 9½", vegetable		225.00	Plate, 11¼", sandwich	16.00	42.00
Creamer	9.00	22.00	Saucer	2.00	7.00
Cup	5.00	20.00	Sugar	9.00	22.00
Mayonnaise, w/ladle, liner	22.00		Tidbit, 2-tier	17.50	
Plate, 6", bread and butter	3.50	11.00			

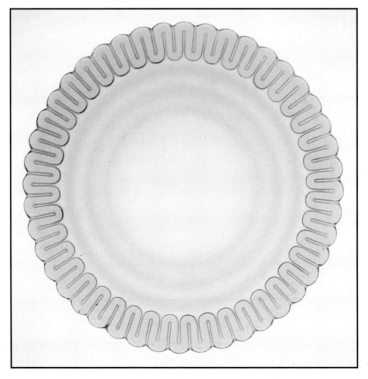

Please refer to Foreword for pricing information

COIN GLASS LINE #1372, FOSTORIA GLASS COMPANY, 1958-1982

Colors: amber, blue, crystal, green, Olive and red.

Coin glass is rapidly becoming a hot collectible in today's markets. With that sentence I opened a can of worms in the first edition of this book. Even though I have had hundreds of letters thanking me for finally providing a price guide for Fostoria's Coin Glass, I was sorry that I had included the pattern before the book was ever off the press. I included Coin because it was becoming an increasingly desirable collectible—so desirable, in fact, that Lancaster Colony, who now owns the Fostoria moulds, began remaking it! I don't mean moulding a few pieces, but producing a whole line in many of the original colors!

I have put an asterisk (*) by all pieces that have been newly made, but I realize even that could change by the time this book becomes available. Obviously, this has set prices in disarray. The quandary I now have is how to handle it. If you collect Fostoria Coin, never has the following been truer. **Know your dealer! Ask him if he can date the piece; remember, if the price sounds too good to be true, it probably is!**

Thankfully, the blue and green colors currently being manufactured are different shades than those originally made. I have photographed these new colors on the bottom of page 46 with the original green and blue colors shown on page 45. The blue lamp minus shade was one of a pair I bought in an antique mall in Ohio last year for an outrageously low price! There are still bargains to be found!

The Olive Green is sometimes referred to as avocado, but Olive was the official name. The green that is most desired is often called "emerald" by collectors. This color is represented by the jelly and cruet set shown on bottom of page 45.

You will find some crystal with gold decorated coins. This sells for about double the price of normal crystal if the gold is not worn. It is almost impossible to sell with worn or faded gold.

	Amber	Blue	Crystal	Green	Olive	Ruby
Ash tray, 5" #1372/123	17.50	25.00	18.00	30.00	17.50	22.50
Ash tray, 7½", center coin #1372/119	20.00		25.00	35.00		25.00
Ash tray, 7½", round #1372/114	25.00	40.00	25.00	45.00	30.00	20.00
Ash tray, 10" #1372/124	30.00	50.00	25.00	55.00	30.00	
Ash tray, oblong #1372/115	15.00	20.00	10.00	25.00	25.00	
Ash tray/cover, 3" #1372/110	20.00	25.00	25.00	30.00		
Bowl, 8", round #1372/179	30.00	50.00	25.00	70.00	25.00	45.00
Bowl, 8½", ftd. #1372/199	60.00	85.00	50.00	100.00	50.00	70.00
Bowl, 8½", ftd. w/cover #1372/212	100.00	150.00	85.00	175.00		
*Bowl, 9", oval #1372/189	30.00	55.00	30.00	70.00	30.00	50.00
*Bowl, wedding w/cover #1372/162	70.00	90.00	55.00	125.00	55.00	85.00
Candle holder, 4½", pr. #1372/316	30.00	50.00	40.00	50.00	30.00	50.00
Candle holder, 8", pr. #1372/326	60.00		50.00		50.00	95.00
Candy box w/cover, 4⅛" #1372/354	30.00	60.00	30.00	75.00	30.00	60.00
*Candy jar w/cover, 6⁵⁄₁₆" #1372/347	25.00	50.00	25.00	75.00	25.00	50.00
*Cigarette box w/cover, 5¾" x 4½" #1372/374	50.00	75.00	40.00	100.00		
Cigarette holder w/ash tray cover #1372/372	50.00	75.00	45.00	90.00		
Cigarette urn, 3⅜", ftd. #1372/381	25.00	45.00	20.00	50.00	20.00	40.00
Condiment set, 4 pc. (tray, 2 shakers and cruet) #1372/737	210.00	270.00	130.00		205.00	
Condiment tray, 9⅝", #1372/738	60.00	75.00	40.00		75.00	
*Creamer #1372/680	11.00	16.00	10.00	30.00	15.00	16.00
Cruet, 7 oz. w/stopper #1372/531	65.00	100.00	50.00	150.00	80.00	
*Decanter w/stopper, pint, 10³⁄₁₆" #1372/400	120.00	160.00	80.00	325.00	120.00	
*Jelly #1372/448	17.50	25.00	15.00	35.00	15.00	25.00
Lamp chimney, coach or patio #1372/461	50.00	60.00	40.00			
Lamp chimney, hndl., courting #1372/292	45.00	65.00				
Lamp, 9¾", hndl., courting, oil #1372/310	105.00	160.00				
Lamp, 10⅛", hndl., courting, electric #1372/311	100.00	160.00				
Lamp, 13½", coach, electric #1372/321	125.00	185.00	95.00			
Lamp, 13½", coach, oil #1372/320	125.00	185.00	95.00			

Please refer to Foreword for pricing information

COIN GLASS #1372 (Cont.)

	Amber	Blue	Crystal	Green	Olive	Ruby
Lamp, 16⅝", patio, electric #1372/466	150.00	260.00	125.00			
Lamp, 16⅝", patio, oil #1372/459	150.00	260.00	125.00			
Nappy, 4½" #1372/495			18.00			
*Nappy, 5⅜", w/hndl. #1372/499	20.00	30.00	15.00	40.00	18.00	30.00
Pitcher, 32 oz., 6 5/16" #1372/453	50.00	105.00	50.00	150.00	50.00	80.00
Plate, 8", #1372/550			20.00		20.00	40.00
Punch bowl base #1372/602			150.00			
Punch bowl, 14", 1½ gal., #1372/600			150.00			
Punch cup #1372/615			30.00			
*Salver, ftd., 6½" tall #1372/630	110.00	150.00	90.00	250.00	115.00	
Shaker, 3¼", pr. w/chrome top #1372/652	30.00	45.00	25.00	90.00	30.00	45.00
Stem, 4", 5 oz. wine #1372/26			30.00		45.00	60.00
Stem, 5¼", 9 oz., sherbet, #1372/7			20.00		40.00	60.00
Stem, 10½ oz., goblet #1372/2			30.00		45.00	85.00
*Sugar w/cover #1372/673	35.00	45.00	25.00	60.00	30.00	45.00
Tumbler, 3⅝", 9 oz. juice/old fashioned #1372/81			27.50			
Tumbler, 4¼", 9 oz. water, scotch & soda #1372/73			27.50			
Tumbler, 5⅛", 12 oz. ice tea/high ball #1372/64			35.00			
Tumbler, 5⅜", 10 oz. double old fashioned #1372/23			22.00			
Tumbler, 5 3/16", 14 oz. ice tea #1372/58			30.00		40.00	75.00
*Urn, 12¾", ftd., w/cover #1372/829	80.00	125.00	75.00	200.00	80.00	100.00
Vase, 8", bud #1372/799	22.00	40.00	20.00	60.00	25.00	45.00
Vase, 10", ftd. #1372/818			45.00			

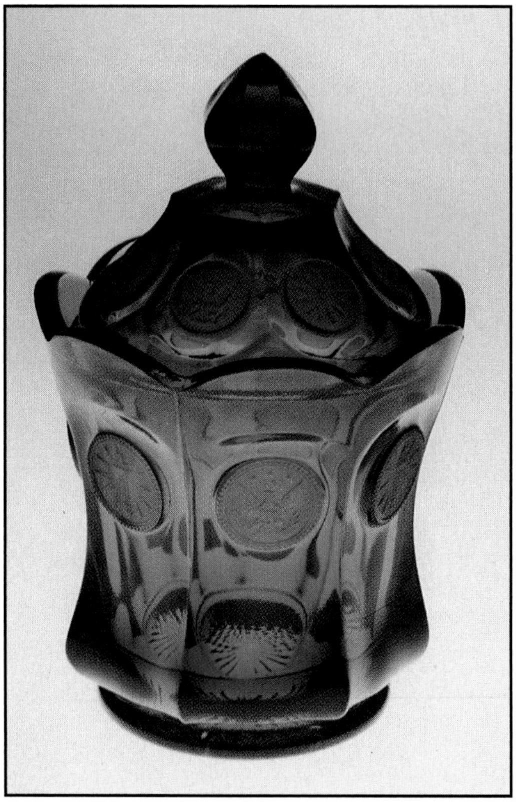

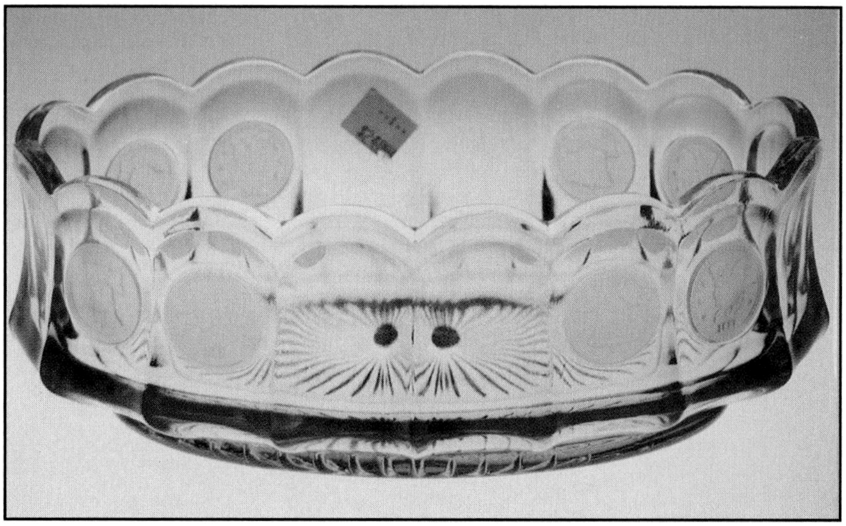

CORSAGE PLATE ETCHING #325, FOSTORIA GLASS COMPANY 1935-1960

Color: Crystal.

Corsage had its beginnings before the 40's decade, but most of its production falls within the era depicted by this book. Observe the "ice cream cone" bouquet of flowers in this design. It is sometimes confused with Fostoria's Mayflower pattern that has a cornucopia of flowers in its main design. Turn to page 135 so you can compare these two patterns both new to this edition.

Corsage is one of few Fostoria patterns found on several different dinnerware blanks. The creamer and sugar pictured are #2440 or Lafayette blank as are the cup and saucer and a few other serving pieces. The individual creamer and sugar are found on #2496 which is known as Baroque. I can't think of any other pattern that has different blanks for two sizes of sugars. Notice that there are many other pieces on Baroque. Oddly enough, the basic plates are from the #2337 line that has plain round plates. The larger cake plate and the 13" torte plate are on the Lafayette line.

I found all this amusing as I researched this pattern for the book. You will have fun ferreting out the different blanks on which Corsage is etched. I know I did!

	Crystal		Crystal
Bowl, #869, finger	22.00	Plate, 10", hdld., cake, #2496	32.50
Bowl, 4", #4119, ftd.	20.00	Plate, 11", cracker, #2496	25.00
Bowl, 4⅝", 3 corner, #2496	17.50	Plate, 13", torte, #2440	45.00
Bowl, 7⅜" 3 ftd., bon bon, #2496	15.00	Plate, 16", #2364	75.00
Bowl, 9", hdld., #2536	65.00	Relish, 2 part, #2440	27.50
Bowl, 9½", ftd., #2537	125.00	Relish, 2 part, #2496	22.50
Bowl, 10", hdld., #2484	55.00	Relish, 3 part, #2440	35.00
Bowl, 12", flared, #2496	50.00	Relish, 3 part, #2496	32.50
Bowl, 12½", oval, #2545, "Flame"	35.00	Relish, 4 part, #2419	42.50
Candelabra, 2 light w/prisms, #2527	65.00	Relish, 4 part, #2496	37.50
Candlestick, 5½", #2496	30.00	Relish, 5 part, #2419	57.50
Candlestick, 5½", #2535	35.00	Sauce bowl, 6½", oval, #2440	65.00
Candlestick, 6¾", duo, #2545, "Flame"	37.50	Sauce tray, 8½", oval, #2440	35.00
Candlestick, duo, #2496	35.00	Saucer, #2440	5.00
Candlestick, trindle, #2496	42.50	Stem, #6014, 3¾", 1 oz., cordial	45.00
Candy, w/lid, 3 part, #2496	85.00	Stem, #6014, 3¾", 4 oz., oyster cocktail	17.50
Celery, #2440	30.00	Stem, #6014, 4½", 5½ oz., low sherbet	16.00
Comport, 3¼", cheese	17.50	Stem, #6014, 5¼", 3 oz., wine	30.00
Comport, 5½", #2496	22.50	Stem, #6014, 5⅜", 5½ oz., high sherbet	22.00
Creamer, #2440	17.50	Stem, #6014, 5", 3½ oz., cocktail	22.00
Creamer, ind., #2496	12.50	Stem, #6014, 7⅜", 9 oz., water	27.50
Cup, #2440	18.00	Stem, #6014, 7⅞", 4 oz., claret	35.00
Ice Bucket, #2496	65.00	Sugar, #2440	17.50
Mayonnaise, 2 part, #2440	25.00	Sugar, ind., #2496	12.50
Mayonnaise, 3 pc., #2496½	37.50	Tid bit, 3 footed, #2496	15.00
Pickle, #2440	22.00	Tray, 6½", ind. sug/cr., #2496½	12.50
Pitcher	225.00	Tumbler, #6014, 4¾", 5 oz., ftd. juice	17.50
Plate, 6½", #2337	8.00	Tumbler, #6014, 5½", 9 oz., ftd. water	21.00
Plate, 7½", #2337	10.00	Tumbler, #6014, 6", 12 oz., ftd. ice tea	25.00
Plate, 8½",	12.50	Vase, 8", bud, #5092	45.00
Plate, 9½", #2337	37.50	Vase, 10", ftd., #2470	110.00
Plate, 10½", cake, hdld., #2440	32.50		

CROCHETED CRYSTAL IMPERIAL GLASS COMPANY, 1943-early 1950's

Color: Crystal.

Crocheted Crystal was made by Imperial exclusively for Sears, Roebuck and Company. The listing below is from the fall 1943 Sears catalogue. In order to show you the stemware in this pattern, I have included a couple of ads showing these on pages 52-53. My thanks to Dan Tucker for use of his ads. The Narcissus bowl will be added to my listing since it was omitted previously.

I first started looking at this pattern because the shapes and styles reminded me of Laced Edge, also made by Imperial. Some of the pieces I have pictured are not in the listing below, although they have all the characteristics of the pattern. I do not have all the Sears catalogue listings from this era; so there may be additional pieces not in my list. The footed bowl in the foreground of the top photograph may be a part of this pattern; but the bowl behind it probably is not. In the bottom photograph the center handled plate and ruffled bowl in the back may not be correct, but they are great "go-with" items if not.

In that bottom photo is a punch bowl with closed handled cups, although the catalogue ad shows open handled ones. I suspect these cups came both ways. There is no punch liner, but the 14" plate will do in a pinch. The single candleholder next to the double one, which is so commonly seen, is shaped like the Narcissus bowl. Even though it is not listed, I have no doubts that this is truly Crocheted Crystal.

An astounding thing I encountered while trying to buy pieces of this pattern was the divergence of prices. No one seemed to know what it was, but they all had elevated prices because it was "pretty good glass" or "elegant looking glass."

I have never understood how vendors can come up with a momentous price when they have no idea what they are pricing. A guess based upon what was paid, I understand; but attempting to tell someone what something is when one has no idea, is a mistake! It's better to put nothing on the label but a price. That way, one avoids looking foolish, when a piece of Imperial is labeled "Heisey" or "Cambridge" just because they've heard that those are good glass company names! Yes, I've been "informed" pieces of this pattern were made by both aforesaid companies, and the prices asked were commensurate with the company names!

	Crystal		Crystal
Basket, 6"	27.50	Mayonnaise plate, 7½"	7.50
Basket, 9"	37.50	Plate, 8", salad	7.50
Basket, 12"	60.00	Plate, 9½"	12.50
Bowl, 7", Narcissus	35.00	Plate, 13", salad bowl liner	20.00
Bowl, 10½", salad	27.50	Plate, 14"	22.50
Bowl, 11", console	27.50	Plate, 17"	37.50
Bowl, 12", console	30.00	Punch bowl, 14"	65.00
Buffet set, 14" plate, ftd. sauce bowl, ladle	35.00	Punch cup closed hdld.	5.00
Cake stand, 12", ftd.	40.00	Punch cup, open hdld.	7.00
Candleholder, 4½", 2-lite	17.50	Relish, 11½", 3 pt.	25.00
Candleholder (Narcissus bowl shape)	25.00	Stem, 4½", 3½ oz., cocktail	12.50
Celery, 10", oval	22.50	Stem, 5½", 4½ oz., wine	17.50
Cheese & cracker, 12" plate, ftd. dish	35.00	Stem, 5", 6 oz., sherbet	10.00
Creamer	12.50	Stem, 7⅛", 9 oz., water goblet	14.00
Epergne, 11", ftd. bowl, center vase	130.00	Sugar	12.50
Hors d'oeuvre dish, 10½", 4 pt., round	30.00	Tumbler, 6", 6 oz., ftd. fruit juice	8.50
Lamp, 11", hurricane	35.00	Tumbler, 7⅛", 12 oz., ftd. iced tea	15.00
Mayonnaise bowl, 5¼"	12.50	Vase, 8"	17.50
Mayonnaise ladle	5.00		

CROCHETED CRYSTAL

Our choice and yours . . . Harmony House *Crocheted Crystal*

Your table deserves fine hand-made crystal, and this is it. Harmony House Crocheted Crystal . . . unusually elegant, unusually low priced . . . exclusive with Sears. You'll want it for yourself, and you'll choose it for impressive gifts. All pieces (except stemware) have graceful "crocheted" openwork edges.

4-piece Salad Set

A With this set you'll add sparkle to salads, flatter your dining table. Bowl, 10½-in. diam.; plate, 13-in. diam.; glass serving fork, spoon.
35 E 01732—Shpg. wt., 7 lbs . . . 4-piece set **$2.65**

Charming Epergne Centerpiece

B Filled with colorful fruit or flowers, this beautiful epergne will brighten your living room or add a graceful touch to your dining table or buffet. Sparkling, footed crystal glass bowl, 11 inches in diameter, with removable vase. Overall height, 11 inches. Shipping weight, 7 pounds.
35 E 01727 . . . . . . Complete centerpiece **$2.89**

Graceful Cake Stand

C This beautiful cake stand will even do justice to your prize cakes—and it's equally good for holding smaller tid-bits like cookies, candies, and fruit. Overall diam., 12 in. Height, 4 in.
35 E 1729—Shipping weight, 5 pounds . . Each **$1.49**

Lovely 3-piece Console Set

D Glittering crystal and glowing candle-light add charm and glamour to any occasion. Here is a 3-piece console set, consisting of two exquisitely styled crystal glass twin candle-holders, each about 4½ inches high, and a lovely crystal glass bowl, about 11 inches in diameter. Candles not incl.
35 E 01739—Shpg. wt., 6 lbs . . . . . 3-piece set **$1.45**

Matched Crocheted Stemware

E Start your collection of crocheted crystal with this 12-piece set, which includes the most popular, most-used pieces. All have strikingly beautiful shapes and decorated stems. Set of four goblets, four sherbets and four 8-inch salad plates. Makes a romantic gift any bride would treasure.
35 E 01751—Shpg. wt., 10 lbs . . . 12-piece set **$5.79**

Add more stemware from time to time from open stock
35 E 1750—State pieces.

	Height	Shpg. wt.	Each	Six for
Goblet . . . . . Size 9 oz	7½ in .	1 lb	.55c	3.25
Sherbet . . . . . Size 6 oz	5 in	1 lb	.55c	3.25
Wine . . . Size 4½ oz	5½ in	1 lb	.55c	3.25
Iced Tea . . . Size 12 oz	7½ in	1 lb	.55c	3.25
Salad Plate . Size 8-in. diam. . . .		2 lbs	.38c	2.19

Narcissus Bowl

F Just the thing for growing narcissus or other bulbs; you'll like it, too, for candies, preserves and salted nuts. Deep bowl, 4½-in. high, 7 in. diam.
35 E 1714—Shipping weight, 3 pounds 8 ounces **85c**

14-piece Punch Set

G If you're one who plays hostess often, this set will prove practical—really invaluable. It adds a festive touch to any occasion, and is wonderful for holiday entertaining. Cups hook over the edge of the bowl, which can also be used for salads. 4-qt. bowl, 14 in. in diam.; 12 six-ounce cups; glass ladle.
35 E 01719—Shpg. wt., 18 lbs . . . 14-piece set **$5.75**
35 E 1720—Set of 12 cups only. Shpg. wt., 8 lbs **$2.89**

3-Piece Mayonnaise Set

H Bowl 5¼-in. diam.; plate 7½-in. diam.; ladle.
35 E 1705—Shipping weight, 3 lbs. 8 oz . . Set **89c**

Exquisite Crocheted Plates

J Use the 9½-inch size for place plates; 14-inch size plate for cake; 17-inch size for sandwiches.
35 E 01701—9½-in. Shpg. wt., 9 lbs . . Set of six **$2.59**
35 E 01703—14-in. Shpg. wt., 5 lbs . . . . Each 1.25
35 E 01704—17-in. Shpg. wt., 8 lbs . . . . Each 3.45

3-piece Buffet Set

K Ideal for serving snacks that require sauces. 14-in. serving plate, removable bowl for sauce, and ladle.
35 E 01736—Shipping weight, 6 pounds . . . Set **$1.65**

Hors d'oeuvre Dish

L Useful relish dish with four handy partitions.
35 E 1716—Diam. 10½ in. Shpg. wt., 3 lbs . . . **98c**

Crocheted Crystal can be added to your Easy Terms order . . . see inside back cover

"DAISY," NUMBER 620 INDIANA GLASS COMPANY

Colors: crystal, 1933-40; fired-on red, late 30's; amber, 1940's; dark green and milk glass, 1960's, 1970's, 1980's.

"Daisy" is one of the few patterns that fit both my 1930's and 1950's glassware books; so a decision had to be made as to placement. Since more collectors search for the amber or green "Daisy," I decided that it best fit this book instead of *The Collector's Encyclopedia of Depression Glass.* Know that the crystal was made in 1930's, but there are few collectors for that today.

Shortly after we photographed the shelf set up, I finally found the amber grill plate with the indent for the cream soup. It never fails to amaze me how many times that has happened in the past. It's been four years since we last photographed "Daisy" without turning up that one missing amber piece; and two weeks after this photo session, a stack of those plates were sitting in an antique mall just begging for a home! They were not cheap enough to buy for resale, but I had to have one for photography. The pattern shot below shows this indented grill plate in green. Note how large the ring is. It is much larger than the base of a cup, but fits the base of the cream soup perfectly.

Avocado colored "Daisy" was marketed by Indiana as "Heritage" in the 1960's through 1980's and not under the name "Daisy" or No. 620 as it was when it was first produced in the late 1930's. I mention this because Federal Glass Company also made a "Heritage" pattern that is rare in green. Federal's green is the brighter, normally found Depression Glass color and not the avocado colored green shown here. You can see that rare color on page 116.

Amber "Daisy" is one of the few amber colored patterns that continues to have its admirers. "Daisy" prices have invariably increased. Besides the indented grill plate, the 12 oz. footed tea, relish dish, 9⅜" berry and cereal bowls are all scarce, not rare. Perfect (without inner rim roughness) cereal bowls have become the most difficult pieces to find, taking that honor away from the ice tea.

There are a few pieces of fired-on red "Daisy" being found. A reader's letter last year said that her family had a red set that was acquired in 1935. That helps date this production. There is a pitcher in a fired-on red being found with the No. 618 tumblers. This pitcher does not belong to either pattern per se, but was sold with both of these Indiana patterns. Thus, it's a legitimate "go-with" pitcher.

	Crystal	Green	Red, Amber
Bowl, 4½", berry	4.50	6.00	9.00
Bowl, 4½", cream soup	4.50	6.00	12.00
Bowl, 6", cereal	10.00	12.00	30.00
Bowl, 7⅜", deep berry	7.50	9.00	15.00
Bowl, 9⅜", deep berry	13.00	16.00	32.00
Bowl, 10", oval vegetable	9.50	11.00	16.00
Creamer, footed	5.50	5.00	8.00
Cup	4.00	4.00	6.00
Plate, 6", sherbet	2.00	2.00	3.00
Plate, 7⅜", salad	3.50	3.50	7.00
Plate, 8⅜", luncheon	4.00	4.50	6.00
Plate, 10⅜", grill	5.50	7.50	10.00
Plate, 9⅜", dinner	5.50	6.50	9.00
Plate, 10⅜", grill w/indent for cream soup		15.00	22.00
Plate, 11½", cake or sandwich	6.50	7.50	14.00
Platter, 10¾"	7.50	8.50	15.00
Relish dish, 8⅜", 3 part	12.00		32.00
Saucer	1.50	1.50	2.00
Sherbet, footed	5.00	5.50	9.00
Sugar, footed	5.50	5.00	8.00
Tumbler, 9 oz., footed	9.50	9.50	18.00
Tumbler, 12 oz., footed	20.00	22.00	37.50

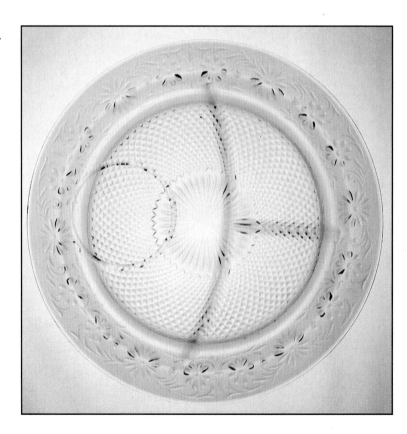

Please refer to Foreword for pricing information

DEWDROP JEANNETTE GLASS COMPANY, 1953-1956

Color: Crystal.

Dewdrop is one of those patterns that evokes emotional differences in collectors. Some feel it is wonderful, while others consider it junk. You either love or hate it. If you like the pattern, your hopes are to find someone who has a bunch and thinks it is worthless.

At least the butter dish had a top for this photography session. I notice the punch bowl base is missing in the photograph for some reason. Maybe it was left unpacked in the box. That is almost as bad as missing pieces in my listings when they are in the photograph.

Many collectors are buying the lazy susan in this pattern to get the missing ball bearings for their Shell Pink lazy susan. These ball bearings are interchangeable. While in Seattle last year, I bought the Dew Drop lazy susan set and let the lady keep the glass pieces. She looked astonished, but the ball bearings travel much better by airline than those big glass items. Besides, I had just bought the Shell Pink set minus the ball bearing in Chattanooga on my way to Florida! The boxed lazy susan below is an original. The Shell Pink lazy susan came in the same decorated floral box, but with pink flowers.

I have included a photo of the iced tea tumbler since it did not get in the photographs. The snack sets were sold as TV snack trays in sets of four. I have seen several boxed sets of these in my travels.

Dewdrop will not break your bank account now, so buy it. Someday you will not be sorry! Besides, nearly all crystal patterns make wonderful table settings.

	Crystal		Crystal
Bowl, 4¾"	4.00	Plate, snack, w/indent for cup	4.00
Bowl, 8½"	11.00	Punch bowl base	9.00
Bowl, 10⅜"	16.50	Punch bowl, 6 qt.	24.00
Butter, w/cover	27.50	Relish, leaf shape w/hndl.	8.00
Candy dish, w/cover, 7", round	20.00	Sugar, w/cover	13.00
Creamer	8.00	Tray, 13", lazy susan	22.00
Cup, punch or snack	4.00	Tumbler, 9 oz., water	12.00
Pitcher, ½ gallon	25.00	Tumbler, 15 oz., iced tea	16.00
Plate, 11½"	16.00		

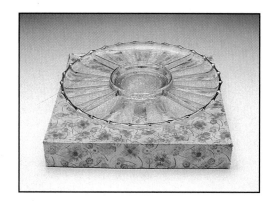

EMERALD CREST FENTON ART GLASS COMPANY, 1949-1955

Color: White with green edge.

Emerald Crest, introduced in 1949, was listed in Fenton catalogues until January 1955. That means production was finished at least by the end of 1955. This popular line followed the Aqua Crest (blue trimmed), started in 1941, and Silver Crest (crystal trimmed) started in 1943. Prices for Aqua Crest fall between that of Emerald Crest and Silver Crest (priced on pages 208 and 210).

Thanks for all the communications I have received approving the addition of Fenton patterns in this book. I appreciate the time and help I have had obtaining accurate price listings for Emerald Crest and Silver Crest. Most mayonnaise sets are found with crystal spoons, but a green spoon was made. It is rarely found. You can see two green spoons in the mustards. The green stopper for the oil bottle is also difficult to locate.

Some pieces of Emerald Crest have two different line numbers on them. Originally, this line was #680, and all pieces carried that designation. In July, 1952, Fenton began issuing a Ware Number for each piece. That is why you see two separate numbers for the different sized plates.

	White w/Green		White w/Green
Basket, 5" #7236	77.50	Mayonnaise set, 3 pc. w/gr. ladle #7203	85.00
Basket, 7" #7237	97.50	Mustard, w/lid and spoon	77.50
Bowl, 5", finger or deep dessert #7221	18.00	Oil bottle, w/green stopper #680, #7269	90.00
Bowl, 5½", soup #680, #7230	37.50	Pitcher, 6" hndl., beaded melon #7116	55.00
Bowl, 8½", flared #680	40.00	Plate, 5½" #680, #7218	15.00
Bowl, 9½" #682	57.50	Plate, 6½" #680, #7219	16.00
Bowl, 10" salad #7220	75.00	Plate, 8½" #680, #7217	32.50
Bowl, dessert, shallow #7222	20.00	Plate, 10" #680, #7210	40.00
Bowl, ftd., tall, square #7330	75.00	Plate, 12" #680, #7212	47.50
Cake plate, 13" high ftd. #680, #7213	80.00	Plate, 12" #682	47.50
Cake plate, low ftd. #5813	67.50	Plate, 16", torte #7216	65.00
Candle holder, flat saucer base, pr. #680	75.00	Saucer #7208	13.00
Comport, 6", ftd., flared #206	37.50	Sherbet, ftd. #7226	22.50
Comport, ftd., double crimped	37.50	Sugar, clear reeded hndls. #7231	36.00
Creamer, clear reeded hndls. #7231	42.50	Tidbit, 2 tier bowls, 5½" & 8½"	65.00
Cup #7208	37.00	Tidbit, 2 tier bowls, 8½" & 10"	85.00
Flower pot w/attached saucer #7299	67.50	Tidbit, 2 tier plates #7297	57.50
Mayonnaise bowl, #7203	32.50	Tidbit, 3 tier plates #7298	77.50
Mayonnaise ladle, crystal #7203	5.00	Vase, 4½", fan #36, #7355	23.00
Mayonnaise ladle, green, #7203	35.00	Vase, 6¼", fan #36, #7357	30.00
Mayonnaise liner, #7203	12.00	Vase, 8", bulbous base #186	62.00
Mayonnaise set, 3 pc. w/crys. ladle #7203	55.00		

ENGLISH HOBNAIL LINE NO. 555 WESTMORELAND GLASS COMPANY, 1920's-1983

Colors: amber, crystal and crystal with various color treatments.

English Hobnail has been in my Depression era book since 1972; but crystal and amber English Hobnail pattern were made until Westmoreland closed in 1983. Thus, I am pricing amber and crystal in this book. Even though crystal with amber or black feet and some shades of amber were made before 1940, pricing is fairly consistent for all these colors that essentially fit the time structure of this book. Milk glass was made very late. You can double the price listed for any fruit decorated milk glass. Ruby flashed is difficult to sell at regular crystal prices.

The icer shown next to the comport (sweetmeat) on the top of page 61 is not in any of the catalogue listings I have. There were eight of these in a mall in Chattanooga, Tennessee, but I could only buy one for photography since the price (I thought) was prohibitive to buy them all for resale. However, I found a collector in Texas (through another dealer) who wanted the icers; and so, I went back and bought the others. I have only run on to a couple of others since then; they are fairly unusual. Sometimes rarely found items do not sell because the right collector does not come along; and sometimes they do not sell because there are few collectors of that pattern or color! Rarity does not always determine price, but demand does!

Item	Amber/Crystal	Item	Amber/Crystal	Item	Amber/Crystal
Ash tray, 3"	5.00	Bowl, 11", bell	30.00	Cup, demitasse	16.00
Ash tray, 4½"	7.00	Bowl, 11", rolled edge	30.00	Decanter, 20 oz.	50.00
Ash tray, 4½", sq.	7.50	Bowl, 12", celery	17.50	Egg cup	10.00
Basket, 5", hdld.	15.00	Bowl, 12", flange or console	30.00	Hat, high	15.00
Basket, 6", tall, hdld.	35.00	Bowl, 12", flared	30.00	Hat, low	12.50
Bon bon, 6½", hdld.	12.50	Bowl, 12", oval crimped	35.00	Ice tub, 4"	17.50
Bottle, toilet, 5 oz.	17.50	Bowl, cream soup	10.00	Ice tub, 5½"	35.00
Bowl, 4", rose	15.00	Candelabra, 2-lite	17.50	Icer, sq. base,	
Bowl, 4½", finger	7.50	Candlestick, 3½", rnd. base	8.00	w/patterned insert	42.50
Bowl, 4½", round nappy	7.00	Candlestick, 5½", sq. base	15.00	Lamp, 6½", electric	30.00
Bowl, 4½", sq. ftd., finger	9.00	Candlestick, 9", rnd. base	22.50	Lamp, 9½", electric	40.00
Bowl, 4½", sq. nappy	7.00	Candy dish, 3 ftd.	30.00	Lamp, candlestick	
Bowl, 5", round nappy	9.50	Candy, ½ lb. and cover,		(several types)	30.00
Bowl, 5½", bell nappy	11.50	cone shaped	22.50	Lampshade, 17"	160.00
Bowl, 6", crimped dish	12.50	Chandelier, 17" shade		Marmalade w/cover	17.50
Bowl, 6", rose	17.50	w/200+ prisms	395.00	Mayonnaise, 6"	10.00
Bowl, 6", round nappy	10.00	Cheese w/cover, 6"	35.00	Mustard, sq. ftd., w/lid	15.00
Bowl, 6", sq. nappy	10.00	Cheese w/cover, 8¾"	50.00	Nut, individual, ftd.	6.00
Bowl, 6½", grapefruit	11.00	Cigarette box and cover,		Oil bottle, 2 oz., hdld.	20.00
Bowl, 6½", round nappy	12.00	4½"x2½"	17.50	Oil bottle, 6 oz., hdld.	30.00
Bowl, 6½", sq. nappy	12.50	Cigarette jar w/cover, rnd.	12.50	Oil-vinegar combination, 6 oz.	37.50
Bowl, 7", 6 pt.	15.00	Cigarette lighter		Parfait, rnd. ftd.	15.00
Bowl, 7", oblong spoon	17.50	(milk glass only)	11.00	Pitcher, 23 oz., rounded	45.00
Bowl, 7", preserve	13.50	Coaster, 3"	5.00	Pitcher, 32 oz., straight side	50.00
Bowl, 7", round nappy	13.00	Compote, 5", round, rnd. ftd.	12.00	Pitcher, 38 oz., rounded	60.00
Bowl, 7½", bell nappy	14.00	Compote, 5", sq. ftd., round	12.50	Pitcher, 60 oz., rounded	65.00
Bowl, 8", 6 pt.	22.50	Compote, 5½", ball stem,		Pitcher, 64 oz., straight side	75.00
Bowl, 8", cupped, nappy	20.00	sweetmeat	25.00	Plate, 5½", rnd.	4.50
Bowl, 8", ftd.	25.00	Compote, 5½", bell	14.00	Plate, 6", sq.	5.00
Bowl, 8", hexagonal ftd.,		Compote, 5½", sq. ftd., bell	15.00	Plate, 6", sq. finger bowl liner	5.00
2-hdld.	35.00	Compote, 6", honey, rnd. ftd.	15.00	Plate, 6½", depressed center, rnd.	6.00
Bowl, 8", pickle	12.50	Compote, 6", sq. ftd., honey	15.00	Plate, 6½", round.	6.00
Bowl, 8", round nappy	20.00	Compote, 8", ball stem,		Plate, 6½, rnd. finger bowl liner	6.50
Bowl, 9", bell nappy	25.00	sweetmeat	35.00	Plate, 8", rnd.	7.50
Bowl, 9", celery	15.00	Creamer, hexagonal, ftd.	8.50	Plate, 8", rnd., 3 ftd.	12.50
Bowl, 9½", round crimped	27.50	Creamer, low, flat	7.50	Plate, 8½", plain edge	8.00
Bowl, 10", flared	30.00	Creamer, sq. ftd.	8.50	Plate, 8½", rnd.	8.00
Bowl, 10", oval crimped	35.00	Cup	6.00	Plate, 8¾", sq.	8.00

ENGLISH HOBNAIL

	Amber/Crystal		Amber/Crystal		Amber/Crystal
Plate, 10½", grill, rnd	12.50	Stem, 5 oz., rnd. claret	12.50	Tumbler, 7 oz., sq. ftd., juice	9.00
Plate, 10", rnd.	12.50	Stem, 5 oz., sq. ftd., oyster cocktail	9.00	Tumbler, 8 oz., rnd., ball, water	10.00
Plate, 10", sq.	12.50	Stem, 8 oz., rnd. water goblet	10.00	Tumbler, 8 oz., water	10.00
Plate, 12", sq.	20.00	Stem, 8 oz., sq. ftd., water goblet	10.00	Tumbler, 9 oz., rnd., ball, water	10.00
Plate, 15", sq.	30.00	Stem, sherbet, low, one ball, rnd ftd.	6.00	Tumbler, 9 oz., rnd., ftd. water	10.00
Plate, 14", rnd., torte	27.50	Stem, sherbet, rnd. low foot	7.00	Tumbler, 9 oz., sq. ftd., water	10.00
Plate, 20½", rnd., torte	50.00	Stem, sherbet, sq. ftd., low	7.00	Tumbler, 10 oz., ice tea	12.00
Plate, cream soup liner, rnd.	5.00	Stem, champagne, two ball, rnd ftd.	8.00	Tumbler, 11 oz., rnd., ball, ice tea	10.00
Puff box, w/ cover, 6", rnd.	17.50	Stem, sherbet, high, two ball, rnd ftd.	9.00	Tumbler, 11 oz., sq. ftd., ice tea	12.00
Punch bowl	175.00	Stem, sherbet, rnd. high foot	9.00	Tumbler, 12 oz., ice tea	12.50
Punch bowl stand	50.00	Stem, sherbet, sq. ftd., high	9.00	Tumbler, 12½ oz., rnd. ftd. iced tea	10.00
Punch cup	6.50	Sugar, hexagonal, ftd.	8.50	Urn, 11", w/cover	30.00
Punch set (bowl, stand, 12 cups, ladle)	325.00	Sugar, low, flat	7.50	Vase, 6½", ivy bowl, sq., ftd., crimp top	27.50
Relish, 8", 3 part	15.00	Sugar, sq. ftd.	8.50	Vase, 6½", sq., ftd., flower holder	20.00
Saucer, demitasse, rnd.	10.00	Tid-bit, 2 tier	22.50	Vase, 7½", flip	25.00
Saucer, demitasse, sq.	10.00	Tumbler, 1½ oz., whiskey	11.00	Vase, 7½", flip jar w/cover	50.00
Saucer, rnd.	2.00	Tumbler, 3 oz., whiskey	10.00	Vase, 8", sq. ftd.	35.00
Saucer, sq.	2.00	Tumbler, 5 oz., ginger ale	8.00	Vase, 8½", flared top	37.50
Shaker, pr., rnd. ftd.	20.00	Tumbler, 5 oz., old fashioned cocktail	10.00	Vase, 10" (straw jar)	57.50
Shaker, pr., sq. ftd.	20.00	Tumbler, 5 oz., rnd. ftd., ginger ale	8.00		
Stem, 1 oz., rnd. ftd., cordial	13.00	Tumbler, 5 oz., sq. ftd., ginger ale	8.00		
Stem, 1 oz., rnd., ball, cordial	16.00	Tumbler, 7 oz., rnd. ftd. juice	9.00		
Stem, 1 oz., sq. ftd., cordial	13.00				
Stem, 2 oz., rnd. ftd., wine	10.00				
Stem, 2 oz., sq. ftd., wine	10.00				
Stem, 2¼ oz., rnd. ball, wine	9.00				
Stem, 3 oz., rnd. cocktail	8.00				
Stem, 3 oz., sq. ftd., cocktail	8.00				
Stem, 3½ oz., rnd. ball, cocktail	7.00				

Westmoreland's Handmade "English Hobnail" Crystal
Catalog No. 555

WESTMORELAND GLASS COMPANY *Handmade Glassware of Quality*
GRAPEVILLE, PENNSYLVANIA

Since 1889

Westmoreland's Handmade "English Hobnail" Crystal—Line No. 555

WESTMORELAND'S "English Hobnail" Crystal Pattern is handmade in one hundred and thirty-seven open stock items. It is fashioned in three Line Numbers: Line 555 with round foot; Line No. 555/2 has square plates and all stemware items are made with square foot. Line No. 555/3 stemware is barrel-shape, with ball stem and round foot. All three versions are identical in pattern, except for difference in foot as illustrated on the following pages. The various items of all three Lines intermix charmingly, and provide a wide choice for complete luncheon or dinner service.

555/12½ oz. Ice Tea, ftd.   555/9 oz. Tumbler, ftd.   555/7 oz. Tumbler, ftd.   555 Parfait   555 Sherbet High foot.   555 Sherbet Low foot.   555/3 oz. Cocktail   555/8 oz. Goblet

555/5 oz. Claret   555/2 oz. Wine   555 Cordial   555 Old Fashioned Cocktail   1½ oz. Whiskey. Also 3 oz.   555/5 oz. Ginger Ale   555/8 oz. Tumbler   555/10 oz. Ice Tea   555/12 oz. Ice Tea

555/2 oz. Oil   555/6 oz. Oil   555/6 oz. Oil-Vinegar Comb.   555/20 oz. Decanter   555/1 qt. Jug Also in ½ Gal.   555/38 oz. Jug. Also 23 oz., 60 oz.

555 Sugar & Cream Set, footed.   555 Sugar & Cream Set, Low.   555 Salt and Pepper   555/5½ Bell Compote

Westmoreland's Handmade "English Hobnail" Crystal—Line No. 555

555/10" Plate

555/8" Plate
Also 6½", 5½"

555/7" Pie Plate

555/1/8½" Plate
Plain Edge.

555/6½" Plate,
Depressed Center

555 Cream Soup
555 Cream Soup plate

555 Cup & Saucer

555/4½" Finger Bowl
555/6½" Finger Bowl, Plate

555/10½" Grill Plate,
3 part

555/8" Relish, 3 part

555/6" Mayo

555/6"
Nappy, Square

555/5½" Nappy, Bell

555/8" Nappy, Round

555/6"
Nappy, Round

555/5"
Nappy, Round

555/4½"
Nappy, Round

555/7½" Nappy, Bell

555/11" Bowl, Bell

555/12" Bowl, Flared

555/½ lb. Candy
and Cover

555/5" Compote,
Round, footed

555/6" Honey, footed

555/12" Bowl, Oval Crimped
Also in 10"

ENGLISH HOBNAIL

Westmoreland's Handmade "English Hobnail" Crystal—Line No. 555

555/4½x2½" Cigarette Box & Cover

High Hat

Low Hat

555/4½" Ash Tray.

555 Ind. Nut, ftd.

3" Ash Tray

555 3" Coaster

555/6½" Grapefruit

555/6½" Bon Bon, H'ld.

555/8" Pickle

555/6" Crimped Dish

555/6" Rose Bowl

4" Rose Bowl

555/8"/6 Pt. Bowl. Also in 7"

555/2-Lite Candelabra

555/6" Basket, Tall Handled.

555/6" Three-Footed Covered Dish

555 Marmalade and Cover

555/3½" Candlestick

555/9½" Bowl, Round, Crimped

555/12" Celery, Also 9"

555/14" Torte Plate, Also in 20½"

555/15 Piece Punch Set

Westmoreland's Handmade "English Hobnail" Crystal—Line No. 555/2

555/2/11 oz. Ice Tea, ftd.

555/2/9 oz. Tumbler, ftd.

555/2/7 oz. Tumbler, ftd.

555/2/5 oz. Ginger Ale

555/2/8 oz. Goblet

555/2/3 oz. Cocktail

555/2 Sherbet, Low

555/2 Sherbet, High

555/2/2 oz. Wine

555/2 Cordial

555/2 Oyster Cocktail

555/2 Mustard

555/2 Salt and Pepper

555/2 Cream and Sugar, footed

555/2/5" Compote, Round

555/2/5½" Compote, Bell

555/2/6" Honey, ftd.

555/2/5½" Candlestick

555/2/4½" Nappy, Sq.

555/2 Finger Bowl, footed

555/2/10" Square Plate

555/2 Cup and Saucer

555/2/4½" Ash Tray, Sq.

555 Finger Bowl
555/2/6" Sq. Plate

555/2/6" Cheese and Cover. Also 8¾"

555/2/8¾" Square Plate

555/2/6" Square Plate

555/2/6½" Flower Holder, footed

555/2/6½" Ivy Ball, Crimp Top, ftd.

Westmoreland's Handmade "English Hobnail" Crystal—Line No. 555/3

555/3/11 oz. Ice Tea, ftd.   555/3/8 oz. Goblet   555/3/9 oz. Tumbler   555/3/5 oz. Ginger Ale, ftd.   555/3 Champagne   555/3 Sherbet, High Foot

555/3/2¼ oz. Wine   555/3/1 oz. Cordial   555/3/11" Urn and Cover or 8" Vase.   555/3/3½ oz. Cocktail   555/3 Sherbet, Low Foot.

Westmoreland's Handmade "English Hobnail" Crystal

WESTMORELAND has been making their "English Hobnail" Crystal reproductions for more than fifty years. Each piece is made by hand by the same meticulous methods and with the same precise attention to detail that were employed two generations ago.

The scintillating beauty of Westmoreland's old "English Hobnail" Crystal Pattern has long been cherished in many homes. Its charm is a part of gracious living, and the inherent loveliness of its distinctive design increases with long association and use.

"English Hobnail" is adaptable to any decor. It is equally at home in a provincial or modern setting. The wide choice of plates and stemware items make selection a delight. Because it is an open stock pattern you can add to your original selection as you may wish.

WESTMORELAND GLASS COMPANY

GRAPEVILLE, PENNSYLVANIA

Handmade Glassware of Quality

Since 1889

FIRE-KING DINNERWARE "ALICE"
ANCHOR HOCKING GLASS CORPORATION, early 1940's

Colors: Jade-ite, white w/trims of blue or red.

You will find "Alice" with white plates and with white trimmed in red or blue. Some of the red trimmed pieces fade to pink; and there are two shades of blue trimmed pieces being found. I promised to show the red trimmed pieces this time, but they did not seem to surface when it came time for photography.

Each year during my travels I buy glass for photography. That glassware is packed by book category: Depression, 50's, Elegant or Kitchen. When a photo session approaches, all of this glass is unpacked (usually by Cathy and her mom) and sorted into separate patterns. Sometimes a piece or two out of the melange doesn't end up where it belongs!

Dinner plates are still the pieces to own in this little "Alice" pattern. Obviously, few people bought the plates to go with the cup and saucers that were packed in oatmeal boxes. That was the reason that Hocking's Forest Green Sandwich has six easily found small pieces with all the larger pieces difficult to find. They, too, were packed in "Crystal Wedding Oats." The larger pieces were not premiums; the marketing procedure obviously failed (in these cases) at stimulating equal sales of the rest of the pattern.

	Jade-ite	White/Blue trim	White/Red trim
Cup	3.50	12.00	15.00
Plate, 9½"	20.00	20.00	22.50
Saucer	2.00	3.00	5.00

Please refer to Foreword for pricing information

FIRE-KING DINNERWARE CHARM
ANCHOR HOCKING GLASS CORPORATION, 1950-1954

Colors: Azur-ite, Jade-ite, Forest Green and Royal Ruby.

Charm refers to the square shaped dishes made by Anchor Hocking from 1950 through 1954. The Jade-ite and Azur-ite were advertised alongside the Forest Green and Royal Ruby; however, the color names of Forest Green and Royal Ruby prevailed on those squared shapes instead of Charm. **Prices for those colors will be found under their respective color names instead of under the pattern name Charm.**

Jad-ite continues to elude collectors. There seem to be enough Azur-ite pieces to supply collectors' needs, but this squared shape is the hardest Jade-ite to find. At present, the platter and dinner plates are very elusive. I recently sold a platter to a lady who had been searching for one for three years. Azur-ite dinner plates abound in my area, and they are, frankly, hard to sell there. Take them west and they "fly" off the table at shows. It is remarkable how some patterns remained in one geographical area, and are relatively scarce in others.

The 8⅜" plate is listed in a 1950 catalogue as a dinner plate, but later as a luncheon plate. Evidently, catalogue writers at Hocking felt that 8⅜" was a very small dinner plate and changed its designation after the first year.

	Azur-ite	Jad-ite
Bowl, 4¾", dessert	4.50	9.00
Bowl, 6", soup	13.00	20.00
Bowl, 7⅜", salad	10.00	20.00
Creamer	6.00	14.00
Cup	3.50	9.00
Plate, 6⅝", salad	4.00	4.50
Plate, 8⅜", luncheon	5.00	9.00
Plate, 9¼", dinner	13.00	25.00
Platter, 11" x 8"	13.00	28.00
Saucer, 5⅜"	1.50	2.50
Sugar	6.50	14.00

Please refer to Foreword for pricing information

FIRE-KING DINNERWARE FLEURETTE and HONEYSUCKLE
ANCHOR HOCKING GLASS CORPORATION, 1958-1960

Color: White w/decal.

Fleurette first appeared in Anchor Hocking's 1959-1960 catalogue printed in April 1958, with Honeysuckle showing up the following year. Both patterns seem to have given way to Primrose by the 1960-1961 catalogue. Both Fleurette and Honeysuckle are in shorter supply than Primrose.

I have enclosed catalogue sheets for Fleurette on pages 73-75 and Honeysuckle on page 72. The photograph below represents all the Honeysuckle I have been able to find in two years. I did see one large set for sale, but I didn't need an eight piece setting to photograph.

Note on page 74 the various sized sets of Fleurette that were available: 16 pc., 19 pc., 35 pc., and 53 pc. On page 75, you can see the actual selling prices of these sets when they were first issued.

There were three sizes of tumblers listed for the Honeysuckle set, but none were listed for Fleurette. If you run into a tumbler of each size, let me know since I need them for photography!

	Fleurette	Honeysuckle		Fleurette	Honeysuckle
Bowl, 4⅝", dessert	2.00	2.00	Platter, 9" x 12"	12.00	12.00
Bowl, 6⅝", soup plate	3.50	5.00	Saucer, 5¾"	.50	.50
Bowl, 8¼", vegetable	9.00	10.00	Sugar	3.00	3.00
Creamer	4.00	4.00	Sugar cover	3.00	3.00
Cup, 5 oz., snack	2.00		Tumbler, 5 oz., juice		5.00
Cup, 8 oz.	3.50	4.00	Tumbler, 9 oz., water		5.00
Plate, 6¼", bread and butter	1.50		Tumbler, 12 oz., iced tea		8.00
Plate, 7⅜", salad	2.50	3.00	Tray, 11"x 6", snack	2.50	
Plate, 9⅛", dinner	3.50	5.00			

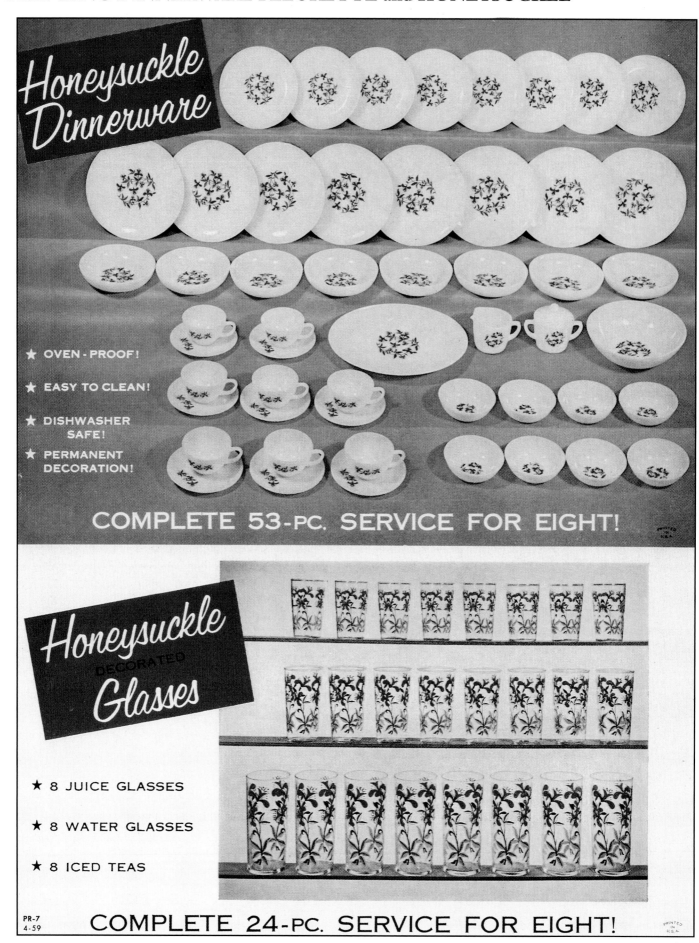

Honeysuckle Dinnerware

★ OVEN - PROOF!

★ EASY TO CLEAN!

★ DISHWASHER SAFE!

★ PERMANENT DECORATION!

COMPLETE 53-PC. SERVICE FOR EIGHT!

Honeysuckle DECORATED Glasses

★ 8 JUICE GLASSES

★ 8 WATER GLASSES

★ 8 ICED TEAS

PR-7
4-59

COMPLETE 24-PC. SERVICE FOR EIGHT!

FLEURETTE® DINNERWARE

W4679/58 — W4629/58

W4674/58

W4637/58 — W4638/58 — W4641/58

PACKING

W4679/58—8 oz. Cup	6 doz. — 25 lbs.
W4629/58—5¾" Saucer	6 doz. — 27 lbs.
W4674/58—4⅝" Dessert	6 doz. — 21 lbs.
W4637/58—6¼" Bread & Butter Plate	3 doz. — 16 lbs.
W4638/58—7⅜" Salad Plate	3 doz. — 23 lbs.
W4641/58—9⅛" Dinner Plate	3 doz. — 39 lbs.

W4667/58

Fleurette
Prepacked Sets
are shown on
Page 3.

W4647/58

W4667/58— 6⅝" Soup Plate	3 doz. — 27 lbs.
W4647/58—12 x 9" Platter	1 doz. — 20 lbs.

W4678/58

See Prepacked
Serva-Snack Set
on Page 3.

W4653/58 — W4654/58

W4678/58—8¼" Vegetable Bowl	1 doz. — 15 lbs.
W4653/58— Sugar & Cover	2 doz. — 16 lbs.
W4654/58— Creamer	2 doz. — 12 lbs.

HEAT-PROOF

FLEURETTE® PREPACKED SETS

W4600/4—16 Pce. Starter Set
Each Set in Gift Display Carton,
4 Sets to Shipping Carton — 37 lbs.
COMPOSITION:
Four W4679/58 Cups
Four W4629/58 Saucers
Four W4674/58 Desserts
Four W4641/58 Dinner Plates

W4600/2—35 Pce. Dinner Set
Each Set in Shipping Carton — 21 lbs.
COMPOSITION:
Six W4679/58 Cups   One W4678/58 Vegetable Bowl
Six W4629/58 Saucers   One W4647/58 Platter
Six W4674/58 Desserts   One W4653/58 Sugar & Cover
Six W4638/58 Salad Plates   One W4654/58 Creamer
Six W4641/58 Dinner Plates

W4600/1—19 Pce. Luncheon Set (Not Illustrated)
Each Set in Gift Carton, 4 Sets to Shipping Carton — 41 lbs.
COMPOSITION:
Four W4679/58 Cups   Four W4641/58 Dinner Plates
Four W4629/58 Saucers   One W4653/58 Sugar & Cover
Four W4674/58 Desserts   One W4654/58 Creamer

W4600/3—53 Pce. Dinner Set (Not Illustrated)
Each Set in Shipping Carton — 32 lbs.
COMPOSITION:
Eight W4679/58 Cups   Eight W4641/58 Dinner Plates
Eight W4629/58 Saucers   One W4678/58 Vegetable Bowl
Eight W4674/58 Desserts   One W4647/58 Platter
Eight W4638/58 Salad Plates One W4653/58 Sugar & Cover
Eight W4667/58 Soup Plates One W4654/58 Creamer

SERVA-SNACK SET

W4600/9—8 Pce. Snack Set
Each Set in Die-Cut Display Carton,
6 Sets to Shipping Carton — 48 lbs.
COMPOSITION:
Four 5 oz. Cups
Four 11 x 6" Rectangular Trays

(See Crystal Serva-Snack Sets on Page 10.)

PROMOTE PREPACKED SETS

HEAT-PROOF

74

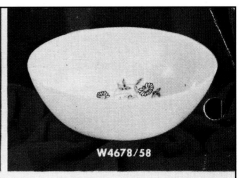

Fleurette

W4674/58

W4678/58

HEAT-PROOF

W4647/58

W4667/58

W4653/58

W4679/58 — W4629/58

W4654/58

Anchorglass ®

OPEN STOCK

	Per Doz. Net Pkd.	Doz. Ctn.	Wt. Ctn.
W4679/58— 8 oz. Cup	$ .90	6	25#
W4629/58— 5¾" Saucer	.90	6	28#
W4674/58— 4⅝" Dessert	.90	6	21#
W4637/58— 6¼" B & B Plate	1.20	3	16#
W4638/58— 7⅜" Salad Plate	1.50	3	23#
W4667/58— 6⅝" Soup Plate	1.60	3	24#
W4641/58— 9⅛" Dinner Plate	1.80	3	39#
W4678/58— 8½" Vegetable Bowl	2.40	1	14#
W4647/58—12 x 9" Platter	3.60	1	20#
W4653/58— Sugar & Cover	1.50	2	11#
W4654/58— Creamer	1.25	2	12#

SETS

W4600/4—16 PCE. STARTER SET $1.55 Set   4 Sets   39#
(Each Set in Gift Display Ctn.)
COMPOSITION: Four each Cups, Saucers, Desserts and Dinner Plates

W4600/1—19 PCE. LUNCHEON SET   1.75 Set   4 Sets   40#
(Each Set in Gift Carton)
COMPOSITION: Four each Cups, Saucers, Desserts and Dinner Plates. One Sugar & Cover and one Creamer.

W4600/2—35 PCE. DINNER SET   3.95 Set   1 Set   21#
(Each Set in Shipping Carton)
COMPOSITION: Six each Cups, Saucers, Desserts, Salad Plates and Dinner Plates. One each Vegetable Bowl, Platter, Sugar & Cover and Creamer.

W4600/3—53 PCE. DINNER SET   6.00 Set   1 Set   32#
(Each Set in Shipping Carton)
COMPOSITION: Eight each Cups, Saucers, Desserts, Salad Plates, Soup Plates and Dinner Plates. One each Vegetable Bowl, Platter, Sugar & Cover and Creamer.

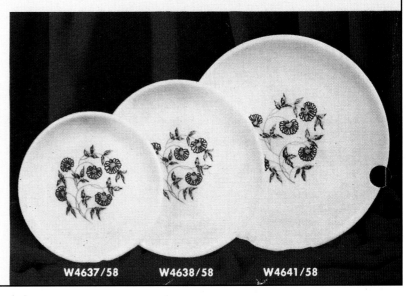
W4637/58   W4638/58   W4641/58

75

FIRE-KING DINNERWARE "GAME BIRD"
ANCHOR HOCKING GLASS CORPORATION, 1959-1962

Color: White w/decal decoration.

Anchor Hocking called these both "Wild Bird" and "Game Bird," but the "Game Bird" seemed more applicable when I was making a name designation for use in the first *Collectible Glassware from the 40's, 50's, 60's*. Since that time, other authors have used the name; so I guess my choice "stimulated" their work.

You will find the following birds on this pattern: Canada Goose, Ringed-Necked Pheasant, Ruffled Grouse and Mallard Duck. I have catalogue sheets of mugs, cereals and ash trays listed for 1960-1961, but as you can see below, there are many more pieces available than those.

After a recent pilgrimage to Oklahoma, I found that this pattern must have "flocked" into southwestern Missouri and Oklahoma. Either through promotional sales or give-aways, this area is inundated with "Game Bird."

The Ringed Neck Pheasant is the only "game" in town if you are looking for serving pieces. No one has notified me of any other "Game Bird" decoration on the sugar, creamer, 8¼" vegetable or platter. It is possible to collect a whole set of Pheasant decorated dinnerware, but no other bird can be collected in a full set as far as I can determine.

Prices on this little pattern have escalated due to the number of collectors searching for these feathered friends. Mugs and tumblers are the most sought items after serving pieces. Unfortunately, there aren't enough of these feathered friends to suit everyone looking for them! One man told me you couldn't beat these mugs for morning coffee!

	White w/decals		White w/decals
Ash tray, 5¼"	8.00	Plate, 7⅜", salad	4.00
Bowl, 4⅝", dessert	4.00	Plate, 9⅛", dinner	6.50
Bowl, 5", soup or cereal	7.50	Platter, 12" x 9"	17.50
Bowl, 8¼", vegetable	18.00	Sugar	8.00
Creamer	8.00	Sugar cover	3.00
Mug, 8 oz.	8.00	Tumbler, 11 oz., iced tea	9.00

Please refer to Foreword for pricing information

Anchorwhite heat-resistant Mugs and Bowls

With authentic game bird decorations

Colorful game bird decorations lend a touch of rustic charm to these practical Anchorwhite mugs and bowls. The mugs are as ideal for in-home use as they are for outdoors. Versatile, too, they're perfect for coffee as well as for cocoa, hot chocolate and milk. The cereal-soup bowls, with their matching decorations, will brighten up any table setting. Both mugs and bowls are heat-resistant and safe to use with hot liquids and foods.

ANCHORGLASS

No.	Size	Item	Doz. Ctn.	Lbs. Ctn.
W1212/5931	8 oz.	Ruffed Grouse Mug	4	27
W1212/5932	8 oz.	Ring-Necked Pheasant Mug	4	27
W1212/5933	8 oz.	Canada Goose Mug	4	27
W1212/5934	8 oz.	Mallard Duck Mug	4	27
W291/5931	5"	Ruffed Grouse Bowl	4	27
W291/5932	5"	Ring-Necked Pheasant Bowl	4	27
W291/5933	5"	Canada Goose Bowl	4	27
W291/5934	5"	Mallard Duck Bowl	4	27

ANCHOR HOCKING GLASS CORPORATION
Lancaster, Ohio, U.S.A.

FIRE-KING DINNERWARE JADE-ITE RESTAURANT WARE
ANCHOR HOCKING GLASS CORPORATION, 1950-1956

Jade-ite collectors are adding to their other Hocking sets with the Restaurant Ware line. Several pieces are in increasingly short supply due to avid gatherings of this line. The smaller platter (9½") is rapidly disappearing. The 5-compartment plate and the oval partitioned plates (already discontinued before 1953) are not being seen as regularly as many collectors would wish. Thankfully, not every collector wants these pieces.

This Restaurant Ware line of Anchor Hocking is being sought also for its adaptability to microwave use. As far as I know, any of these pieces can be used this way. Remember to put the dish in the microwave for just a little time to see if it gets hot as you would test any other dish. "Jane Ray" collectors started the rush on this Jade-ite and now there is not enough of this short-lived pattern to go around.

You can see a catalogue sheet on page 79 to show you the differences in the three sizes of cups and the mug. This mug seems to come in both thick and thin styles.

	Jade-ite		Jade-ite
Bowl, 4¾", fruit G294	5.00	Plate, 8⅞", oval partitioned G211	10.00
Bowl, 8 oz., flanged rim, cereal G305	12.00	Plate, 8", luncheon G316	5.00
Bowl, 10 oz., deep G309	8.00	Plate, 9⅝", 3-compartment G292	6.00
Bowl, 15 oz., deep G300	10.00	Plate, 9⅝", 5-compartment G311	12.00
Cup, 6 oz., straight G215	5.00	Plate, 9¾", oval, sandwich G216	10.00
Cup, 7 oz., extra heavy G299	6.00	Plate, 9", dinner G306	8.00
Cup, 7 oz., narrow rim G319	6.00	Platter, 9½", oval G307	15.00
Mug, coffee, 7 oz. G212	7.00	Platter, 11½", oval G308	12.00
Plate, 5½", bread/butter G315	2.00	Saucer, 6" G295	2.00
Plate, 6¾", pie or salad G297	4.00		

Please refer to Foreword for pricing information

JADE-ITE *Fire-King** RESTAURANT WARE

Reg. U. S. Pat. Off. INEXPENSIVE ● HEAT-RESISTANT ● RUGGED ● STAIN-RESISTANT ● SANITARY ● COLORFUL

A COMPLETE SERVICE FOR MASS FEEDING ESTABLISHMENTS

Cat. No.	Description	Actual Size or Capacity	Std. Pkg.	Weight
G215	Cup (Straight)	6 oz.	4 doz.	35#
G299	Cup (Extra Heavy)	7 oz.	4 doz.	36#
G319	Cup (Narrow Rim)	7 oz.	4 doz.	32#
G295	Saucer	6″	4 doz.	31#
G212	Coffee Mug (Extra Heavy)	7 oz.	4 doz.	48#
G294	Fruit	4 ¾″	6 doz.	30#
G305	Grapefruit—Cereal	8 oz.	4 doz.	37#
G309	Bowl	10 oz.	4 doz.	30#
G300	Bowl	15 oz.	4 doz.	43#
G315	B & B Plate	5 ½″	4 doz.	30#
G297	Pie or Salad Plate	6 ¾″	4 doz.	35#
G316	Luncheon Plate	8″	2 doz.	26#
G306	Dinner Plate	9″	2 doz.	31#
G292	3-Compartment Plate	9 ⅝″	2 doz.	38#
G211	Oval Partitioned Plate	8 ⅞″	2 doz.	23#
G307	Oval Platter	9 ½″	2 doz.	24#
G308	Oval Platter	11 ½″	1 doz.	20#
G311	5-Compartment Plate	9 ⅝″	2 doz.	37#

*REG. U. S. PAT. OFF.

PRINTED IN U.S.A.

ANCHOR HOCKING GLASS CORP.
LANCASTER, OHIO, U. S. A.

FIRE-KING DINNERWARE "JANE RAY"
ANCHOR HOCKING GLASS CORPORATION, 1945-1963

Colors: Ivory, Jade-ite, Peach Lustre, white and white trimmed in gold.

"Jane Ray" is a name that collectors have called this pattern. A 1947 chain store listing of glassware by Anchor Hocking lists this as "Jade-ite Heat Proof Tableware," which is the only real name known. This listing also records the vegetable bowl as 8⅛" instead of 8¼" as listed in later catalogues. I have never seen a variance in these, but there may be.

"Jane Ray" has always been synonymous with Jade-ite. In truth, I had it listed in only Jade-ite in my first book. Notice that there *are* other colors! It is highly likely that a complete set can be found in Ivory. I have seen pieces other than the plate, cup, saucer and dessert bowls shown below. However, I have only found the demitasse cup and saucers in Peach Lustre and white; but there may be other pieces available. Let me know if you find some!

"Jane Ray" is one of the most collected Anchor Hocking patterns from this era. It was listed in catalogues for almost twenty years. As with "Bubble" pattern, there was an abundance of "Jane Ray" made. A Jade-ite set is still possible to attain in this dinnerware, though many collectors are using the Restaurant Ware line to supplement "Jane Ray." Demitasse sets are the most difficult pieces to find with collectors grudgingly giving over thirty dollars for them. Remember that the demitasse saucers are harder to find than the cups. In that regard, these may be the Iris demitasse sets of tomorrow! Platters, vegetable and soup bowls are also becoming scarce for this normally easy to find pattern.

Availability, as with blue "Bubble" and green Block years ago, puts this pattern in front of many new collectors. Prices are climbing, however, due to the ever increasing demand and the dilemma of locating some pieces. If you like this pattern, start collecting now and jump at buying the harder to find pieces when you discover them! You won't be sorry!

	Ivory/White	Jade-ite		Ivory/White	Jade-ite
Bowl, 4⅞", dessert	3.50	4.50	Plate, 7¾", salad	7.00	6.00
Bowl, 5⅞", oatmeal	7.50	7.50	Plate, 9⅛", dinner	9.00	7.50
Bowl, 7⅝", soup plate	10.00	14.00	Platter, 9" x 12"	12.00	12.00
Bowl, 8¼", vegetable	12.00	14.00	Saucer	1.50	1.50
Cup	4.00	3.00	Saucer, demitasse	20.00	25.00
Cup, demitasse	15.00	15.00	Sugar	5.00	4.00
Creamer	7.50	4.50	Sugar cover	2.50	6.00

Please refer to Foreword for pricing information

FIRE-KING DINNERWARE PEACH LUSTRE/GRAY LAUREL

ANCHOR HOCKING GLASS CORPORATION, 1952-1963

"The New Sensation" is how Peach Lustre color/pattern was described in a 1952 catalogue. This "laurel leaf" design was also made as Gray Laurel in 1953. A 1953 catalogue is the only time that Gray Laurel is mentioned in Anchor Hocking records. Gray will undoubtedly turn out to be scarce when compared to the quantity of Peach Lustre ("laurel leaf" design) that was listed continuously until the 1963 catalogue. Page 82 is taken from a 1954 catalogue. From its introduction until its demise in 1963, the name Peach Luster was used for the color and not just the pattern.

The 11" serving plate was discontinued as of 8-25-60. It is the most difficult piece to find especially with good color. That is the major distraction to both of these patterns — the colors wear through. If much used, each of these colors will show white streaks.

Gray Laurel has three sizes of tumblers that were made to go with it. These tumblers are "complementary decorated" with gray and maroon bands. There is a 5 ounce juice, a 9 ounce water and a 13 ounce iced tea. To date, I have not spotted any of these. Have you?

Catalogue numbers are the same for each pattern with Gray Laurel having a "K" prefix and Peach Lustre using an "L" prefix.

Crystal stemware like that shown under Bubble and "Boopie" was also engraved with a "Laurel" cutting to go with these patterns.

	Gray Laurel	Peach Lustre		Gray Laurel	Peach Lustre
Bowl, 4⅞", dessert	4.00	3.00	Plate, 7⅜", salad	4.00	3.00
Bowl, 7⅝", soup plate	6.00	6.00	Plate, 9⅛", dinner	7.50	4.00
Bowl, 8¼", vegetable	10.00	8.50	Plate, 11", serving	14.00	12.00
Creamer, ftd.	4.50	3.50	Saucer, 5¾"	.75	.75
Cup, 8 oz.	4.00	3.50	Sugar, ftd.	4.50	3.50

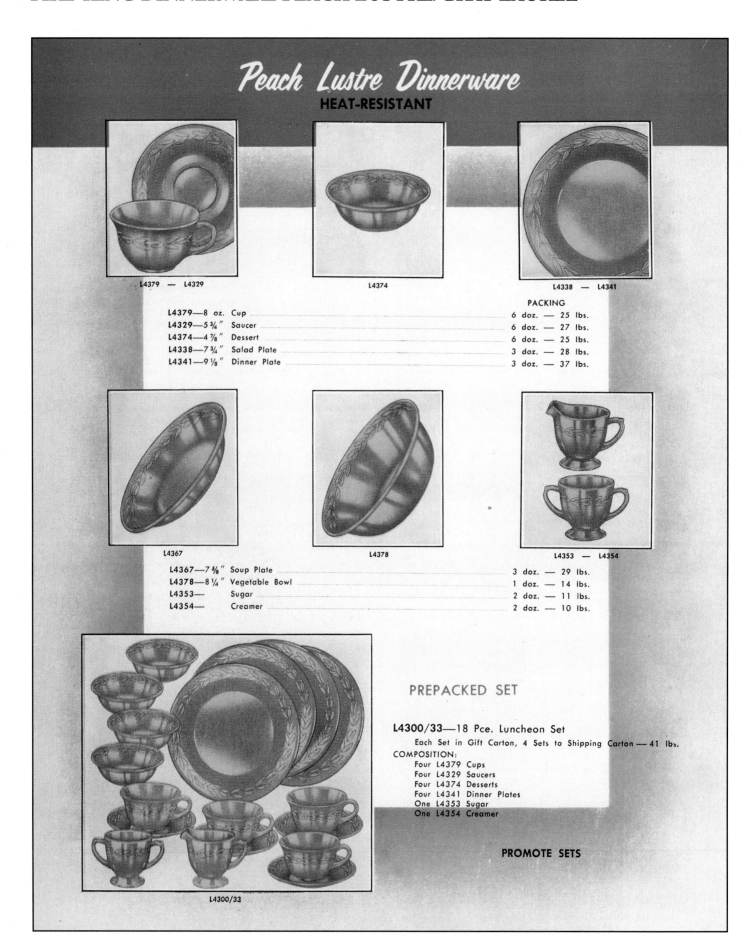

Peach Lustre Dinnerware
HEAT-RESISTANT

L4379 — L4329

L4374

L4338 — L4341

PACKING

L4379—8 oz. Cup	6 doz.	— 25 lbs.
L4329—5 ¾" Saucer	6 doz.	— 27 lbs.
L4374—4 ⅞" Dessert	6 doz.	— 25 lbs.
L4338—7 ¾" Salad Plate	3 doz.	— 28 lbs.
L4341—9 ⅛" Dinner Plate	3 doz.	— 37 lbs.

L4367

L4378

L4353 — L4354

L4367—7 ⅝" Soup Plate	3 doz.	— 29 lbs.
L4378—8 ¼" Vegetable Bowl	1 doz.	— 14 lbs.
L4353— Sugar	2 doz.	— 11 lbs.
L4354— Creamer	2 doz.	— 10 lbs.

PREPACKED SET

L4300/33—18 Pce. Luncheon Set
Each Set in Gift Carton, 4 Sets to Shipping Carton — 41 lbs.
COMPOSITION:
Four L4379 Cups
Four L4329 Saucers
Four L4374 Desserts
Four L4341 Dinner Plates
One L4353 Sugar
One L4354 Creamer

PROMOTE SETS

L4300/33

FIRE-KING DINNERWARE & OVENWARE PRIMROSE

ANCHOR HOCKING GLASS CORPORATION, 1960-1962

Primrose was the pattern that Anchor Hocking used to bridge the gap between dinnerware and ovenware usage. Primrose was made for both with pieces designed for either job. Although many of Anchor Hocking's lines were issued as dinnerware, they are marked ovenware on the bottom to let customers know that they were "heat-proof" and could be "pre-warmed" in the oven.

Recently, in southern Illinois, I found two sets of Primrose that had white tumblers instead of the crystal ones shown here from the boxed set. I offered almost as much for the tumblers as the dealer was asking for the sets, but I had to buy the complete sets to get her to part with the tumblers. Until then, I thought only the "Game Bird" tumblers could be found in white. These tumblers will fetch a minimum price of twice that found in crystal Primrose. Tumblers in either style are the most difficult pieces to find in this pattern.

Primrose seems to be the pattern that Hocking tried to thrust on the public more than they did Fleurette and Honeysuckle; but Primrose may not have been as successful as many earlier Fire-King patterns. It was only listed in the 1960-1961 and 1961-1962 catalogues. From the availability I see in the ovenware line, it might be scarce — or, as with the blue Fire-King ovenware, many housewives may still be using it instead of parting with it to buy newer wares.

All casserole covers are clear crystal Fire-King. All pieces of ovenware were guaranteed against oven breakage for two years. Dealers would exchange a new item for the broken pieces. The one quart casserole, baking pan and oval casserole were all sold with a brass finished candle warmer and candle. I have received numerous letters saying that those brass holders are still working as they were intended!

The deep loaf pan was sold as a baking pan by adding a crystal glass cover. All the crystal glass lids are harder to find than their respective bottoms. Lids always did have a tendency to be dropped — or overlooked at sales.

White w/decal		White w/decal		White w/decal	
Bowl, 4⅝", dessert	2.25	Casserole, 2 qt., knob cover	12.50	Plate, 7⅜", salad	2.50
Bowl, 6⅝", soup plate	6.00	Creamer	4.00	Plate, 9⅛", dinner	5.00
Bowl, 8¼", vegetable	8.00	Cup, 5 oz., snack	2.50	Platter, 9" x 12"	12.00
Cake pan, 8", round	9.00	Cup, 8 oz.	3.00	Saucer, 5¾"	1.00
Cake pan, 8", square	9.00	Custard, 6 oz., low or dessert	3.00	Sugar	3.50
Casserole, pt., knob cover	6.50	Pan, 5" x 9", baking, w/cover	13.00	Sugar cover	3.00
Casserole, ½ qt., oval,		Pan, 5" x 9", deep loaf	12.00	Tray, 11" x 6", rectangular, snack	4.00
au gratin cover	14.00	Pan, 6½" x 10½", utility baking	9.00	*Tumbler, 5 oz., juice (crystal)	5.00
Casserole, 1 qt., knob cover	10.00	Pan, 8" x 12½", utility baking	12.50	*Tumbler, 9 oz., water (crystal)	5.50
Casserole, 1½ qt., knob cover	10.00	Plate, 6¼", bread and butter	1.50	*Tumbler, 13 oz., iced tea (crystal)	6.50

*Double price for white

New Primrose Anchorglass Ovenware

Number	Size	Item	Doz. Ctn.	Lbs. Ctn.
W424/62	6 Oz.	Dessert	4	15
W405/62	1 Pt.	Casserole, Cover	1	16
W406/62	1 Qt.	Casserole, Cover	½	14
W407/62	1½ Qt.	Casserole, Cover	½	19
W467/62	1½ Qt.	Oval Casserole, Au Gratin Cover	½	19
W408/62	2 Qt.	Casserole, Cover	½	21
W450/62	8″	Round Cake Pan	½	12
W452/62	8″	Square Cake Pan	½	17
W409/62	5″ x 9″	Deep Loaf Pan	½	11
W410/62	6½″ x 10½″	Utility Baking Pan	½	15
W411/62	8″ x 12½″	Utility Baking Pan	½	23
W469/62	5″ x 9″	Baking Pan and Cover	½	21
W400/245*		8 Pc. Set	4 Sets	34
W400/246**		11 Pc. Set	4 Sets	53

*Composition: One each 1 qt. Casserole, Cover, 10½″ Utility Baking Pan, 8″ Round Cake Pan; four 6 oz. Desserts, Gift Ctn.

**Composition: One each 1½ qt. Casserole, Cover, 5″ x 9″ Deep Loaf Pan, 8″ x 12½″ Utility Baking Pan, 8″ Square Cake Pan; six 6 oz. Desserts, Gift Ctn.

FIRE-KING OVEN GLASS ANCHOR HOCKING GLASS CORPORATION, 1942-1950'S

Colors: Sapphire blue, crystal; some Ivory and Jade-ite.

Fire-King is one of the most easily recognized patterns in this book! Nearly every family still has a piece or two! It was the ovenware that was recognized for its durability. Fire-King had a two year guarantee. All you had to do was take the broken pieces to your local dealer and your piece was replaced at no charge.

Fire-King is grand for standard ovens, but it tends to develop heat cracks from sudden temperature changes when used in the microwave. We learned that the hard way!

Collectors prefer the casseroles with pie plate covers to those with knobbed covers. The 8 oz. nurser is not as available as the 4 oz.

The skillet and nipple cover on page 87 are shown compliments of Anchor-Hocking's photographer. The skillets are still in hiding, but a few nipple covers have surfaced. These blue covers are embossed "BINKY'S NIP CAP U.S.A." (and not Fire-King). The boxed display set on page 88 was found in a Rhode Island consignment shop for $2.00. Unfortunately, not by me! Bargains still exist!

The dry cup measure has ounce measurements up the side and no spout for pouring. Without these measurements on the side, it is the normally found mug! These mugs come in two styles — thick and thin. Speaking of different styles, the 6 oz. custard cup can be found in three different styles.

The reason that juice saver pie plate is so high in price comes from the fact that most were heavily used. Many are deeply marred. To obtain the price below, this pie plate has to be mint!

The prices with asterisks under Ivory listing are for Jade-ite items with the Fire-King embossing. All the Ivory is plain with no design. You will find plain Ivory and Jade-ite mugs, but they hold eight oz. and not seven. The Jade-ite mug with the embossed Fire-King pattern is rare!

All listings below are from Anchor Hocking's Catalogue "L" with some additional catalogue items shown on page 89.

There are two styles of table servers being found; and you can find a casserole lid on a Bersted Mfg. Co. popcorn popper. One of these can be seen in my book on *Kitchen Glassware of the Depression Era*.

	Ivory	Sapphire		Ivory	Sapphire
Baker, 1 pt., 4½" x 5"		5.50	Loaf pan, 9⅛" x 5⅛", deep	13.50	20.00
Baker, 1 pt., round	4.00	5.00	Mug, coffee, 7 oz., 2 styles	*27.50	23.00
Baker, 1 qt., round	6.00	7.00	Nipple cover		175.00
Baker, 1½ qt., round	6.00	12.00	Nurser, 4 oz.		16.00
Baker, 2 qt., round	8.50	12.50	Nurser, 8 oz.		27.50
Baker, 6 oz., individual	3.00	5.00	Percolator top, 2⅛"		5.00
Bowl, 4⅜", individual pie plate		14.00	Pie plate, 8⅜", 1½" deep		7.50
Bowl, 5⅜", cereal or deep dish pie plate	6.50	15.00	Pie plate, 9⅝", 1½" deep		9.50
Bowl, measuring, 16 oz.		23.00	Pie plate, 9", 1½" deep	7.00	8.50
Cake pan (deep), 8¾" (½ roaster)		22.50	Pie plate, 10⅜", juice saver	*75.00	100.00
Cake pan, 9"	13.00		Refrigerator jar & cover, 4½" x 5"	**9.00	11.00
Casserole, 1 pt., knob handle cover	8.50	12.00	Refrigerator jar & cover, 5⅛" x 9⅛"	**18.00	32.50
Casserole, 1 qt., knob handle cover	10.00	12.50	Roaster, 8¾"		50.00
Casserole, 1 qt., pie plate cover		16.00	Roaster, 10⅜"		75.00
Casserole, 1½ qt., knob handle cover	12.00	13.00	Table server, tab handles (hot plate)	10.00	16.00
Casserole, 1½ qt., pie plate cover		17.00	Utility bowl, 6⅞", 1 qt.		12.00
Casserole, 2 qt., knob handle cover	13.50	20.00	Utility bowl, 8⅜", 1½ qt.		16.00
Casserole, 2 qt., pie plate cover		25.00	Utility bowl, 10⅛"		18.00
Casserole, individual, 10 oz.		13.00	Utility pan, 8⅛" x 12½", 2 qt.		35.00
Cup, 8 oz. measuring, 1 spout		17.00	Utility pan, 10½" x 2" deep	12.50	22.50
Cup, 8 oz., dry measure, no spout		195.00			
Cup, 8 oz., measuring, 3 spout		20.00	*Jade-ite w/embossed design		
Custard cup or baker, 5 oz.	3.00	3.25	**Jade-ite		
Custard cup or baker, 6 oz.	3.25	4.00			

Please refer to Foreword for pricing information

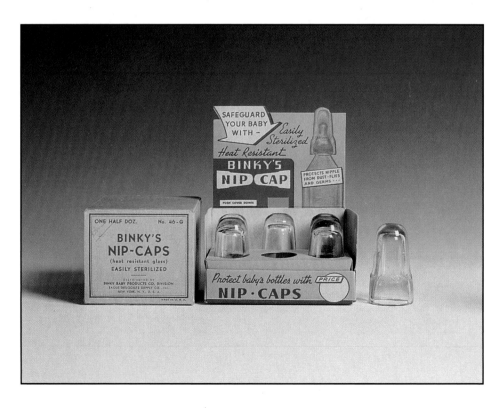

FIRE - KING OVEN GLASS

Housewives prefer to cook in glass for they are then able to actually see their foods cooking, eliminating the possibility of improperly cooked foods. Glass is also more easily cleaned than metal utensils, saving time and labor.

A three-fold purpose—bake, serve, and store in the same dish. Fire-King oven glass is not only suitable for oven cooking but makes ideal serving dishes for the table and in addition is safe and practical for refrigerator use.

Not only does Fire-King possess unusual cooking qualities but it is attractive, a complement to any table, and above all—the lowest priced oven glass on the market.

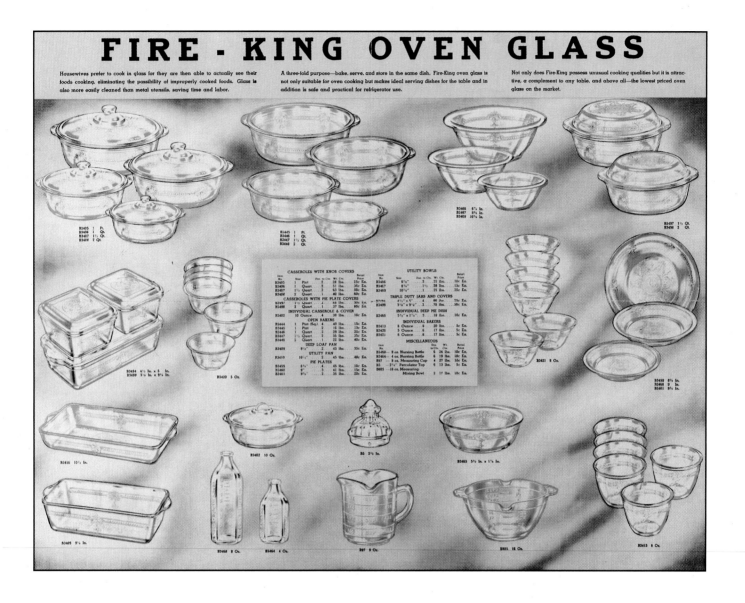

FIRE-KING OVEN WARE, TURQUOISE BLUE
ANCHOR HOCKING GLASS CORPORATION, 1957-1958

Color: Turquoise Blue.

Turquoise Blue was advertised as dinnerware, but all pieces are marked ovenware except for the egg plate. Most of Anchor Hocking's other dinnerware is also marked ovenware. This let the customer know that the glassware could be pre-warmed in the oven before serving. Turquoise Blue has become as popular a pattern as the Fire-King Sapphire blue oven glass.

When you use a pattern for five years as we did this one, various observations about buying or using it come to mind. The 10" serving plates are rarely found and not available in quantity. As far as I am concerned, it is an ideal size for a dinner plate! (The normal 9" dinner with its upturned edges did not hold enough for my boys!) Soup and cereal bowls are not commonly found and are probably under priced in today's market. My teenagers always used the 8" vegetable bowl for soup or cereal; so, we were always searching for them. Even though Marc is now 22 and in college, those are his favorite bowls! He joyfully garnered a couple more for Christmas this year. He ought to have a service for eight in that bowl by now.

The batter bowl was never shown in catalogues. There have been few of these reported and big prices are being asked. I do not believe Anchor Hocking only made eight of these as one dealer tried to tell his customer. Nobody knows how many pieces of a particular piece of glass were made!

The 5¾" ash tray was discontinued before the 1957-58 catalogue was out of print. It should be rarer than the smaller ones, ash tray collectors. There were special promotions of the three-part relish, egg plate and the snack sets with 22K gold decorations. Do not put these gold edged pieces in the microwave because the gold causes sparks. All other pieces worked well in our microwave. The 10" will warm a complete dinner (or snack for a teenager)!

Cups, saucers, 9" dinner plates, creamer and sugar are easily found. Mugs are the next easiest pieces to accumulate. The 6⅛" and 7" plates are not quite as hard to find as the 10" plates, but they are both uncommon.

The 6⅛" plates may be as rare as the 10". Since most collectors only buy one 10" plate and six, eight or twelve of the smaller ones, there are not as many of the smaller ones to go around. Numerous collectors have told me they have never seen either one! Although the 9" plate with cup indent is not as plentiful as the dinner plate, it does not command the price of the dinner since not every buyer wants to own snack sets… yet! The 1 qt. round mixing bowl and the 3 qt. tear shaped mixing bowls are the most difficult sizes to find in these bowl sets. However, the 1 qt. tear shaped bowl is always the first to sell at shows. Many people want these to use as small serving dishes.

	Blue		Blue
Ash tray, 3½"	6.50	Bowl, round, mixing, 3 qt.	14.00
Ash tray, 4⅝"	9.00	Bowl, round, mixing, 4 qt.	16.00
Ash tray, 5¾"	13.00	Creamer	6.00
Batter bowl, w/spout	200.00	Cup	4.00
Bowl, 4½", berry	6.00	Egg plate, 9¾"	15.00
Bowl, 5", cereal	12.50	Mug, 8 oz.	10.00
Bowl, 6⅝", soup/salad	15.00	Plate, 6⅛"	12.00
Bowl, 8", vegetable	15.00	Plate, 7"	11.00
Bowl, tear, mixing, 1 pt.	12.00	Plate, 9"	7.00
Bowl, tear, mixing, 1 qt.	17.00	Plate, 9", w/cup indent	6.00
Bowl, tear, mixing, 2 qt.	20.00	Plate, 10"	27.50
Bowl, tear, mixing, 3 qt.	22.00	Relish, 3 part, 11⅛"	12.00
Bowl, round, mixing, 1 qt.	12.00	Saucer	1.00
Bowl, round, mixing, 2 qt.	10.00	Sugar	6.00

Please refer to Foreword for pricing information

TURQUOISE-BLUE TABLEWARE — HEAT-PROOF

B4079 — B4029

B4074

B4037 — B4038 — B4041 — B4046

PACKING

B4079—	8 oz. Cup		6 doz. —	24 lbs.
B4029—	5¾″ Saucer		6 doz. —	32 lbs.
B4074—	4⅝″ Dessert		6 doz. —	23 lbs.
B4037—	6¼″ Bread & Butter Plate		3 doz. —	18 lbs.
B4038—	7¼″ Salad Plate		3 doz. —	23 lbs.
B4041—	9″ Dinner Plate		3 doz. —	42 lbs.
B4046—	10″ Serving Plate		1 doz. —	18 lbs.

See Mixing Bowls on Page 27, Mug and Bowl on Page 23 and Ash Trays on Page 41.

B4067

B4078

B4053 — B4054

B4067—	6⅝″ Soup Plate		3 doz. —	26 lbs.
B4078—	8¼″ Vegetable Bowl		1 doz. —	17 lbs.
B4053—	Sugar		2 doz. —	11 lbs.
B4054—	Creamer		2 doz. —	11 lbs.

B4000/18

PREPACKED SETS

B4000/18—12 Pce. Starter Set
Each Set in Display Style Carton, 6 Sets to Shipper — 48 lbs.
COMPOSITION: Four Each B4079 Cups, B4029 Saucers and B4041 Dinner Plates

B4000/19—18 Pce. Luncheon Set
Each Set in Gift Carton, 4 Sets to Shipper — 40 lbs.
COMPOSITION: Four Each B4079 Cups, B4029 Saucers, B4074 Desserts, and B4041 Dinner Plates; One Each B4053 Sugar and B4054 Creamer

B4000/21—34 Pce. Dinner Set
Each Set in Shipping Carton — 20 lbs.
COMPOSITION: Six Each B4079 Cups, B4029 Saucers, B4074 Desserts, B4038 Salad Plates and B4041 Dinner Plates; One Each B4078 Vegetable Bowl, B4046 Serving Plate, B4053 Sugar and B4054 Creamer

B4000/22—52 Pce. Dinner Set
Each Set in Shipping Carton — 32 lbs.
COMPOSITION: Eight Each B4079 Cups, B4029 Saucers, B4074 Desserts, B4038 Salad Plates, B4067 Soup Plates and B4041 Dinner Plates; One Each B4078 Vegetable Bowl, B4046 Serving Plate, B4053 Sugar and B4054 Creamer

FIRE-KING OVEN WARE, "SWIRL"
ANCHOR HOCKING GLASS CORPORATION, 1950's

Colors: Azur-ite, Ivory, Ivory trimmed in gold or red, white or white trimmed in gold, and Pink.

Repeating from the last edition, I looked at the many "swirled" patterns that Anchor Hocking made starting with 1950, and spent a whole day trying to find a way to organize them into some sequence of order that made a little sense. Initially, colors determined name and not pattern which has been a major problem with Anchor Hocking. There were also two distinct swirled patterns and even a change in sugar styles. Finally, I came up with the following for this book: Swirls of the 1950's and Swirls of the 1960's.

The first "Swirl," introduced in 1950, was Azur-ite which is the light blue shown on top of page 95; that was followed by Sunrise (red trimmed, shown on bottom of page 95). In 1953 Ivory White was introduced; but in the mid 1950's, this became known as Anchorwhite. If you find a flat white sugar or creamer, it is Ivory White; but finding a footed creamer or sugar means it is Anchorwhite. Golden Anniversary was introduced in 1955 by adding 22K gold trim to Ivory White; and Pink was not introduced until 1956.

Note the footed sugar and creamer in pink on the bottom of page 95. These do not have the typical white exteriors normally found on the bottoms of this pattern. Tumblers were made to go with only the pink as far as I can find out. The tumbler pictured is from an original boxed set.

	Anchorwhite Ivory White	Golden Anniversary	Azur-ite/Pink Sunrise
Bowl, 4⅞", fruit or dessert	2.50	2.75	4.00
Bowl, 7¼", vegetable			12.00
Bowl, 7⅝", soup plate	2.75	3.00	8.00
Bowl, 8¼", vegetable	5.00	5.00	14.00
Creamer, flat	3.50		7.00
Creamer, ftd.	2.75	3.25	
Cup, 8 oz.	2.75	3.00	5.00
Plate, 7⅜", salad	2.50	2.50	4.00
Plate, 9⅛", dinner	3.00	4.00	6.50
Plate, 11", serving			15.00
Platter, 12" x 9"	6.00	6.50	15.00
Saucer, 5¾"	.50	.50	1.00
Sugar lid, for flat sugar	2.50		5.00
Sugar lid, for ftd. sugar	2.50		
Sugar, flat, tab handles	3.50		6.00
Sugar, ftd., open handles	3.00	3.50	
Tumbler, 5 oz., juice			4.50
Tumbler, 9 oz., water			6.00
Tumbler, 12 oz., iced tea			6.50

GOLDEN ANNIVERSARY DINNERWARE

W4100/57

W4100/57—18 Pce. Luncheon Set
Each Set in Gift Carton, 4 Sets to Shipping Carton — 41 lbs.
COMPOSITION:
Four W4179/50 Cups	Four W4141/50 Dinner Plates
Four W4129/50 Saucers	One W4153/50 Sugar
Four W4174/50 Desserts	One W4154/50 Creamer

W4100/58—34 Pce. Dinner Set (Not illustrated)
Each Set in Shipping Carton — 23 lbs.
COMPOSITION:
Six W4179/50 Cups	One W4178/50 Vegetable Bowl
Six W4129/50 Saucers	One W4147/50 Platter
Six W4174/50 Desserts	One W4153/50 Sugar
Six W4138/50 Salad Plates	One W4154/50 Creamer
Six W4141/50 Dinner Plates	

W4100/59—52 Pce. Dinner Set (Not illustrated)
Each Set in Shipping Carton — 35 lbs.
COMPOSITION:
Eight W4179/50 Cups	Eight W4141/50 Dinner Plates
Eight W4129/50 Saucers	One W4178/50 Vegetable Bowl
Eight W4174/50 Desserts	One W4147/50 Platter
Eight W4138/50 Salad Plates	One W4153/50 Sugar
Eight W4167/50 Soup Plates	One W4154/50 Creamer

OPEN STOCK

W4179/50 — W4129/50   W4174/50   W4138/50 — W4141/50   W4167/50

PACKING

W4179/50—	Cup	6 doz. —	26 lbs.
W4129/50—	Saucer	6 doz. —	28 lbs.
W4174/50—4 7/8"	Dessert	6 doz. —	24 lbs.
W4138/50—7 3/4"	Salad Plate	3 doz. —	26 lbs.
W4141/50—9 1/8"	Dinner Plate	3 doz. —	40 lbs.
W4167/50—7 5/8"	Soup Plate	3 doz. —	29 lbs.

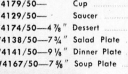

W4178/50   W4147/50   W4153/50 — W4154/50

W4178/50— 8 1/4"	Vegetable Bowl	1 doz. —	15 lbs.
W4147/50—12 x 9"	Platter	1 doz. —	21 lbs.
W4153/50—	Sugar	2 doz. —	10 lbs.
W4154/50—	Creamer	2 doz. —	10 lbs.

HEAT-PROOF   **ANCHORWHITE — 22 K. GOLD TRIMMED**

PINK Anchorglass® DINNERWARE

M4179 — M4129

M4174

M4138 — M4141 — M4146

M4167

		PACKING
M4179— 8 oz. Cup		6 doz. — 25 lbs.
M4129— 5¾" Saucer		6 doz. — 32 lbs.
M4174— 4⅞" Dessert		6 doz. — 25 lbs.
M4138— 7¾" Salad Plate		3 doz. — 27 lbs.
M4141— 9⅛" Dinner Plate		3 doz. — 38 lbs.
M4146—11" Serving Plate		1 doz. — 20 lbs.
M4167— 7⅝" Soup Plate		3 doz. — 29 lbs.

DESIGNED FOR BEAUTY — PRICED FOR EVERYDAY VOLUME SALES.

M4177 — M4178

M4143 — M4144

M4177—7¼" Vegetable Bowl		1 doz. — 11 lbs.
M4178—8¼" Vegetable Bowl		1 doz. — 15 lbs.
M4143— Sugar & Cover		2 doz. — 11 lbs.
M4144— Creamer		2 doz. — 12 lbs.

Each Piece comes with a beautiful Pink, Black and Gold
label reading "PINK HEAT-PROOF ANCHORGLASS."

See Listing of Prepacked Sets on Page 2.

— HEAT-PROOF —

FIRE-KING OVEN WARE, "SWIRL"
ANCHOR HOCKING GLASS CORPORATION, 1960's-1975

Colors: White, white trimmed in gold, Jade-ite, and iridized Lustre.

Anchorwhite "Swirl" continued to be made into the early 1960's. In 1963, Hocking changed the "Swirl" design by making the edge more predominately scalloped. This new design with the 22K gold edge was called Golden Shell and it was made into the late 1970's. Pages 98 and 99 show catalogue pages of this new design. Note the taller, footed creamer and sugar in this line.

You can see the major differences in Golden Anniversary (page 94) and Golden Shell (page 99) by studying these catalogue reprints. These two patterns do not blend as well as other analogous patterns since the serving pieces are decidedly more scalloped on the Golden Shell's serving pieces. The cups, creamers and sugars are also shaped so they do not mate well.

Using this new "Swirl" design, Anchor Hocking introduced a Jade-ite set in 1964. The catalogue called it an "English Regency style." You can see an example of this pattern on the bottom of page 102. To continue Hocking's confusing ways of not naming patterns, this pattern's name was only Jade-ite. It was shown in catalogues until 1972.

In 1966, Lustre Shell was introduced and manufactured until the late 1970's. This iridized color was the same used for Peach Lustre, introduced in 1952. Since Peach Lustre was discontinued in 1963, someone at Hocking must have missed spraying on that color. Of course, marketing gurus may have decided the public needed an iridized color again. This Lustre wears off easily; so look for pieces that were used sparingly.

The soup bowl was sized upward from 6⅜" to 7⅝" with the reintroduction of this color. Lustre was Anchor Hocking's name for the color and shell was the design. Now why didn't they add shell to the Jade-ite and solve our name problems thirty years later? Jade-ite Shell should have been the name!

A demitasse cup and saucer were introduced to the Lustre shell line in 1972. As with other Fire-King patterns, the demitasse saucers are harder to find than the cups.

On page 100 and 101 are two photographs of "Swirl" with hand painted scenes. I thought the glass was priced right for what it was and the few pieces of hand painted Pyrex in with the Anchor Hocking didn't deter me from buying it. No one has contacted me about having any information on the J. Kinney who painted this ware.

	Golden Shell	Jade-ite "Shell"	Lustre Shell
Bowl, 4¾", dessert	1.75	3.00	3.00
Bowl, 6⅜", cereal	2.50	4.00	4.50
Bowl, 7⅝", soup plate	5.00	6.50	5.00
Bowl, 6⅜", soup	4.00	5.00	
Bowl, 8½", vegetable	5.50	7.50	8.00
Creamer, ftd.	3.50	5.50	5.50
Cup, 8 oz.	3.25	4.00	4.00
Cup, 3¼ oz., demitasse			7.00
Saucer, 4¾", demitasse			5.50
Plate, 7¼", salad	2.50	2.75	3.50
Plate, 10", dinner	4.00	6.00	7.00
Plate, 11", serving			10.00
Platter, 9½" x 13"	8.00	13.00	
Saucer, 5¾"	.50	.50	.50
Sugar, ftd.	2.75	6.00	6.00
Sugar cover	4.00	4.00	4.00

FIRE-KING OVEN WARE, "SWIRL"

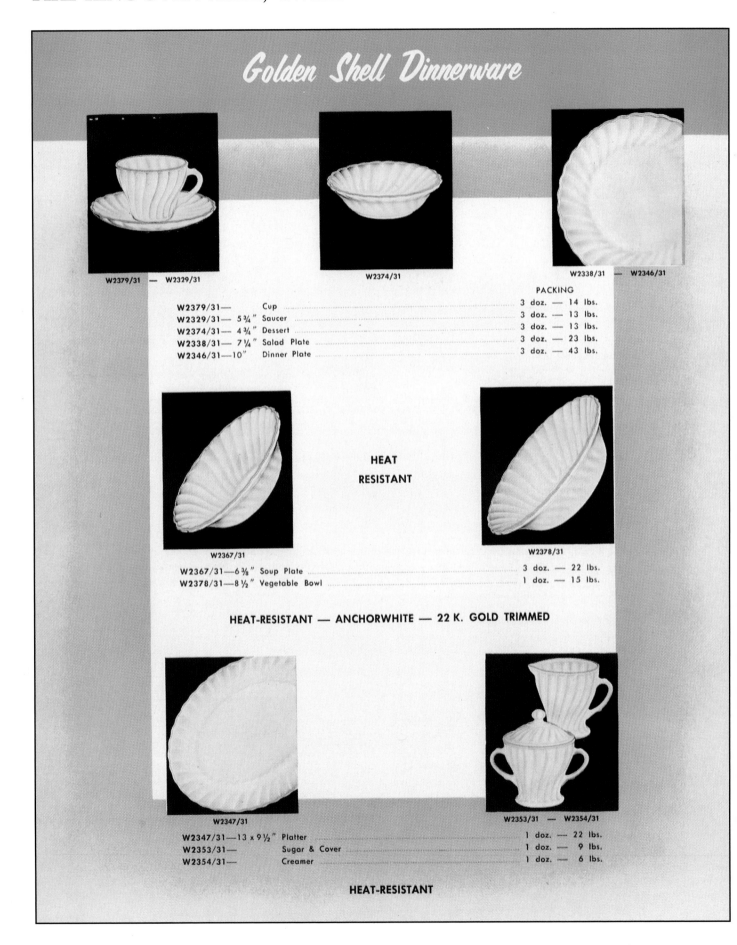

Golden Shell Dinnerware

W2379/31 — W2329/31   W2374/31   W2338/31 — W2346/31

		PACKING
W2379/31—	Cup	3 doz. — 14 lbs.
W2329/31— 5¾"	Saucer	3 doz. — 13 lbs.
W2374/31— 4¾"	Dessert	3 doz. — 13 lbs.
W2338/31— 7¼"	Salad Plate	3 doz. — 23 lbs.
W2346/31—10"	Dinner Plate	3 doz. — 43 lbs.

HEAT
RESISTANT

W2367/31   W2378/31

W2367/31—6⅜"	Soup Plate	3 doz. — 22 lbs.
W2378/31—8½"	Vegetable Bowl	1 doz. — 15 lbs.

HEAT-RESISTANT — ANCHORWHITE — 22 K. GOLD TRIMMED

W2347/31   W2353/31 — W2354/31

W2347/31—13 x 9½"	Platter	1 doz. — 22 lbs.
W2353/31—	Sugar & Cover	1 doz. — 9 lbs.
W2354/31—	Creamer	1 doz. — 6 lbs.

HEAT-RESISTANT

98

Golden Shell Dinnerware Sets

16-PIECE
STARTER
SET
GIFT-BOXED

ANCHORWHITE
EDGED
WITH 22 K.
GOLD

W2300/1—16 Pce. Starter Set

Each Set in Gift Display Box, 4 Sets to Shipping Carton — 38 lbs.

COMPOSITION:
Four W2379/31 Cups
Four W2329/31 Saucers
Four W2374/31 Desserts
Four W2346/31 Dinner Plates

HEAT-RESISTANT

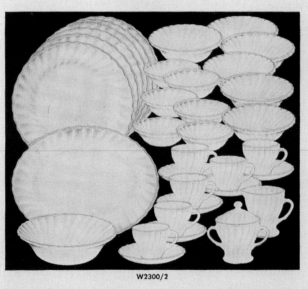

W2300/2

35-PIECE
SET
WITH 22 K. GOLD

53-PIECE
SET LISTED
BELOW

W2300/2—35 Pce. Dinner Set

Each Set in Shipping Carton — 23 lbs.

COMPOSITION:
Six   W2379/31 Cups
Six   W2329/31 Saucers
Six   W2374/31 Desserts
Six   W2367/31 Soups
Six   W2346/31 Dinner Plates
One   W2378/31 Vegetable Bowl
One   W2347/31 Platter
One   W2353/31 Sugar & Cover
One   W2354/31 Creamer

W2300/3—53 Pce. Dinner Set

Each Set in Shipping Carton — 33 lbs.

COMPOSITION:
Eight W2379/31 Cups
Eight W2329/31 Saucers
Eight W2374/31 Desserts
Eight W2338/31 Salad Plates
Eight W2367/31 Soups
Eight W2346/31 Dinner Plates
One   W2378/31 Vegetable Bowl
One   W2347/31 Platter
One   W2353/31 Sugar & Cover
One   W2354/31 Creamer

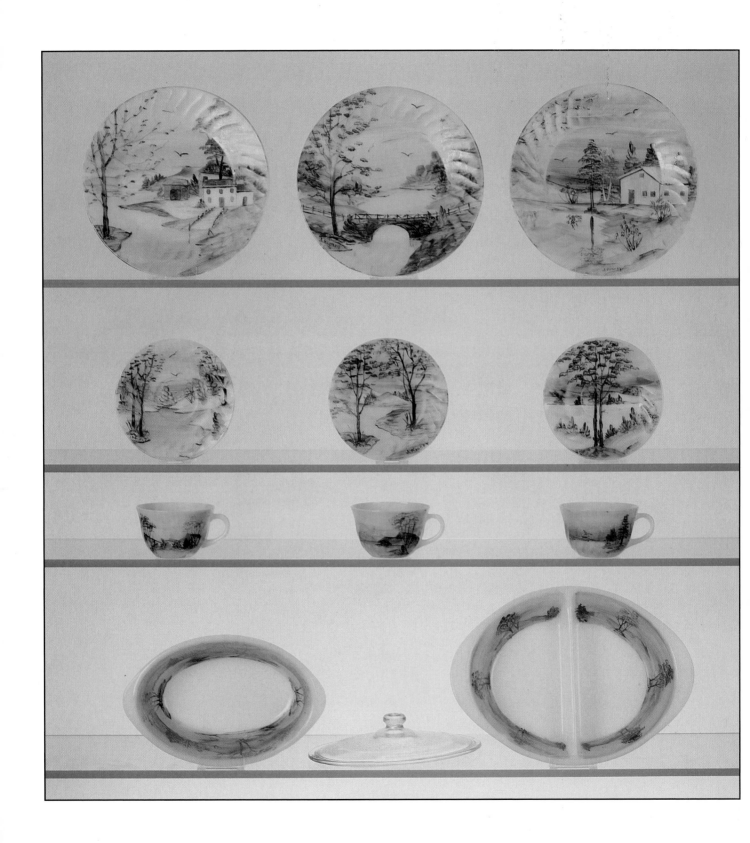

FIRE-KING OVEN WARE, "SWIRL"

FIRE-KING OVEN WARE, WHEAT & BLUE MOSAIC
ANCHOR HOCKING GLASS CORPORATION, 1962-late 1960's

I have been able to find a few pieces of Blue Mosaic in Florida as I travel. For those who wrote me about the sugar and creamer not being shown, I should point out that they are solid blue as is the cup shown. They do not have Mosaic pattern. The snack tray in this pattern is oval and not rectangular as are most of Fire-King patterns. The same blue cup accompanies the snack tray as is shown on a saucer in the photograph. No designed cups were made as far as I can determine. This short lived Anchor Hocking pattern was shown only in a 1967 catalogue.

Production of wheat began in 1962 and was one of Anchor Hocking's most productive lines of the 1960's. Like Sapphire blue Fire-King in the 1940's, everyone has seen the Wheat pattern of the 1960's!

Both the oval and round 1½ quart casseroles and the 10½" baking pan were used with candle warmers. These candle warmers were brass finished with walnut handles and candle. A few of these warmers have been seen with prices in the $4.00 to $5.00 range. Most of these were never used as they are being found with the candles intact! I had a couple of letters stating that these warmers worked very well and that replacement candles can be found at most kitchenware stores.

	Wheat	Blue Mosaic		Wheat	Blue Mosaic
Bowl, 4⅝", dessert	2.50	3.50	Cup, 8 oz.	3.00	
Bowl, 6⅝", soup plate	4.50	5.50	Custard, 6 oz., low or dessert	2.50	
Bowl, 8¼", vegetable	6.00	12.00	Pan, 5" x 9", baking, w/cover	14.00	
Cake pan, 8", round	9.00		Pan, 5" x 9", deep loaf	8.00	
Cake pan, 8", square	9.00		Pan, 6½" x 10½" x 1½",		
Casserole, 1 pt., knob cover	5.00		utility baking	10.00	
Casserole, 1 qt., knob cover	7.50		Pan, 8" x 12½" x 2",		
Casserole, 1½ qt., knob cover	9.50		utility baking	12.00	
Casserole, 1½ qt., oval,			Plate, 7⅜", salad	2.50	4.00
au gratin cover	12.50		Plate, 10", dinner	4.00	6.00
Casserole, 2 qt., knob cover	12.50		Platter, 9" x 12"	10.00	16.00
Casserole, 2 qt., round,			Saucer, 5¾"	1.00	1.50
au gratin cover	14.00		Sugar	3.00	6.00
Creamer	4.00	6.00	Sugar cover	3.50	3.50
Cup, 5 oz., snack	3.00		Tray, 11" x 6", rectangular, snack	3.50	
Cup, 7½ oz.		4.50	Tray, 10" x 7½", oval, snack		3.50

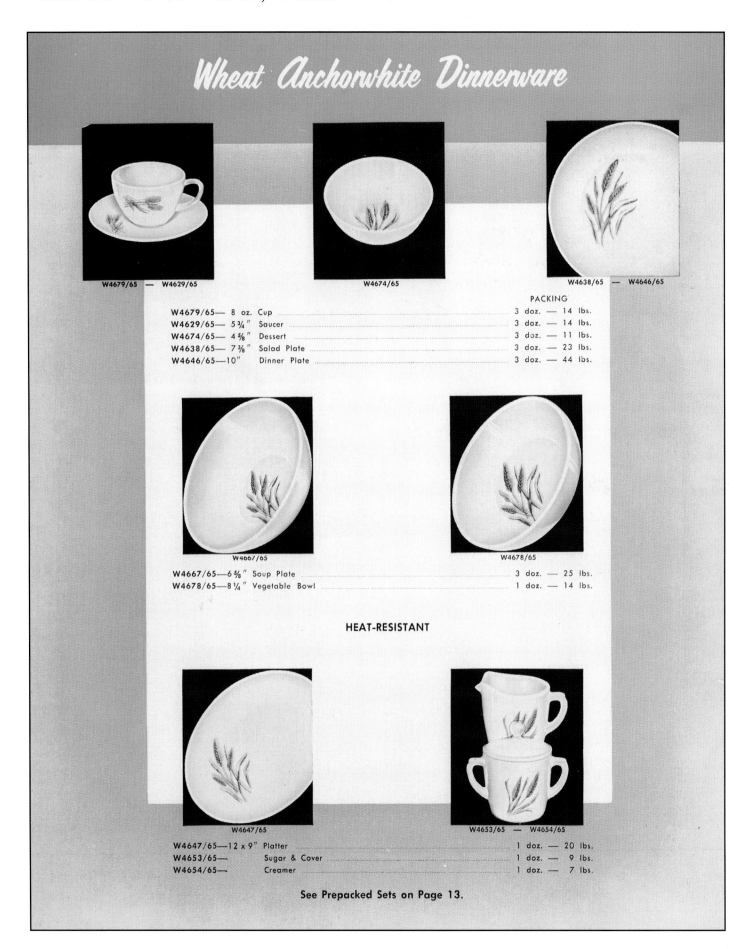

Wheat Anchorwhite Dinnerware

W4679/65 — W4629/65

W4674/65

W4638/65 — W4646/65

				PACKING
W4679/65—	8 oz.	Cup	....	3 doz. — 14 lbs.
W4629/65—	5¾"	Saucer	....	3 doz. — 14 lbs.
W4674/65—	4⅝"	Dessert	....	3 doz. — 11 lbs.
W4638/65—	7⅜"	Salad Plate	....	3 doz. — 23 lbs.
W4646/65—	10"	Dinner Plate	....	3 doz. — 44 lbs.

W4667/65

W4678/65

W4667/65—6⅝"	Soup Plate	....	3 doz. — 25 lbs.
W4678/65—8¼"	Vegetable Bowl	....	1 doz. — 14 lbs.

HEAT-RESISTANT

W4647/65

W4653/65 — W4654/65

W4647/65—12 x 9"	Platter	....	1 doz. — 20 lbs.
W4653/65—	Sugar & Cover	....	1 doz. — 9 lbs.
W4654/65—	Creamer	....	1 doz. — 7 lbs.

See Prepacked Sets on Page 13.

Wheat Dinnerware Sets

W4600/46—16 Pce. Starter Set

Each Set in Gift Display Carton, 4 Sets to Shipping Carton — 38 lbs.

COMPOSITION:
- Four W4679/65 Cups
- Four W4629/65 Saucers
- Four W4674/65 Desserts
- Four W4646/65 Dinner Plates

W4600/47—35 Pce. Dinner Set

Each Set in Shipping Carton — 23 lbs.

COMPOSITION:
- Six W4679/65 Cups
- Six W4629/65 Saucers
- Six W4674/65 Desserts
- Six W4667/65 Soup Plates
- Six W4646/65 Dinner Plates
- One W4678/65 Vegetable Bowl
- One W4647/65 Platter
- One W4653/65 Sugar & Cover
- One W4654/65 Creamer

W4600/48—53 Pce. Dinner Set

Each Set in Shipping Carton — 34 lbs.

COMPOSITION:
- Eight W4679/65 Cups
- Eight W4629/65 Saucers
- Eight W4674/65 Desserts
- Eight W4638/65 Salad Plates
- Eight W4667/65 Soup Plates
- Eight W4646/65 Dinner Plates
- One W4678/65 Vegetable Bowl
- One W4647/65 Platter
- One W4653/65 Sugar & Cover
- One W4654/65 Creamer

HEAT-RESISTANT

8-PCE. SNACK SET

W4600/49—8 Pce. Snack Set

Each Set in Die-Cut Display Box,
6 Sets to Shipping Carton — 48 lbs.

COMPOSITION:
- Four 5 oz. Cups
- Four 11 x 6" Rectangular Trays

**Crystal Clear Serva-Snack Sets
are shown on Page 7.**

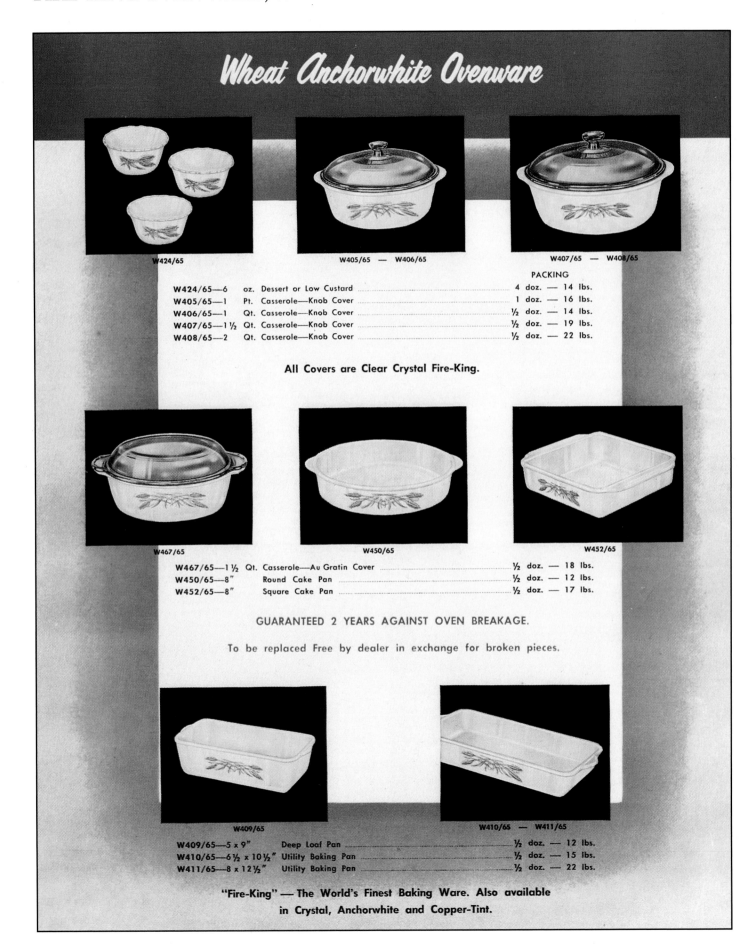

Wheat Anchorwhite Ovenware

W424/65

W405/65 — W406/65

W407/65 — W408/65

PACKING

W424/65—6	oz.	Dessert or Low Custard	4 doz.	14 lbs.
W405/65—1	Pt.	Casserole—Knob Cover	1 doz.	16 lbs.
W406/65—1	Qt.	Casserole—Knob Cover	½ doz.	14 lbs.
W407/65—1½	Qt.	Casserole—Knob Cover	½ doz.	19 lbs.
W408/65—2	Qt.	Casserole—Knob Cover	½ doz.	22 lbs.

All Covers are Clear Crystal Fire-King.

W467/65

W450/65

W452/65

W467/65—1½	Qt.	Casserole—Au Gratin Cover	½ doz.	18 lbs.
W450/65—8"		Round Cake Pan	½ doz.	12 lbs.
W452/65—8"		Square Cake Pan	½ doz.	17 lbs.

GUARANTEED 2 YEARS AGAINST OVEN BREAKAGE.

To be replaced Free by dealer in exchange for broken pieces.

W409/65

W410/65 — W411/65

W409/65—5 x 9"	Deep Loaf Pan	½ doz.	12 lbs.
W410/65—6½ x 10½"	Utility Baking Pan	½ doz.	15 lbs.
W411/65—8 x 12½"	Utility Baking Pan	½ doz.	22 lbs.

"Fire-King" — The World's Finest Baking Ware. Also available in Crystal, Anchorwhite and Copper-Tint.

Wheat Ovenware Sets

W400/315—Round Casserole & Candlewarmer Set

Each Set in Gift Carton, 4 Sets to Shipping Carton — 20 lbs.
COMPOSITION:
  One W407/65 Casserole & Crystal Cover
  One Brass Finished Candlewarmer
    (Candle included)

W400/313—8 Pce. Ovenware Set

Each Set in Gift Carton, 4 Sets to Shipping Carton — 34 lbs.
COMPOSITION:
  One W406/65 Casserole—Knob Cover
  One W410/65 Utility Baking Pan
  One W450/65 Round Cake Pan
  Four W424/65 Desserts or Custards

"Fire-King" — The World's Finest Baking Ware. Also available in Crystal, Anchor-white and Copper-Tint.

W400/317—Oval Casserole & Candlewarmer Set

Each Set in Gift Carton, 4 Sets to Shipping Carton — 19 lbs.
COMPOSITION:
  One W467/65 Oval Casserole & Crystal Cover
  One Brass Finished Candlewarmer
    (Candle included)

W400/314—11 Pce. Ovenware Set

Each Set in Gift Carton, 4 Sets to Shipping Carton — 53 lbs.
COMPOSITION:
  One W407/65 Casserole—Knob Cover
  One W409/65 Deep Loaf Pan
  One W411/65 Utility Baking Pan
  One W452/65 Square Cake Pan
  Six W424/65 Desserts or Custards

W400/316—Baking Pan & Candlewarmer Set

Each Set in Gift Carton, 4 Sets to Shipping Carton — 18 lbs.
COMPOSITION:
  One W410/65 Utility Baking Pan
  One Brass Finished Twin Candlewarmer
    (Candle included)

HEAT-RESISTANT

FLORAGOLD, "LOUISA" JEANNETTE GLASS COMPANY, 1950's

Colors: Iridescent, some Shell Pink, ice blue and crystal.

Floragold is one of the patterns that was formerly in *The Collector's Encyclopedia of Depression Glass.* This pattern was made long after the Depression era. Floragold is often confused with an old Carnival glass pattern called Louisa. Some "antique dealers," who do not sell much glassware, will price this early 1950's glassware "out of sight." Carnival glass collectors most often accept glassware made through the 1920's. The rose bowl in Carnival "Louisa" is often offered for sale as Floragold which turns the confusion around the other way. If you ever have occasion to see this bowl, you will understand why there is some confusion about what pattern it really is!

If you are buying a vase or the 15 oz. tumblers, make sure that they are a strong iridized color. For such a large investment, you do not need a weakly sprayed-on color. This color is made by applying an iridized spray over crystal and reheating. Heating it too hotly burned out the color! That rarely found vase was made by taking a 15 oz. tumbler and fluting the top. These large, 15 oz. tumblers can be found in crystal selling in the $10.00 to 12.00 range; add the iridized spray and you have to add another zero on that price. Evidently, many of these tumblers were never sprayed. I seem to find more crystal tumblers than iridized ones in my travels! Occasionally, you will see a crystal vase. That is enough to make you want to learn how to iridize glassware!

There are two different 5¼" comports in Floragold. Both of these are pictured in the first edition of my *Very Rare Glassware of the Depression Years* book. One has a ruffled top, and the other has a plain top. You can see the ruffled style below.

Because cups were sold without saucers in two separate ways, there is an abundance of cups in Floragold. The large bowl and the pitcher were both sold with twelve cups as "egg nog" sets for the Christmas market. Each set sold added another dozen cups to production; so, today, saucers have a right to be scarce. Someone walked out of our booth in an antique mall with 12 Floragold saucers, leaving the cups! (If you stoop to stealing collectibles, you need more than glass can provide. Seek counseling!) That 5¼" saucer has no cup ring and is the same as the sherbet plate.

Perfect tops to shakers are hard to find. Cracked tops are not acceptable to most collectors. They were made of plastic, and many were broken by tightening them too much. Only white or brown plastic tops are originals. Each top is worth $15.00, which makes the tops more than half the price of the shakers!

Ice blue, crystal, red-yellow, Shell Pink and iridized large comports were made in the late 1950's and into the early 1970's. See Shell Pink for a look at the shape of this piece. All the other colored comports are selling in the $10.00 to $12.00 range and sitting on the shelf from $15.00 up. That iridized comport I saw for sale at a flea market for $175.00 has been reduced to $100.00 with no takers.

	Iridescent		Iridescent
Ash tray/coaster, 4"	5.50	Tid-bit, wooden post	32.50
Bowl, 4½", square	5.50	Tumbler, 10 oz., footed	18.00
Bowl, 5½", round cereal	35.00	Tumbler, 11 oz., footed	18.00
Bowl, 5½", ruffled fruit	8.00	Tumbler, 15 oz., footed	100.00
Bowl, 8½", square	13.00	Vase or celery	385.00
Bowl, 9½", deep salad	40.00		
Bowl, 9½", ruffled	8.00	* Shell pink $20.00	
Bowl, 12", ruffled large fruit	7.00	**Tops $15.00 each included in price	
Butter dish and cover, ¼ lb. oblong	25.00		
Butter dish and cover, round, 6¼" sq. base	42.50		
Butter dish bottom	14.00		
Butter dish top	28.50		
Butter dish and cover, round, 5½" sq. base	650.00		
Candlesticks, double branch, pr.	47.50		
Candy dish, 1 handle	11.00		
Candy or Cheese dish and cover, 6¾"	50.00		
*Candy, 5¼" long, 4 feet	7.50		
Comport, 5¼", plain top	575.00		
Comport, 5¼", ruffled top	675.00		
Creamer	9.00		
Cup	6.00		
Pitcher, 64 oz.	35.00		
Plate or tray, 13½"	22.00		
Plate or tray, 13½", with indent	50.00		
Plate, 5¼", sherbet	12.00		
Plate, 8½", dinner	37.50		
Platter, 11¼"	22.00		
**Salt and pepper, plastic tops	47.50		
Saucer, 5¼" (no ring)	12.00		
Sherbet, low, footed	15.00		
Sugar	6.50		
Sugar lid	10.00		

Please refer to Foreword for pricing information

FOREST GREEN ANCHOR HOCKING GLASS COMPANY CORPORATION, 1950-1967

Color: Forest Green.

Forest Green is the color made by Anchor Hocking and not a pattern. Forest Green was used for the square Charm blank (1950), but the glassware became better known by its color. Even Hocking's "Bubble" was called Forest Green as you can see by the catalogue sheet on page 21.

The bottom of page 20 shows some stemware that was sold along with Bubble. These have been called "Boopie" by collectors, but the prices of the Forest Green "Boopie" have steadily declined while the "Bubble" stemware shown on page 21 has increased in price. I think it has more to do with the abundance of "Boopie" being found than any other reason. These lines are both priced below.

The oval vegetable in Forest Green is scalloped along the edges and has a swirled effect on the sides. See this bowl in the foreground at the top of page 111. Several large quantities of this oval bowl and the platter have appeared recently and the price for both has softened to some extent. It is hard to convince customers that these pieces are hard to find when some dealers insist on setting them out in a stack of twenty or more after they attain a copious supply. I have seen this several times. This is bad marketing!

Forest Green 6" soup bowls and dinner plates are seldom found. At least one catalogue listing had the 8⅜" plate as a dinner plate, so perhaps that is why 9¼" dinners are so hard to acquire. That dinner had been erroneously listed at 10" previously. Were the larger plates made as an afterthought or were they made first and dropped? Look for scratches on these plates; prices are for mint condition plates!

You will find many odd dark green pieces on the market. To be truly Forest Green, it must have been made by Anchor Hocking!

Notice the 9 oz. tumblers in the bottom picture. The metal caps were covers for dairy products such as cottage cheese. In my former Kentucky area, it was Sealtest brand dairy products. A reader reported finding a box of twenty-four 7 oz. tumblers in a box marked, "Clover Honey Delight, Packed by National Honey Packers Mt. Sterling Illinois."

The large quantity of 4" ball ivy vases testifies to successful sales of Citronella candles that were packed in these vases. The bottom picture shows a boxed set of two "mosquito repellent" candles that originally sold for $1.19. Having been in Florida the last few years makes me want to discover a few cases of these for my boat dock and porch. Since my office is the screened porch, I have had a problem with my computer and lights on after dark. Working fourteen to sixteen hour days, I have not found a way to only work in daylight hours. Furthermore, I have to fish occasionally! Mosquitoes often cover the windows on the outside until there is no more room! It takes a vacuum cleaner to dispose of all the bodies. (Blind mosquitoes they may be called, but they congregate at my lights!)

Decorated tumblers such as "A Bicycle for Two" will bring a dollar or two more than regular tumblers when they sell. Undecorated tumblers sell faster to collectors!

The paperweight below was one of five I unearthed a few years back. They were obviously from this era and may have been promotional items from Anchor Hocking!

	Green		Green		Green
Ash tray, 3½", square	4.00	Stem, 6 oz., sherbet	9.00	Tumbler, 10 oz., ftd., 4½"	6.50
Ash tray, 4⅝", square	5.00	*Stem, 6 oz., sherbet	6.00	Tumbler, 11 oz.	7.00
Ash tray, 5¾", square	7.50	*Stem, 9 oz., goblet	10.00	Tumbler, 13 oz., iced tea	7.50
Ash tray, 5¾", hexagonal	8.00	Stem, 9½ oz., goblet	13.00	Tumbler, 14 oz., 5"	7.50
Batter bowl w/spout	22.50	*Stem, 14 oz., iced tea	14.00	Tumbler, 15 oz., long boy	10.00
Bowl, 4¾", dessert	5.50	Sugar, flat	6.50	Tumbler, 15 oz., tall iced tea	12.00
Bowl, 5¼" deep	8.50	Tumbler, 5 oz., 3½"	4.00	Tumbler, 32 oz, giant iced tea	17.00
Bowl, 6", soup	17.00	Tumbler, 7 oz.	4.00	Vase, 4" ivy ball	4.00
Bowl, 6", mixing	9.00	Tumbler, 9 oz, table	5.00	Vase, 6⅜"	5.00
Bowl, 7⅜", salad	12.00	Tumbler, 9 oz, fancy	6.00	Vase, 9"	7.00
Bowl, 8½", oval vegetable	21.00	Tumbler, 9½ oz., tall	6.50		
Creamer, flat	6.50			* "Boopie"	
Cup (square)	5.00				
Pitcher, 22 oz.	22.50				
Pitcher, 36 oz.	25.00				
Pitcher, 86 oz., round	29.00				
Plate, 6¾", salad	5.00				
Plate, 6⅝", salad	5.00				
Plate, 8⅜", luncheon	6.50				
Plate, 9¼", dinner	28.00				
Platter, 11", rectangular	22.00				
Punch bowl	22.50				
Punch bowl stand	22.50				
Punch cup (round)	2.25				
Saucer, 5⅜"	1.50				
Sherbet, flat	7.50				
*Stem, 3½ oz., cocktail	10.00				
*Stem, 4 oz., juice	10.00				
Stem, 4½ oz., cocktail	12.50				
Stem, 5½ oz., juice	12.50				

Please refer to Foreword for pricing information

GOLDEN GLORY FEDERAL GLASS COMPANY, 1959-66; 1978-79

Color: White with 22K gold decorations.

Golden Glory, a small Federal pattern, is beginning to frequent collecting circles. The 22K gold decorations wear easily and detergent will fade them. This makes for difficulty in finding mint condition pieces, unless you can run across ones that were rarely used or still boxed. Dishes were bought to be used, and using them caused wear marks and deterioration that collectors today have to take into account.

Cathy and I ran into a stack of dinner plates and saucers in an antique mall in Mississippi. As the proprietor was wrapping them, I heard her tell a co-worker that she wished she had spotted them first. They were priced reasonably enough to use and she didn't need cups anyway. I offered her a deal on them, but she couldn't handle missing them at a bargain price and giving me a little profit! This set had been used in a church. I guess the coffee drinkers dropped a passel of cups!

Originally, there were a dozen pieces catalogued. When reissued in 1978, there were three pieces added. This later issue included the larger 10" dinner plate, the smaller 6⅝" soup and the 11¼" round platter. Dropped from the reissue were the oval platter, larger soup, sugar, creamer and tumblers.

According to an avid collector, the hardest to find pieces are the 8¼" vegetable bowl, tumblers and the 7¾" salad plate. I have had little luck in spotting a platter, so they may not be very common either!

Bowl, 4⅞", dessert	4.50	Plate, 10", dinner	6.50
Bowl, 6⅜", soup	8.00	Platter, 11¼", round	12.00
Bowl, 8½", vegetable	12.00	Platter, 12", oval	10.00
Bowl, 8", rimmed soup	8.00	Saucer	.50
Creamer	4.00	Sugar	3.00
Cup	3.00	Sugar lid	3.00
Plate, 7⅔", salad	3.00	Tumbler, 9 oz., ftd.	8.00
Plate, 9⅛", dinner	5.00	Tumbler, 10 oz., 5"	9.00

HARP JEANNETTE GLASS COMPANY, 1954-1957

Colors: crystal, crystal with gold trim, and cake stands in Shell Pink, pink, iridescent white and ice blue.

I figured that the Harp cake stand varieties had been completely catalogued and the collector of Harp cake stands had reached the end of the line. However, two new colors have been added to the list making twelve types with eight colors for now. The new colors are platinum (similar to the ash tray/coaster in the foreground of the picture below) and red. The platinum one is the flat edged variety, but the style of the red was not recorded. You can see two styles of ice blue below. The ruffled, gold trimmed crystal and an iridescent one are also pictured. Note the color variations on the blue. The Shell Pink Harp cake stand can be seen under that pattern. The twelve varieties of cake stands are as follows:

> 1,2. Crystal with smooth or ruffled rim
> 3,4. Either of above with gold trim
> 5. Iridescent with smooth rim
> 6,7. White or Shell Pink (opaque) with beads on rim and foot
> 8,9. Ice blue with beads on foot and smooth or ruffled rim
> 10. Pink transparent
> 11. Platinum decorated with smooth rim
> 12. Red

The Harp cake stand is reminiscent of late 1800's and early 1900's glassware. Most patterns after that time had cake plates instead of a stand.

Lately, plate, cup and saucer prices have increased. With so many new collectors starting on smaller sized patterns, the demand for basic pieces has doubled the prices in the last few years. There is simply not enough of this smaller pattern to provide everyone a set who wishes one. Many collectors love this pattern to use for their bridge parties. With the cake stand, cups, saucers and the 7" plates, it's ideal for small parties.

Many pieces are found with gold trims which bothers some collectors. An art gum eraser will take care of that problem with a little elbow grease!

As reported in the last book, the vase does stand 7½" and not 6" as it had previously been listed! I had a telephone report of a different style vase, today! Keep your eyes open for this.

	Crystal		Crystal
Ash tray/coaster	5.00	Plate, 7"	12.00
Coaster	4.50	Saucer	7.50
Cup	15.00	**Tray, 2-handled, rectangular	32.50
*Cake stand, 9"	21.00	Vase, 7½"	22.00

* Ice blue, white, pink or Shell Pink - $32.00
** Shell Pink $52.50

113

HEATHER ETCHING #343, FOSTORIA GLASS COMPANY 1949-1976

Colors: crystal

Heather is another Fostoria pattern that was introduced in my *Elegant Glassware of the Depression Era* because of reader requests. I am now transferring it here where it belongs. Heather is one of those patterns that is now being divided among family, and second and third generation family members are seeking replacements for pieces missing or long since broken.

All pieces in this pattern that do not have a line number below are etched on the Century blank #2630. My photo arrangers insist on standing the salver up so you can see the pattern. It is the large 12¼" piece in the top photograph. You may think of it as a cake stand, but it was listed by Fostoria as a salver. To the immediate right of the salver is the covered candy and beside that is the preserve stand. That should keep you from mixing these up if you find them!

In the bottom photo are two rarely seen items. In the foreground is a crescent salad plate and in the back is the #2470, 10" footed vase. I have tried to give as accurate a listing for this pattern as possible from old catalogues, but I'm sure there are additional pieces. Supply me with your information please and I'll try to pass it along. (Pictures with measurements are helpful!)

Basket, 10¼" x 6½", wicker hdld.	75.00	
Bowl, 4½", hdld.	12.00	
Bowl, 5", fruit	14.00	
Bowl, 6", cereal	25.00	
Bowl, 6¼", snack, ftd.	14.50	
Bowl, 7⅛", 3 ftd., triangular	20.00	
Bowl, 7¼", bonbon, 3 ftd.	18.00	
Bowl, 8", flared	32.50	
Bowl, 9", lily pond	35.00	
Bowl, 9½", hdld., serving bowl	35.00	
Bowl, 9½", oval, serving bowl	40.00	
Bowl, 10", oval, hdld.	40.00	
Bowl, 10½", salad	45.00	
Bowl, 10¾", ftd., flared	42.50	
Bowl, 11, ftd., rolled edge	47.50	
Bowl, 11¼", lily pond	42.50	
Bowl, 12", flared	45.00	
Butter, w/cover, ¼ lb.	42.50	
Candlestick, 4½"	18.00	
Candlestick, 7", double	32.50	
Candlestick, 7¾", triple	40.00	
Candy, w/cover, 7"	32.50	
Comport, 2¾", cheese	18.00	
Comport, 4⅜"	22.50	
Cracker plate, 10¾"	30.00	
Creamer, 4¼"	10.00	
Creamer, individual	10.00	
Cup, 6 oz., ftd.	15.00	
Ice Bucket	70.00	
Mayonnaise, 3 pc.	37.50	
Mayonnaise, 4 pc., div. w/2 ladles	42.50	
Mustard, w/spoon, cover	32.50	
Oil, w/stopper, 5 oz.	50.00	
Pickle, 8¾"	18.00	
Pitcher, 6⅛", 16 oz.	70.00	
Pitcher, 7⅛", 48 oz.	125.00	
Plate, 6", bread/butter	6.00	
Plate, 7½", crescent salad	42.50	

Plate, 7½", salad	8.50
Plate, 8½", luncheon	12.50
Plate, 8", party, w/indent for cup	30.00
Plate, 9½", small dinner	30.00
Plate, 10", hdld., cake	30.00
Plate, 10½", dinner, large center	40.00
Plate, 10½", snack tray, small center	30.00
Plate, 14", torte	45.00
Plate, 16", torte	65.00
Platter, 12"	52.50
Preserve, w/cover, 6"	45.00
Relish, 7⅜", 2 part	20.00
Relish, 11⅛", 3 part	30.50
Salt and pepper, 3⅛", pr.	47.50
Salver, 12¼", ftd. (like cake stand)	52.50
Saucer	4.50
Stem, #6037, 4", 1 oz., cordial	42.00
Stem, #6037, 4", 4½ oz., oyster cocktail	18.00
Stem, #6037, 4¾", 7 oz., low sherbet	14.00
Stem, #6037, 5", 4 oz., cocktail	20.00
Stem, #6037, 6⅛", 6 oz., parfait	25.00
Stem, #6037, 6⅜", 9 oz., low goblet	26.00
Stem, #6037, 6", 4 oz., claret-wine	32.50
Stem, #6037, 6", 7 oz., saucer champagne	18.00
Stem, #6037, 7⅞", 9 oz., goblet	26.00
Sugar, 4", ftd.	10.00
Sugar, individual	10.00
Tid bit, 8⅛", 3 ftd., upturned edge	27.50
Tid bit, 10¼", 2 tier, metal hdld.	45.00
Tray, 7⅛", for ind. sug/cr.	15.00
Tray, 9½", hdld., muffin	33.00

Tray, 9⅛", hdld., utility	33.00
Tray, 11½", center hdld.	37.50
Tumbler, #6037, 4⅞", 5 oz., ftd., juice	20.00
Tumbler, #6037, 6⅛", 12 oz., ftd., tea	25.00
Vase, 5", #4121	45.00
Vase, 6", bud	22.50
Vase, 6", ftd. bud, #6021	40.00
Vase, 6", ftd., #4143	55.00
Vase, 7½", hdld.	75.00
Vase, 8", flip, #2660	95.00
Vase, 8", ftd., bud, #5092	85.00
Vase, 8½", oval	75.00
Vase, 10", ftd., #2470	115.00

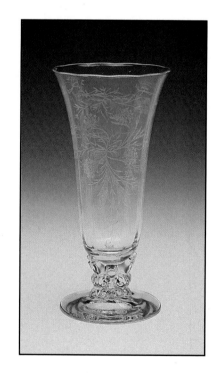

HERITAGE FEDERAL GLASS COMPANY, 1940-1955

Colors: crystal, some pink, blue, green and cobalt.

Heritage is another of the smaller patterns that new collectors seem to notice. Because of new collectors' demand, prices for crystal creamers, sugars and 8½" berry bowls continue to rise. These are the most difficult pieces to find. The sugar turns up with a little more frequency than the creamer for some reason. I have only seen one 8½" berry bowl for sale in the last few years. It was quickly snapped up by an eager collector. Where did these bowls go? They used to be considered common!

The reproduction berry bowls are so poorly made that they are causing little trouble for collectors. Why anyone would want to remake this little pattern is beyond my comprehension. Reproductions of Heritage bowls were marketed by McCrory's, and other similar stores. These were made in amber, crystal and green. Many are marked "MC" in the center. I say "many" because not all reports from readers have mentioned this mark. In any case, the smaller berry bowls are selling three for $1.00 and the larger for $1.59 each. The pattern on these pieces is not very good and should not fool even beginning collectors. Just compare the fully designed hobs in the photograph to the sparsely designed hobs on the reproductions. The green being found is much darker and closer to the 1970's avocado green. Amber was never made originally; so that is no problem.

Pink, blue and green berry bowls all remain elusive. These are truly rare! It is a shame that only berry bowl sets were made in these colors. Colored Heritage would have driven collectors wild!

Heritage was advertised as late as 1954 in some of the women's magazines.

Crystal Heritage sets can be assembled more easily than sets of many other patterns due to a lack of pieces. There are only ten separate pieces to find; so the only limitation you have is whether to search for a six, eight or twelve place setting. Thankfully, you only have to find one creamer and one large berry bowl no matter how many place settings you collect. Some collectors are buying several of the larger fruit bowls and ignoring the harder to find berry bowl.

Refer to Daisy for an explanation of Indiana's green Heritage pattern.

	Crystal	Pink	Blue Green
Bowl, 5", berry	8.00	40.00	50.00
Bowl, 8½", large berry	35.00	110.00	185.00
Bowl, 10½", fruit	14.00		
Cup	7.00		
Creamer, footed	25.00		
Plate, 8", luncheon	9.00		
Plate, 9¼", dinner	12.00		
Plate, 12", sandwich	13.00		
Saucer	4.00		
Sugar, open, footed	22.50		

HOLIDAY, "BUTTONS AND BOWS" JEANNETTE GLASS COMPANY, 1947-mid 1950's

Colors: pink, iridescent; some Shell Pink and crystal.

Collecting Holiday has some distinctive design problems for beginning collectors. There are contrasting styles of Holiday pieces. Collectors need to be aware that there are three styles of cup and saucer sets. One style cup and saucer have a plain center. These are easy to match up and are shown on the left at the bottom of page 117. There are two other styles of cups that have a rayed center. You **can not mix** these together since the base of the cup will not fit the saucer ring of the wrong type. Rayed cups have to go on rayed saucers, but you have to check these for size of the cup bottom. One cup's base is 2" and fits a 2⅛" saucer ring. The other cup's base is 2⅜" and fits a 2½" saucer ring.

There are two styles of 10 oz. tumblers, as can be seen in the picture. The tumbler on the right is flat bottomed, while the one on the left has a small raised foot and is narrower at the bottom. There is no difference in price, but purist collectors need to know that there are variances in pieces. These are just from different moulds, but new collectors sometimes get upset with differences on the same item purchased in different places.

While we are pointing out differences, there are also two styles of sherbets. The one on the right has a rayed foot while the one on the left is plain. The two sherbet plates both have 2¾" centers, but the one on the left has a "beads" effect in the center, while the one on the right has a center ring with a "diamond" effect in the center. These mould variations occur in many patterns, but it is confusing unless you know what to expect. There is no law against mixing styles, but some people do not wish to do so. These confusing items are all shown on the bottom of page 117.

HERITAGE

HOLIDAY, "BUTTONS AND BOWS"

HOLIDAY, "BUTTONS AND BOWS" JEANNETTE GLASS COMPANY, 1947-mid 1950's (Cont.)

If you missed page 117, be sure to refer to it to learn about the different styles of Holiday pieces.

It has become evident that Holiday suffered the same fate as Floral and Doric and Pansy. Some pieces we have difficulty finding in these patterns were exported. Unlike the other patterns that seem to have been sent to England, Holiday was exported to the Philippines. As reported in the ninth *Collector's Encyclopedia of Depression Glass*, iced teas, soups and juices have been found in abundance there. The tumblers were sent in boxes of six to be used as premiums for buying Hershey's chocolate bars. As a footnote, now that the Philippines have been deserted by the Armed Forces, I wonder if there will be any significant quantities of these pieces ever imported from there again. I ran into that collector serviceman who had exported many rare pieces of glassware back to the United States. He still has a shipment tied up in red tape from years ago. I wonder how many of the iced teas were in that lot!

I remember when $10.00 seemed like a high price for these 6" footed tumblers and now $145.00 is the asking price. (I know, our parents walked uphill to school every day — both ways!) If we had invested in these tumblers instead of mutual funds — what would we have today?

There are a few collectors beginning to buy the iridescent pieces of Holiday, not many, but a few!

Holiday console bowls, candlesticks and cake plates remain the most difficult pieces to find (excepting those pieces that were exported.) If you wonder how such a lately manufactured glassware could have so many hard to find pieces, welcome to the club. Evidently, there was little demand for pieces other than the basics. Maybe the serving pieces were premiums. No data has ever surfaced to **explain** these mysteries. Holiday seems to have been a heavily used pattern judging by the multitude of damaged pieces I have examined as I have looked at sets over the years. Be sure to look at the underside of the edges. Those pointed edges are prone to chips, nicks and "chigger bites," an auction term that varies from place to place. (Some auction houses must harbor some big chiggers!) Remember, damaged glass can not be almost mint. The prices listed here are for **mint** condition glassware!

	Pink	Crystal	Iridescent
Bowl, 5⅛", berry	12.00		
Bowl, 7¾", soup	47.50		
Bowl, 8½", large berry	25.00		
Bowl, 9½", oval vegetable	25.00		
*Bowl, 10¾", console	110.00		
Butter dish and cover	37.50		
Butter dish bottom	10.00		
Butter dish top	27.50		
Cake plate, 10½", 3 legged	95.00		
Candlesticks, 3" pr.	95.00		
Creamer, footed	8.00		
Cup, three sizes	8.00		
Pitcher, 4¾", 16 oz. milk	60.00	15.00	22.00
Pitcher, 6¾", 52 oz.	35.00		
Plate, 6", sherbet	6.00		
Plate, 9", dinner	16.00		
Plate, 13¾", chop	95.00		
Platter, 11⅜", oval	20.00		12.50
Sandwich tray, 10½"	17.50		15.00
Saucer, 3 styles	4.00		
Sherbet, 2 styles	6.00		
Sugar	10.00		
Sugar cover	15.00		
Tumbler, 4", 10 oz., flat	20.00		
Tumbler, 4", footed, 5 oz.	40.00		11.00
Tumbler, 4¼", footed, 5¼ oz.		7.50	
Tumbler, 6", footed	145.00		

* Shell Pink $40.00

Please refer to Foreword for pricing information

IRIS, "IRIS AND HERRINGBONE" JEANNETTE GLASS COMPANY, 1928-1932; 1950's; 1970's

Colors: crystal, iridescent; some pink; recently bi-colored red/yellow and blue/green combinations and white.

Newsflash! Iridized Iris tall sherbets recently surfaced and were quickly snatched up by an eager collector. Yes, new discoveries are still being made even after 30 years of serious collecting.

Iris was the most difficult pattern to place in this division between *The Collector's Encyclopedia of Depression Glass* and *Collectible Glassware from the 40's, 50's, 60's* ... since it fits both eras so well. Iridescent Iris belongs entirely within the frame of this 50's book; and although crystal production goes back to 1928 for its start, some crystal was made in the late 1940's, and 1950's; and some pieces, such as candy bottoms and vases, were manufactured as late as the early 1970's. Thus, I have decided to include crystal prices in this book as well.

Two years ago the question I was most asked was, "When are the prices for Iris going to stop increasing?" Perhaps, never, but I can now answer that prices of Iris have begun to slow. All major patterns have had pricing surges, but the one for Iris lasted longer than any I have experienced in my twenty-four years of writing about glassware. Almost all rare pieces have doubled in price in four years. That is astounding at this day and time. It was not unusual for a $10.00 item to go to $20.00 between books, but when $75.00 items go to $165.00 and $40.00 items go to $95.00 with customers fighting to buy them, it is quite a shock! I am seeing more dealers packing some Iris at the end of shows whereas only months ago, they were taking home empty boxes. That probably shows that the higher prices are being resisted by average collectors. Still, at a recent midwest show, I heard one dealer saying he could sell all the Iris he could get his hands on.

Please realize those iridescent candy bottoms are a product of the 1970's when Jeannette made crystal bottoms and iridized or flashed them with two-tone colors such as red/yellow or blue/green. Pictured on the bottom right of 121 is a flashed blue candy bottom. Many of these were sold as vases and, over time, the colors have washed or peeled off making crystal candy bottoms. Some have been stripped of their color to dupe unknowing collectors. These later pieces can be distinguished by the lack of rays on the foot of the dish. All are plain footed. Similarly, white vases were made and sprayed green, red and blue on the outside. Many of these vases have lost the colors on the outside and are now only white. White vases sell in the $10.00-12.00 range.

The 8 oz. water goblet, 5¾", 4 oz. goblet and the demitasse cup and saucer are the most difficult pieces to find in iridescent. The 5¾", 4 oz. goblet is shown in the *Very Rare Glassware of the Depression Era 4th Series*.

Decorated red and gold Iris that turns up on crystal was called "Corsage" and styled by Century in 1946. We know this because of a card attached to a 1946 "Corsage" wedding gift that a reader shared with me. Does anyone know more?

The picture of the bowl advertising "Badcock Furniture will treat you right" shown on the left caused me to receive more mail than anything ever in any of my books. I had not caught on to the fact that Badcock was a still thriving furniture chain! They certainly chose the right glass pattern to use for advertising! It's still doing the job these many years later!

	Crystal	Iridescent	Green/Pink		Crystal	Iridescent	Green/Pink
Bowl, 4½", berry, beaded edge	40.00	9.00		Goblet, 4¼", 4 oz., cocktail	25.00		
Bowl, 5", ruffled, sauce	9.00	25.00		Goblet, 4¼", 3 oz., wine	16.00		
Bowl, 5", cereal	115.00			Goblet, 5¾", 4 oz.	25.00	150.00	
Bowl, 7½", soup	155.00	57.50		Goblet, 5¾", 8 oz.	25.00	165.00	
Bowl, 8", berry, beaded edge	80.00	20.00		**Lamp shade, 11½"	85.00		
Bowl, 9½", ruffled, salad	12.50	13.00	100.00	Pitcher, 9½", footed	37.50	40.00	
Bowl, 11½", ruffled, fruit	15.00	14.00		Plate, 5½", sherbet	14.00	13.00	
Bowl, 11", fruit, straight edge	55.00			Plate, 8", luncheon	100.00		
Butter dish and cover	47.50	40.00		Plate, 9", dinner	50.00	40.00	
Butter dish bottom	13.50	12.00		Plate, 11¾", sandwich	30.00	30.00	
Butter dish top	34.00	28.50		Saucer	12.00	11.00	
Candlesticks, pr.	40.00	42.50		Sherbet, 2½", footed	24.00	14.00	
Candy jar and cover	145.00			Sherbet, 4", footed	22.50	150.00	
Coaster	95.00			Sugar	11.00	11.00	110.00
Creamer, footed	12.00	12.00	110.00	Sugar cover	12.00	12.00	
Cup	15.00	14.00		Tumbler, 4", flat	130.00		
*Demitasse cup	35.00	125.00		Tumbler, 6", footed	18.00	16.00	
*Demitasse saucer	130.00	200.00		Tumbler, 6½", footed	34.00		
Fruit or nut set	65.00			Vase, 9"	27.50	24.00	130.00
Goblet, 4", wine		30.00					

*Ruby, Blue, Amethyst priced as Iridescent
**Colors: $65.00

Please refer to Foreword for pricing information

JAMESTOWN FOSTORIA GLASS COMPANY, 1958-1982

Colors: Amber, amethyst, blue, brown, crystal, green, pink and red.

Jamestown is another of those Fostoria patterns where items other than stems seem to be invisible when you start searching for them. Serving pieces were not promoted by Fostoria for the duration of stemware line; that leaves both collectors and dealers foraging for serving pieces! Not all pieces were made in each color. I have grouped the colors into three pricing groups, though they are pictured in different groups for aesthetic reasons.

Ruby Jamestown has always sold best, but there is not a complete line of the Ruby. A sad note for collectors is that Ruby is again being made and sold in the Fostoria outlet stores. The stems are selling for $16.00 each and that is dropping the prices on the older Ruby items. I guess there is not enough imagination in the glassware industry to come up with new colors or patterns to entice the public.

Many dealers do not stock amber or brown. There is little demand for these colors at present. If you are looking for amber or brown, ask dealers for it. You should be able to find some bargains. In the middle group, crystal is most in demand, but green is beginning to be noticed. I recently received a letter from a collector who had found a set of what she thought were unlisted pieces of Moroccan Amethyst. Those amethyst pieces were Jamestown.

These listings came from two separate Fostoria catalogues. The line numbers on each stem in those catalogues have two different sizes and capacities listed. It is one of the many things that drives me to distraction when writing a book. Which figure do you use? Thus, I have included both stem listings for the purist. Either someone measured incorrectly one year or the sizes were actually changed. If you have pieces with both measurements, please let me know! I have run into this in other companies' catalogues, so I point this out to make you aware of why your measurements could differ from those I have listed.

	Amber/Brown	Amethyst/Crystal/Green	Blue/Pink/Ruby
Bowl, 4½", dessert #2719/421	8.50	13.50	16.00
Bowl, 10", salad #2719//211	21.00	37.50	42.50
Bowl, 10", two hndl. serving #2719/648	21.00	42.50	55.00
Butter w/cover, ¼ pound #2719/300	24.00	45.00	55.00
Cake plate, 9½", hndl. #2719/306	16.00	32.50	37.50
Celery, 9¼" #2719/360	18.00	32.50	37.50
Cream, 3½", ftd. #2719/681	11.00	16.00	24.00
Jelly w/cover, 6⅛" #2719/447	32.50	57.50	80.00
Pickle, 8⅜" #2719/540	21.00	35.00	40.00
Pitcher, 7⁵⁄₁₆", 48 oz., ice jug #2719/456	45.00	95.00	130.00
Plate, 8" #2719/550	8.50	16.00	19.00
Plate, 14", torte #2719/567	26.00	42.50	55.00
Relish, 9⅛", 2 part #2719/620	16.00	32.00	37.50
Salad set, 4 pc. (10" bowl, 14" plate w/wood fork & spoon) #2719/286	55.00	85.00	100.00
Salver, 7" high, 10" diameter #2719/630	55.00	100.00	100.00
Sauce dish w/cover, 4½" #2719/635	18.00	30.00	34.00
Shaker, 3½", w/chrome top. pr. #2719/653	26.00	37.50	47.50
Stem, 4⁵⁄₁₆", 4 oz., wine #2719/26	10.00	20.00	24.00
*Stem, 4¼", 6½ oz., sherbet #2719/7	6.50	12.50	16.00
*Stem, 4⅛", 7 oz., sherbet #2719/7	6.50	12.50	16.00
*Stem, 5¾", 9½ oz., goblet #2719/2	10.00	16.00	16.00
*Stem, 5⅞", 10 oz., goblet #2719/2	10.00	16.00	16.00
Sugar, 3½", ftd. #2719/679	11.00	17.50	24.00
Tray, 9⅜", hndl. muffin #2719/726	26.00	42.50	55.00
Tumbler, 4¼", 9 oz. #2719/73	9.00	21.00	25.00
Tumbler, 4¾", 5 oz., juice #2719/88	9.50	21.00	26.00
Tumbler, 5⅛", 12 oz. #2719/64	9.00	21.00	26.00
Tumbler, 6", 11 oz., ftd. tea #2719/63	10.00	21.00	24.00
Tumbler, 6", 12 oz., ftd. tea #2719/63	10.00	21.00	24.00

*being remade at present

United States Glass Company
TIFFIN, OHIO
KINGS CROWN
Also known as No. 4016 Thumbprint

Sugar

Cream

5" Bread and Butter Plate

Cup and Saucer

10" Dinner Plate

AVAILABLE PLAIN CRYSTAL, DECORATED CRANBERRY OR RUBY

KING'S CROWN, THUMBPRINT LINE NO. 4016 U.S. GLASS (TIFFIN) COMPANY,
late 1800'S - 1960's; INDIANA GLASS COMPANY, 1970's

Colors: Crystal, crystal with ruby or cranberry flash, crystal with gold or platinum.

King's Crown is a pattern that causes some confusion among both old and new collectors. Originally issued as Thumbprint Line No. 4016 by U. S. Glass in the late 1800's, this glassware was also made by Tiffin into the early 1960's. The catalogue reprint shown in this section is from 1955. More problematical, Indiana bought the moulds and changed the design somewhat. Not only does this lend confusion, but there were over twenty other glassware companies who made similar patterns.

For this book I am including the Indiana pieces as well as those made by Tiffin after 1940. You may find additional pieces, but please realize that many of those could be from an earlier time. The Tiffin plates seem to have starred designs in the center while the Indiana ones appear to be plain. I have discovered no hard, fast rules in this confusing pattern! One of the stimulating things about King's Crown is that you never know what piece is lurking round the next corner or in the next booth. However, Cathy, is beginning to groan, "Not another piece of King's Crown!"

I just bought a piece that I thought was the wedding bowl shown in the catalogue reprint on page 131, but this covered bowl is a shade over 7" in diameter. Maybe these came in two sizes or the catalogue was wrong. If you have one in your collection, let me know the diameter of your bowl.

Some pieces are flashed with gold, platinum, blue, green, yellow, cranberry or the ruby. For now, until a market is more clearly established, there will be no price distinction on the different flashed colors. Demand makes ruby the desired color. For crystal, subtract fifty percent of the prices listed. Gold and platinum decorated products were also made at Indiana. Furthermore, iridized Carnival colors, Avocado green, amber and other solid colored items were made by Indiana. In 1976, they also made a smoky blue for the Bicentennial. That identical blue was used in the Tiara Sandwich line that year!

Elongated thumbprint designs were from the original moulds. Some of this elongated style may have been made at Indiana before they changed the moulds, but if the pieces you have show circular thumbprints, you have King's Crown made by Indiana. Also, the Tiffin tumblers are flared at the top while Indiana's are straight. Expect to pay a little less than the prices below for the more recently issued Indiana tumblers.

	Ruby Flashed		Ruby Flashed
Ash tray, 5¼", square	14.00	Plate, 7⅜", mayonnaise liner	12.50
Bowl, 4", finger	17.50	Plate, 7⅜", salad	12.00
Bowl, 4", mayonnaise	16.00	Plate, 9¾", snack w/indent	15.00
Bowl 5¾"	20.00	Plate, 10", dinner	35.00
Bowl, 6", diameter, ftd., wedding or candy	27.50	Plate, 14½", torte	50.00
Bowl, 8¾", 2-hdld., crimped bon bon	40.00	Plate, 24", party	85.00
Bowl, 9¼", salad	56.00	Plate, 24", party server (w/punch ft.)	115.00
Bowl, 10½", ftd., wedding or candy, w/cover	70.00	Punch bowl foot	37.50
Bowl, 11½", 4½" high, crimped	65.00	Punch bowl, 2 styles	185.00
Bowl, 11¼" cone	45.00	Punch cup	8.00
Bowl, 12½", center edge, 3" high	40.00	Punch set, 15 pc. w/foot	325.00
Bowl, 12½", flower floater	40.00	Punch set, 15 pc. w/plate	350.00
Bowl, crimped, ftd.	35.00	Relish, 14", 5 part	65.00
Bowl, flared, ftd.	40.00	Saucer	8.00
Bowl, straight edge	45.00	Stem, 2 oz., wine	7.50
Cake salver, 12½", ftd.	65.00	Stem, 2¼ oz., cocktail	12.50
Candleholder, sherbet type	25.00	Stem, 4 oz., claret	12.00
Candleholder, 2-lite, 5½"	35.00	Stem, 4 oz., oyster cocktail	14.00
Candy box, 6", flat, w/cover	40.00	Stem, 5½ oz., sundae or sherbet	10.00
Cheese stand	17.50	Stem, 9 oz., water goblet	12.00
Compote, 7¼", 9¾" diameter	35.00	Sugar	22.50
Compote, 7½", 12" diameter, ftd., crimped	65.00	Tumbler, 4 oz., juice, ftd.	12.00
Compote, small, flat	18.00	Tumbler, 4½ oz., juice	14.00
Creamer	22.50	Tumbler, 8½ oz., water	13.00
Cup	8.00	Tumbler, 11 oz., ice tea	16.00
Lazy susan, 24", 8½" high, w/ball bearing spinner	125.00	Tumbler, 12 oz., ice tea, ftd.	18.00
Mayonnaise, 3 pc. set	30.00	Vase, 9", bud	30.00
Pitcher	120.00	Vase, 12¼", bud	60.00
Plate, 5", bread/butter	8.00		

Please refer to Foreword for pricing information

KING'S CROWN

KINGS CROWN

Center Edge Bowl 12½″ Diameter 3″ High

2-Lite Candle Holder 5½″ High

Footed Fruit Compote 9¾″ Diameter 7¼″ High

Crimped Bowl 11½″ Diameter 4½″ High

Cone Bowl 11¼″ Diameter 4¾″ High

Page 2   AVAILABLE PLAIN CRYSTAL, DECORATED CRANBERRY OR RUBY

KINGS CROWN

Goblet 9 oz.

Wine 2 oz.

Juice 4 oz.

Claret 4 oz.

Cocktail 2¼ oz.

Oyster Cocktail 4 oz.

Sundae 5½ oz.

Water Tumbler 8½ oz.

Juice Tumbler 4½ oz.

Footed Ice Tea 12 oz.

Ice Tea Tumbler 11 oz.

Finger Bowl 4" Diameter

7⅜" Salad Plate

AVAILABLE PLAIN CRYSTAL, DECORATED CRANBERRY OR RUBY

Page 3

KINGS CROWN

15 pc. Punch Set, with foot
Capacity 12 qts. Diameter 23"

15 pc. Punch Set Flared
Capacity 12 qts. Plate Diameter 23"

Party Server 24" Diameter 8" High

Page 4   AVAILABLE PLAIN CRYSTAL, DECORATED CRANBERRY OR RUBY

KINGS CROWN

Wedding Bowl and Cover
6" Diameter 10½" High

Flower Floater 12½" Diameter

Torte Plate 14" Diameter

Ash Tray 5¼" Square

Footed Cake Salver
12½" Diameter 4¾" High

LIDO PLATE ETCHING #329, FOSTORIA GLASS COMPANY 1937-1960

Color: Crystal, Azure

The renowned Lido is a site of much festivity and celebration. Think of fireworks shooting aloft and you'll be able to remember the design of this pattern.

Lido is a Fostoria pattern that was made in Azure blue as well as crystal. You can see an azure tumbler as the pattern shot on page 133. Azure was discontinued during the middle of World War II. You will not find much of this color, and that is a shame since it is an attractive shade of blue. Blue will fetch up to fifty percent more than the prices for crystal on hard to find items; but there are few collectors searching for it, so basic pieces sell for only a little more than crystal.

I looked at the Lido pitcher on page 133 for several years before I pried the money loose from my checkbook. The dealer only carried it to a couple of shows each year.

All the items without a line number in the listing below are found on #2496 that is known as the Baroque blank. You may find other items with this etching. Let me know what you discover.

Item	Price	Item	Price
Bowl, 4", one hdld., square	13.00	Plate, 9½"	32.50
Bowl, 4⅜", one hdld.	12.00	Plate, 10", hdld. cake	30.00
Bowl, 4⅝", one hdld., 3 cornered	13.00	Plate, 11", cracker	22.50
Bowl, 5", one hdld., flared	12.50	Plate, 14", torte	40.00
Bowl, 6¼", 3 ftd., cupped	20.00	Relish, 6", square, 2 part	17.50
Bowl, 7⅜" 3 ftd., bon bon	15.00	Relish, 10", 3 part	30.00
Bowl, 8½", 2 hdld.	40.00	Saucer	4.00
Bowl, 10½", 2 hdld.	45.00	Shaker, 2¾"	25.00
Bowl, 12", flared	50.00	Stem, #6017, 3⅝", 4 oz., oyster cocktail	20.00
Bowl, 12½", oval, #2545 "Flame"	40.00	Stem, #6017, 3⅞", ¾ oz. cordial	40.00
Bowl, finger, #766	22.00	Stem, #6017, 4½", 6 oz., low sherbet	14.00
Candlestick, 4½", duo	32.50	Stem, #6017, 4⅞". 3½ oz., cocktail	18.00
Candlestick, 4"	15.00	Stem, #6017, 5½", 3 oz., wine	27.50
Candlestick, 5½"	20.00	Stem, #6017, 5½", 6 oz., high sherbet	17.50
Candlestick, 6¾", duo, #2545 "Flame"	37.50	Stem, #6017, 5⅞", 4 oz., claret	30.00
Candy w/cover, 6¼", 3 part	65.00	Stem, #6017, 7⅜", 9 oz., water	22.50
Celery, 11"	22.50	Sugar	9.00
Comport, 3¼", ftd. cheese	17.50	Sugar, individual	10.00
Comport, 4¾"	17.50	Sweetmeat, 6", square, 2 hdld.	17.50
Comport, 5½"	22.50	Tid bit, 8¼", 3 ftd., flat	20.00
Comport, 5¾"	22.50	Tray, 6½" ind. sug/cr., #2496½	12.00
Creamer	10.00	Tumbler, #4132, 2⅛", 1½ oz., whiskey	22.50
Creamer, individual	11.00	Tumbler, #4132, 3½", 4 oz., sham	10.00
Cup, ftd.	15.00	Tumbler, #4132, 3⅛", 7½ oz., old fashioned	15.00
Ice bucket	65.00	Tumbler, #4132, 3¾", 5 oz., sham	10.00
Jelly w/cover, 7½"	55.00	Tumbler, #4132, 3¾", 9 oz., sham	13.00
Mayonnaise, 3 pc. set, 2496½	35.00	Tumbler, #4132, 4⅛", 7 oz., sham	12.00
Oil bottle w/stopper, 3½ oz.	85.00	Tumbler, #4132, 4⅞", 12 oz., sham	15.00
Pickle, 8"	17.50	Tumbler, #4132, 5⅜", 14 oz., sham	17.50
Pitcher, #6011, 8⅞", 53 oz., ftd.	135.00	Tumbler, #6017, 4¾", 5 oz., ftd. juice	14.00
Plate, 6"	6.00	Tumbler, #6017, 5½", 9 oz., ftd. water	18.00
Plate, 7", #2337	9.00	Tumbler, #6017, 6", 12 oz., ftd. ice tea	22.00
Plate, 7½"	9.00	Tumbler, #6017, 6½", 14 oz., ftd.	27.50
Plate, 8½"	12.50		

MAYFLOWER PLATE ETCHING #332, FOSTORIA GLASS COMPANY 1938-1954

Color: Crystal

Mayflower pattern has a cornucopia of flowers as its main design. See the pattern shot of the pitcher on the next page. Mayflower is occasionally confused with Fostoria's Corsage pattern. Refer to page 49 to see the "ice cream cone" bouquet of flowers that makes up Corsage's design so you can compare these two patterns which are newly included in this book.

Most Mayflower etchings are on Fostoria's #2560 blank which is known as Coronet. There are three wavy lines encircling the top of Coronet pieces. You can see this on the relish, comport, creamer and sugar on page 135. Note the handles on the sugar and creamer. These are a dead give away to #2560.

The pitcher is the #4140 jug. This style is rarely found. I bought it from an antique mall in Florida for a little more than the price of the four repaired tumblers that were with it. The dealer may still have those tumblers! The large vase stands 8" tall, but looks much larger due to its wide opening. This is the #2430 vase in the listing.

A "Flame" #2545 oval bowl and single candlestick represent the other blank on which you may find Mayflower. I had a couple of stems, but they seem to have taken a vacation for the photography session. If you find additional pieces than those listed, be sure to drop me a card!

Bowl, finger, #869	20.00	Plate, 6¼", hdld., lemon, #2560	6.00
Bowl, 5", hdld., whip cream, #2560	22.50	Plate, 7½", #2560	10.00
Bowl, 5¾" x 6¼", hdld., bon bon, #2560	20.00	Plate, 8½", #2560	15.00
Bowl, 5½", hdld., sweetmeat, #2560	17.50	Plate, 9½", #2560	37.50
Bowl, 7¼", 3 ftd., bon bon, #2560	22.50	Plate, 10½", hdld. cake, #2560	32.50
Bowl, 8½", hdld., #2560	37.50	Plate, 14", torte #2560	40.00
Bowl, 10", salad, #2560	40.00	Relish, 6½", hdld., 2 part, #2560	20.00
Bowl, 10½", hdld., #2496	40.00	Relish, 10" x 7¾", 3 part, #2560	32.50
Bowl, 11", hdld., #2560	55.00	Saucer, #2560	5.00
Bowl, 11½", crimped, #2560	55.00	Stem, #6020, 3¾", 1 oz., cordial	40.00
Bowl, 12", flared, #2560	45.00	Stem, #6020, 3¾", 4 oz., oyster cocktail	20.00
Bowl, 12½", oval, #2545 "Flame"	50.00	Stem, #6020, 4⅝", 6 oz., low sherbet	15.00
Bowl, 13", fruit, #2560	50.00	Stem, #6020, 4⅞", 3½ oz., cocktail	18.00
Candlestick, 4", #2560½	27.50	Stem, #6020, 5⅜", 3½ oz., wine	30.00
Candlestick, 4½", #2545 "Flame"	22.50	Stem, #6020, 5½", 6 oz., saucer champagne	18.00
Candlestick, 4½", #2560	25.00	Stem, #6020, 5¾", 4½ oz., claret	35.00
Candlestick, 5", duo, #2496	27.50	Stem, #6020, 6⅛", 5½ oz., claret	35.00
Candlestick, 5⅛", duo, #2560	35.00	Stem, #6020, 7¼", 9 oz., water	25.00
Candlestick, 6¾", duo, #2545 "Flame"	40.00	Sugar, #2560	11.00
Celery, 11", #2560	25.00	Sugar, individual, #2560	12.00
Creamer, #2560	12.00	Tray, 7½", individual cr./sug #2560	15.00
Creamer, individual, #2560	12.50	Tray, 10" x 8¼", hdld., muffin, #2560	32.50
Cup, ftd., #2560	17.00	Tumbler, #6020, 4⅞", 5 oz., ftd. juice	17.50
Mayonnaise set, 3 pc., #2560	37.50	Tumbler, #6020, 5¾", 9 oz., ftd. water	20.00
Olive, 6¾", #2560	15.00	Tumbler, #6020, 6⅜", 12 oz., ftd. ice tea	25.00
Pickle, 8¾", #2560	17.50	Vase, 3¾", #2430	50.00
Pitcher, 7½,", 60 oz., flat, #4140	225.00	Vase, 8", #2430	110.00
Pitcher, 9¾", 48 oz., ftd. #5000	225.00	Vase, 10", ftd., #2545, "Flame"	125.00
Plate, 6", #2560	6.00	Vase, 10", ftd., #5100	95.00

MEADOW ROSE PLATE ETCHING #328, FOSTORIA GLASS COMPANY 1936-1982

Colors: Crystal and Azure

Meadow Rose was the pattern most requested to be added to this book. There is little Azure being found. It was discontinued during World War II. Pieces found in Azure will fetch an additional 20%–25% more than crystal.

Those pieces without a mould blank number in the listing below are #2496 or Baroque. Look for the tell-tale fleur-de-lis on this line. Similar in design to Navarre, Meadow Rose was sold alongside its sister pattern for over forty years. Matching stemware service was available until Fostoria's closing.

You will find that pricing for Meadow Rose is similar to Navarre's, but that most items are less in demand than those of Navarre. Today, Meadow Rose collectors are outnumbered dramatically by those searching for Navarre.

If you should happen to find additional pieces in this pattern, please let me know.

Bowl, 4", square, hdld.	11.00	Plate, 10", hdld., cake	47.50
Bowl, 4½", #869, finger	40.00	Plate, 11", cracker	25.00
Bowl, 4⅝", tri-cornered	15.00	Plate, 14", torte	57.50
Bowl, 5", hdld., flared	18.50	Plate, 16", torte, #2364	85.00
Bowl, 6", square, sweetmeat	17.50	Relish, 6", 2 part, square	32.50
Bowl, 7⅜", 3 ftd., bonbon	27.50	Relish, 10" x 7½", 3 part	47.50
Bowl, 8½", hdld.	40.00	Relish, 13¼", 5 part, #2419	85.00
Bowl, 10", oval, floating garden	50.00	Salad dressing bottle, #2083, 6½"	200.00
Bowl, 10½", hdld.	55.00	Salt & pepper, #2375, 3½", ftd., pr.	95.00
Bowl, 12", flared	62.50	Sauce dish liner, 8", oval	27.50
Bowl, 12", hdld., ftd.	62.50	Sauce dish, 6½" x 5¼"	125.00
Bowl, #2545, 12½", oval, "Flame"	55.00	Sauce dish, div. mayo., 6½"	37.50
Candlestick, 4"	20.00	Saucer	6.00
Candlestick, 4½", double	32.50	Stem, #6016, ¾ oz., cordial, 3⅞"	47.50
Candlestick, 5½"	27.50	Stem, #6016, 3¼ oz., wine, 5½"	35.00
Candlestick, 6", triple	40.00	Stem, #6016, 3½ oz., cocktail, 5¼"	25.00
Candlestick, #2545, 6¾", double, "Flame"	45.00	Stem, #6016, 4 oz., oyster cocktail, 3⅝"	27.50
Candy, w/cover, 3 part	100.00	Stem, #6016, 4½ oz., claret, 6"	40.00
Celery, 11"	37.50	Stem, #6016, 6 oz., low sherbet, 4⅜"	24.00
Comport, 3¼", cheese	27.50	Stem, #6016, 6 oz., saucer champagne, 5⅝"	24.00
Comport, 4¾"	30.00	Stem, #6016, 10 oz., water, 7⅝"	30.00
Creamer, 4¾", ftd.	20.00	Sugar, 3½", ftd.	18.00
Creamer, individual	17.50	Sugar, individual	16.00
Cup	18.00	Tid bit, 8¼", 3 ftd., turned up edge	22.00
Ice bucket, 4⅜" high	100.00	Tray, #2375, 11", center hdld.	35.00
Jelly w/ cover, 7½"	65.00	Tray, 6½", 2496½, for ind. sugar/creamer	22.00
Mayonnaise, #2375, 3 piece	67.50	Tumbler, #6016, 5 oz., ftd., juice, 4⅝"	25.00
Mayonnaise, 2496½, 3 piece	67.50	Tumbler, #6016, 10 oz., ftd., water, 5⅜"	25.00
Pickle, 8"	27.50	Tumbler, #6016, 13 oz., ftd., tea, 5⅞"	30.00
Pitcher, #2666, 32 oz.	200.00	Vase, #4108, 5"	75.00
Pitcher, #5000, 48 oz., ftd.	325.00	Vase, #4121, 5"	75.00
Plate, 6", bread/butter	11.00	Vase, #4128, 5"	75.00
Plate, 7½", salad	15.00	Vase, #2470, 10", ftd.	145.00
Plate, 8½", luncheon	20.00		
Plate, 9½", dinner	42.50		

MODERNTONE PLATONITE
HAZEL ATLAS GLASS COMPANY, 1940-early 1950's

Colors: Platonite pastel, white and white decorated.

Searching for pieces of Platonite Moderntone not shown in the first two editions developed into a challenge. With the death of Grannie Bear and the closing of my shop, gathering new pieces stood still for a while. As they were bought Mom enjoyed listing and packing new colors and pieces not pictured in the book. That made my job much easier when it came time for a photography session. Her help is surely missed. I did promise a major overhaul in the pictures; so I hope you appreciate the efforts.

The organization of colors was set up to show the varieties available and not necessarily to help me in pricing. Because there are varying shades that make price differences, I have again chosen color as the predominate factor in laying out the photographs. Children's dishes have a section all their own starting on page 145.

There remains infinitesimal demand for plain white. That could change with the black and white kitchen decor coming into vogue. Shown first in row 4 is a cone shaped tumbler only found in white. The lid states that this tumbler was given free with the purchase of "Lovely" cherry gelatin costing 10¢. Many tumblers of this era were obtained by acquiring some product.

Collectors are enthusiastically searching for white trimmed in red or blue. Exhibit a piece of Blue or Red Willow or Deco trimmed Moderntone (shown on page 139-140) and you will see collectors' eyes illuminate! I have purchased as much Willow decorated Moderntone as I have had the opportunity to find. All the Deco decorated blue pieces on page 139 came out of one set found in Ohio. It is as scarce as hen's teeth!

Pastel colors are the lighter shades of blue, green, pink and yellow. Pastel green is shown on the left atop page 141; pastel pink on the bottom left of page 141, pastel yellow on the top right of page 142, and pastel blue on the right of page 144.

On the bottom of page 141 you may notice that there are two distinct shades of pink. I have been assured by Moderntone collectors that this difference in shade is of no consequence to them. It bothers me to the point that I placed the lighter shades on the far right of the photograph to illustrate my point regarding shades of color. I hope these distinct variations show as well in the printed copy as they do on the working copies of my transparencies.

Observations on Moderntone expressed here have come from gathering at least 4,000 pieces of Platonite and 1,600 pieces of children's sets. That is a sufficient sampling to report a few trends about availability and rarity.

In pastel colors, there is an insignificant price difference on the pieces with white interiors as opposed to those with colored interiors. Over the years, I have found there is more demand for colored interiors than the white. My wife, however, prefers white interiors.

All bowls come with or without rims. Bowls without rims are more difficult to find, but bowls with rims tend to have more inner rim roughness which "turns off" many collectors. Pastel pink 8" bowls with or without rims and yellow 12" platters are easier to find than other pastel colors. These must have been a premium at one time which would account for their abundance.

For discussions of the darker colors of Platonite, turn to page 143.

	Pastel Colors	White or w/stripes	Deco/Red or Blue Willow		Pastel Colors	White or w/stripes	Deco/Red or Blue Willow
Bowl, 4¾", cream soup	6.50	4.00	20.00	Plate, 8⅞", dinner	6.50	3.50	22.00
Bowl, 5", berry, w/rim	5.00	3.00	12.50	Plate, 10½", sandwich	16.00	8.00	
Bowl, 5", berry, wo/rim	6.00			Platter, 11", oval		12.50	30.00
Bowl, 5", deep cereal,				Platter, 12", oval	**15.00	9.00	35.00
w/white	7.50	4.00		Salt and pepper, pr.	16.00	13.00	
Bowl, 5", deep cereal,				Saucer	1.00	1.50	5.00
wo/white	9.00			Sherbet	4.50	2.50	12.50
Bowl, 8", w/rim	*14.00	6.00	30.00	Sugar	5.00	4.00	20.00
Bowl, 8", wo/rim	*20.00			Tumbler, 9 oz.	9.00		
Bowl, 8¾", large berry		7.00	30.00	Tumbler, cone, ftd.		6.00	
Creamer	5.00	4.00	20.00				
Cup	3.50	2.50	20.00				
Mug, 4", 8 oz.		8.00		*Pink $8.50			
Plate, 6¾", sherbet	4.50	2.50	9.00	**Yellow $8.00			

Please refer to Foreword for pricing information

MODERNTONE PLATONITE

MODERNTONE PLATONITE

142

MODERNTONE PLATONITE (Cont.)

HAZEL ATLAS GLASS COMPANY, 1940-early 1950's

Colors: Dark Platonite fired-on colors.

Collecting pastel Platonite will give you few problems in finding some pieces; but collecting the darker, later colors will test your patience! When compared to the quantities of pastel, there is a minute amount of darker colors available. You should be prepared to buy it whenever you find it!

The price list below divides colors into two distinct price groups based upon availability. The first group consists of cobalt blue, turquoise green, lemon yellow and orange. These can be found pictured as follows: cobalt (page 144 left), turquoise (top page 141 center), lemon (top page 142 left) and orange (bottom page 142). You might notice an added "face" to the orange plate. Working long hours near Halloween inspired my help at the photo session to get creative. Enough said! All of these colors can be collected in sets with some difficulty, but they can be found eventually. This group can be found with white or colored interiors. White interiors appear to be more plentiful. It only matters if you do not wish to mix the different color treatments made by Hazel Atlas.

Accumulating a set of any of the other colors, i.e., Chartreuse, Burgundy, Green, Gray, "rust" or "gold" is another matter. As far as I can determine, none of the preceding colors can be found with white interiors. These colors are shown at the top of page 145 except for Chartreuse that can only be seen on the right on page 141. Colors shown on the top of page 145 are as follows from left to right: Burgundy, Green, Gray, "rust" and "gold." Collectors have called the Green incorrectly "forest green" and the Burgundy "maroon." I have also heard the "gold" referred to as "butterscotch" which is a better name as far as I am concerned. As with the pink, some collectors consider the "gold" merely a variation of the "lemon" yellow and not a separate color.

In any case, you have a challenge on your hands if you pick any of the aforementioned colors to collect! Note that several pieces listed under the pastel colors are not listed in the darker colors. So far, cream soups, bowls with rims, sandwich plates and salt and pepper shakers have not been found in any of these colors! Green (dark) tumblers seem to be the color most often found in these later colors. If you find others, let me know.

	Cobalt/Turquoise Lemon/Orange	Burgundy/Chartreuse Green/Gray/Rust/Gold
Bowl, 4¾", cream soup	10.00	
Bowl, 5", berry, w/rim	11.00	
Bowl, 5", berry, wo/rim	8.00	12.00
Bowl, 5", deep cereal, w/white	12.00	
Bowl, 5", deep cereal, wo/white		15.00
Bowl, 8", w/rim	30.00	
Bowl, 8", wo/rim	30.00	35.00
Creamer	8.00	11.00
Cup	7.00	8.00
Plate, 6¾", sherbet	6.00	8.00
Plate, 8⅞" dinner	12.00	13.00
Plate, 10½" sandwich	22.00	
Platter, 12" oval	22.00	30.00
Salt and pepper, pr.	22.50	
Saucer	4.00	5.00
Sherbet	7.00	9.00
Sugar	8.00	11.00
Tumbler, 9 oz.	12.50	*22.50

*Green 16.00

MODERNTONE PLATONITE

MODERNTONE "LITTLE HOSTESS PARTY DISHES"
HAZEL ATLAS GLASS COMPANY, early 1950's

Little Hostess Party Dishes have caught the eye of more than collectors of glassware. Doll collectors and doll dish collectors have also joined the search for our Little Hostess sets. This causes prices to climb even more considering there are collectors from other fields pursuing these little sets.

As a child, my wife received a set as a gift premium from Big Top Peanut Butter. (See top page 147.)

You will notice price increases in the harder to find colors. An all white set has been found in an original box. It is shown in *Very Rare Glassware of the Depression Years - Fourth Series*. Turquoise teapots continue to be more difficult to find than Burgundy. When buying Burgundy teapot tops and bottoms separately, a problem occurs matching the shades of Burgundy.

Notice that some child's cups were also sold as souvenir items. The one shown on page 146 with the pink and black is a souvenir of Canada.

LITTLE HOSTESS PARTY SET	
Pink/Black/White (top 146)	
Cup, ¾", bright pink, white	15.00
Saucer, 3⅞", black, white	12.00
Plate, 5¼", black, bright pink, white	15.00
Creamer, 1¾", bright pink	20.00
Sugar, 1¾", bright pink	20.00
Teapot, 3½", bright pink	75.00
Teapot lid, black	75.00
Set, 16 piece	350.00

LITTLE HOSTESS PARTY SET	
Lemon/Beige/Pink/Aqua	
(bottom 146)	
Cup, ¾", bright pink/aqua/lemon	15.00
Saucer, 3⅞", same	12.00
Plate, 5¼", same	15.00
Creamer, 1¾", pink	20.00
Sugar, 1¾", pink	20.00
Teapot, 3½", brown	75.00

Teapot lid, lemon	75.00
Set, 16 piece	350.00

LITTLE HOSTESS PARTY SET	
Gray/Rust/Gold	
Turquoise (top 147)	
Cup, ¾", Gray, rust	13.00
Cup, ¾", gold, turquoise	13.00
Saucer, 3⅞", all four colors	8.00
Plate, 5¼", same	8.00
Creamer, 1¾", rust	15.00
Sugar, 1¾", rust	15.00
Teapot, 3½", turquoise	62.50
Teapot lid, turquoise	62.50
Set, 16 piece	290.00

LITTLE HOSTESS PARTY SET	
Green/Gray/Chartreuse/	
Burgundy (bottom 147 left)	
Cup, ¾", Green, Gray, Chartreuse	10.00

Cup, ¾", Burgundy	13.00
Saucer, 3⅞", Green,	
Gray & Burgundy, Chartreuse	7.00
Plate, 5¼", Burgundy	10.00
Plate, 5¼", Green, Gray, Chartreuse	8.00
Creamer, 1¾", Chartreuse	12.50
Sugar, 1¾", Chartreuse	12.50
Teapot, 3½", Burgundy	55.00
Teapot lid, Burgundy	60.00
Set, 16 piece	245.00

LITTLE HOSTESS PARTY SET	
Pastel pink/green/blue	
yellow (bottom 147 right)	
Cup, ¾", all four colors	9.00
Saucer, 3⅞", same	7.00
Plate, 5¼", same	10.00
Creamer, 1¾", pink	15.00
Sugar, 1¾", pink	15.00
Set, 14 piece	110.00

Please refer to Foreword for pricing information

MOONSTONE ANCHOR HOCKING GLASS CORPORATION, 1941-1946

Colors: crystal with opalescent hobnails and some green with opalescent hobnails.

Originally, Moonstone was the dividing pattern between *The Collector's Encyclopedia of Depression Glass* and this book. Unfortunately, there are several patterns with rather obscure dates of manufacture and some overlapping time periods that do not make the dividing line of 1940 quite as precise as I would have liked. In any case, Moonstone is truly 1940's glassware. I said that I would remove the photograph of a J. J. Newberry store window display this time, but I received so many letters requesting that I leave the photograph that I did! I wish that more of these types of photographs would surface, but I am afraid that the well is dry!

The 5½" berry bowl (shown in the top right foreground of page 149 and listed as M2775 in the Hocking brochure) is the most difficult piece to find today. There are none of those in the store display photo either! Even though goblets and cups and saucers are also missing in that store window display, they are easily found today.

Ruffled 5½" bowls are more readily found than their straight side counter parts; but even they are not as abundant as once thought. The sandwich plate measures 10¾" instead of 10" as was previously listed. Recently I have seen very few of these in my travels. Moonstone is a pattern that has quietly slipped away from the limelight. Not much of it is seen at shows and there are fewer quantities appearing in the market place.

The green colored Moonstone was issued under the name "Ocean Green" and was made in sets containing goblets, cups, saucers, plates, creamer and sugar. Notice the two pieces shown are slightly different from the standard line in the catalogue pages on 150. I wonder if the pink pictured below had a name. This photograph of Moonstone was furnished by Anchor Hocking of pieces found in their morgue. (Discontinued or experimental items were sometimes stored in some place appropriately called a morgue.) Not long ago, I found a pink, flat 7¼" bowl like the one shown.

Fenton Hobnail pitchers and tumblers make good companion pieces to go with Moonstone sets since there are no pitchers or tumblers to be found in Moonstone, nor are there any shakers. Those found are Fenton. There is no Moonstone cologne bottle about which I must receive a dozen letters a year. The Fenton pieces go well with Moonstone; and, if you would like additional pieces that are similar to your pattern, buy them! The hobs on the Fenton are more pointed than on Moonstone, but the colors match very well. Glass companies often copied successful contemporary wares. That still occurs, today, with successful ideas — or even books!

	Opalescent Hobnail		Opalescent Hobnail
Bowl, 5½", berry	16.00	Cup	8.00
Bowl, 5½", crimped, dessert	9.50	Goblet, 10 oz.	18.00
Bowl, 6½", crimped, handled	10.00	Heart bonbon, one handle	13.00
Bowl, 7¾", flat	12.00	Plate, 6¼", sherbet	6.00
Bowl, 7¾", divided relish	12.00	Plate, 8⅜", luncheon	15.00
Bowl, 9½", crimped	22.00	Plate, 10¾", sandwich	27.50
Bowl, cloverleaf	13.00	Puff box and cover, 4¾", round	24.00
Candle holder, pr.	18.00	Saucer (same as sherbet plate)	6.00
Candy jar and cover, 6"	25.00	Sherbet, footed	7.00
Cigarette jar and cover	22.50	Sugar, footed	9.00
Creamer	9.00	Vase, 5½", bud	12.00

Please refer to Foreword for pricing information

Opalescent "MOONSTONE" Glassware

"MOONSTONE" Glassware

Tableware		DOZ. TO CTN.	WT. OF CTN.
M2779	3⅜" Cup	6	32#
M2729	6¼" Saucer	6	32#
M2713	6 oz. Sherbet	6	32#
M2729	6¼" Sherbet Plate	6	32#
M2775	5½" Dessert	6	32#
M2716	10 oz. Goblet	4	35#
M2740	8⅜" Luncheon Plate	4	44#
Gift Ware			
M2769	7¾" Divided Relish	2	27#
M2766	6½" Crimped Handled Bowl	2	19#
M2755	6¾" Clover Leaf Dish	2	22#
M2772	6½" Heart Bonbon	2	20#
M2767	7¾" Flat Bowl	2	23#
M2753	3¼" Sugar	2	13#
M2754	3¼" Creamer	2	12½#
M2722	4¾" Puff Box & Cover	2	22#
M2799	5" Cigarette Jar & Cover	2	25#
M2782	5½" Vase	2	16#
M2792	6" Candy Jar & Cover	1	20#
M2760	10¾" Sandwich Plate	1	21#
M2768	9½" Crimped Bowl	1	21#
M2765	5½" Crimped Dessert	6	33#
M2781	4¼" Candleholder	2	10#
Suggested Sets - Bulk Packed			
M2700/1	7 Pce. Dessert Set (Bulk Packed in 2 Cartons)	12 Sets	54#
M2700/2	4 Pce. Buffet Set (Bulk Packed in 2 Cartons)	12 Sets	52#

Now Available at Low Prices

150

MOROCCAN AMETHYST HAZEL WARE, DIVISION OF CONTINENTAL CAN, 1960's

Color: Amethyst.

Moroccan Amethyst is the color that is found on several styles and shapes of this Hazel Ware glass. Like Anchor Hocking's Forest Green and Royal Ruby, the color became more important to identifying the glass than the pattern name. Pattern took second place to color!

To have some usable terminology for the different patterns in this color, I will do as we did in Capri. The square or rectangular based pieces (shown on page 152) will be called Colony. For proof, that amber tumbler has a Colony label on it. No "Colony Swirl" has been found in Moroccan. Page 153 shows mostly the Moroccan Swirl with some Octagonal and other miscellaneous styles. All of these patterns occur in Capri which means that the color name will have to precede the pattern derivative. Also at the top of page 154 is a set of "Tulip"-like ash trays. These have sometimes been confused with Dell's Tulip pattern. Note the similarities in the two, but remember there are no ash trays in Dell's Tulip!

The expanded listing shows many new items. One of the most interesting is the Apple shaped salad bowl set found at a flea market south of Pittsburgh. You can see the large and smaller apple shaped bowls on the top of page 154. These pieces have an embossed apple blossom design in the bottom. You may find this salad set in fired on Platonite, but the apple blossom design is missing in the bottom of these bowls. Several of these items on page 154 are shown standing up on 152 and 153. Hopefully, you will find one view to your liking. There is also a floral design in the bottom of the 4½" square ash tray, but it is obliterated by the original Moroccan Amethyst sticker, an item we were reluctant to remove. The 4½", five pointed star candlesticks were an additional find. All these items came from the family of a worker at the Hazel Atlas plant. The seller promised me more pieces the following month, so I drove back the 385 miles to see what else was available. Unfortunately, he did not attend that month as promised.

The top of page 155 shows other colors being found in the swirled design. You will find swirled bowls in green, amber and white! Bowls are usually reasonably priced in these colors. I suspect that they are later productions made to go with the prevalent 1970's Avocado and Harvest Gold colors. Crystal and white stemware are also being found that match the Moroccan designs.

An original box for the amethyst and white punch bowl set is shown on page 155. Notice that this set was called Alpine. The punch cups have open handles to hang onto the side of the punch bowl. I have seen some extravagant prices on this set, but I was able to attain mine for $75.00 by the time I added four missing cups. A "Seashell" snack set in the same two colors was also identified as "Alpine." The amethyst bowl pictured in the center of the punch bowls served not only as a bowl, but also as the punch bowl base. Duality saved making an additional mould.

"The Magic Hour" 4 pc. cocktail set on page 157 features a clock showing six o'clock and says "yours" on one side and "mine" on the other. In this boxed set are two, 2½", 4 oz. tumblers and a spouted cocktail with metal stirring spoon to make up the four pieces. You will find two and three tier tidbit trays made from different pieces in this pattern including bowls, plates and ash trays.

The 7¾" bowl on the bottom right of page 154 is the only piece of this pattern that I have seen with an acid etched design. The dealer who sold it to me said she had found two! Not much of the sprayed red over crystal is being found, but there is also little demand for it at present. Crystal, amber and green pieces may someday be desirable to own; but for now, that does not seem to be the case!

One fun thing about collecting a pattern is finding new pieces not listed! Send me a picture and measurements of what you discover!

	Amethyst		Amethyst
Ash tray, 3¼", triangular	5.50	Goblet, 4¼", 7½ oz., sherbet	7.50
Ash tray, 3¼", round	5.50	Goblet, 4⅜", 5½ oz., juice	9.00
Ash tray, 6⅞", triangular	9.50	Goblet, 5½", 9 oz., water	10.00
Ash tray, 8", square	13.00	Ice bucket, 6"	32.00
Bowl, 4¾", fruit, octagonal	7.50	Plate, 5¾"	4.50
Bowl, 5¾", deep, square	10.00	Plate, 7¼", salad	7.00
Bowl, 6", round	11.00	Plate, 9¾", dinner	9.00
Bowl, 7¾", oval	16.00	Plate, 10", fan shaped, snack w/cup rest	8.00
Bowl. 7¾", rectangular	14.00	Plate, 12", sandwich, w/metal /handle	12.50
Bowl. 7¾", rectangular w/ metal handle	16.00	Saucer	1.00
Bowl, 10¾"	30.00	Tumbler, 4 oz., juice, 2½"	8.50
Candy w/lid short	32.00	Tumbler, 8 oz., old fashion, 3¼"	14.00
Candy w/lid tall	32.00	Tumbler, 9 oz., water	10.00
Chip and dip, 10¾" & 5¾" bowls in metal holder	40.00	Tumbler, 11 oz., water, crinkled bottom, 4¼"	12.00
Cocktail w/stirrer, 6¼", 16 oz., w/lip	30.00	Tumbler, 11 oz., water, 4⅝"	12.00
Cocktail shaker w/lid	30.00	Tumbler, 16 oz., iced tea, 6½"	16.00
Cup	5.00	Vase, 8½", ruffled	37.50
Goblet, 4", 4½ oz., wine	10.00		

MOROCCAN AMETHYST

MOROCCAN AMETHYST

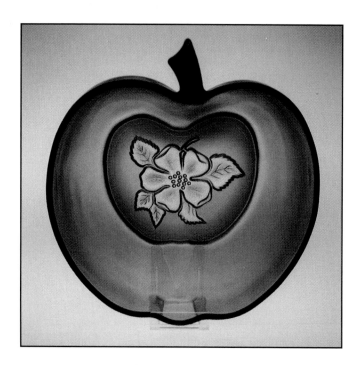

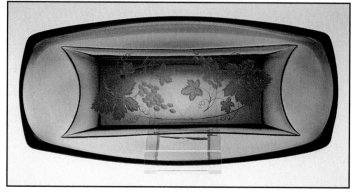

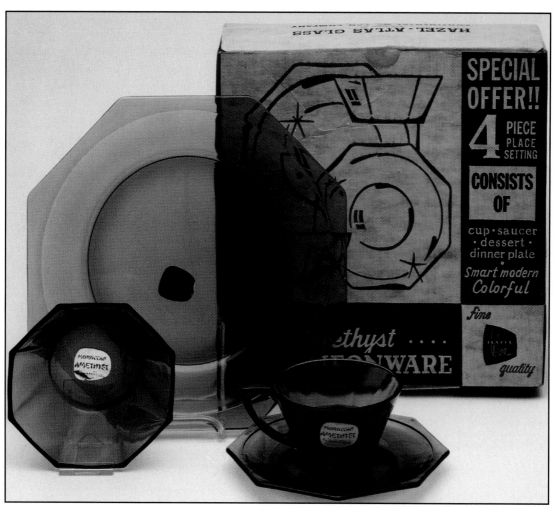

156

NAVARRE PLATE ETCHING #327 FOSTORIA GLASS COMPANY, 1937-1982

Colors: Crystal, blue, pink and rare in green.

Since the biggest distribution of this pattern was after 1937, I have elected to include it in this book. Many of the harder to find pieces were made near the end of Fostoria's reign (late 1970's and early 1980's). Most of these pieces were signed "Fostoria" (acid etched on base) although some carried only a sticker. Most factory "seconds" sold through the outlet stores were not signed.

Shown on page 159 are a few of the later made pieces of Navarre. Top row shows water goblets, magnum and continental champagnes. The second row shows the large claret, regular claret, saucer champagnes, low sherbet, oyster cocktail and bells. The third row shows footed teas, footed water, footed juice, double old fashioned, highball and cordial. The fourth row shows a 10½" footed #2470½ bowl, 3 part candy and a "Flame" oval bowl. The bottom row shows a #2482 triple candlestick, #2440 sugar and creamer, and the "Flame" double candlestick. Parts of several 1982 catalogue sheets are reprinted on page 161 which also display many of those pieces made right at the end of the Navarre production. You will find that gathering a set of Navarre will be time consuming, but it can still be done with time, patience and money!

	Crystal	Blue/Pink		Crystal	Blue/Pink
Bell, dinner	45.00	80.00	Plate, #2440, 10½" oval cake	50.00	
Bowl, #2496, 4", square, hndl.	12.00		Plate, #2496, 14", torte	60.00	
Bowl, #2496, 4⅜", hndl.	12.00		Plate, #2464, 16", torte	90.00	
Bowl, #869, 4½", finger	42.50		Relish, #2496, 6", 2 part, square	32.50	
Bowl, #2496, 4⅝", tri-cornered	15.00		Relish, #2496, 10" x 7½", 3 part	47.50	
Bowl, #2496, 5", hndl., ftd.	18.50		Relish, #2496, 10", 4 part	52.50	
Bowl, #2496, 6", square, sweetmeat	17.50		Relish, #2419, 13¼", 5 part	87.50	
Bowl, #2496, 6¼", 3 ftd., nut	18.50		Salt & pepper, #2364, 3¼", flat, pr.	57.50	
Bowl, #2496, 7⅜", ftd., bonbon	27.50		Salt & pepper, #2375, 3½", ftd., pr.	100.00	
Bowl, #2496, 10", oval, floating garden	55.00		Salad dressing bottle, #2083, 6½"	335.00	
Bowl, #2496, 10½", hndl., ftd.	65.00		Sauce dish, #2496, div. mayo., 6½"	37.50	
Bowl, #2470½, 10½", ftd.	57.50		Sauce dish, #2496, 6½" x 5¼"	125.00	
Bowl, #2496, 12", flared	62.50		Sauce dish liner, #2496, 8", oval	27.50	
Bowl, #2545, 12½", oval, "Flame"	57.50		Saucer, #2440	5.00	
Candlestick, #2496, 4"	20.00		Stem, #6106, ¾ oz., cordial, 3⅞"	47.50	
Candlestick, #2496, 4½", double	35.00		Stem, #6106, 3¼ oz., wine, 5½"	35.00	
Candlestick, #2472, 5", double	42.50		Stem, #6106, 3½ oz., cocktail, 6"	25.00	
Candlestick, #2496, 5½"	30.00		Stem, #6106, 4 oz., oyster cocktail, 3⅝"	27.50	
Candlestick, #2496, 6", triple	45.00		Stem, #6106, 4½ oz., claret, 6"	40.00	60.00
Candlestick, #2545, 6¾", double, "Flame"	50.00		Stem, #6106, 5 oz., continental		
Candlestick, #2482, 6¾", triple	50.00		champagne, 8⅛"	47.50	60.00
Candy, w/cover, #2496, 3 part	115.00		Stem, #6106, 6 oz., cocktail/sherry, 6³⁄₁₆"	37.50	
Celery, #2440, 9"	30.00		Stem, #6106, 6 oz., low sherbet, 4⅜"	24.00	
Celery, #2496, 11"	40.00		Stem, #6106, 6 oz., saucer champagne, 5⅝"	24.00	35.00
Comport, #2496, 3¼", cheese	27.50		Stem, #6106, 6½ oz., large claret, 6½"	37.50	55.00
Comport, #2400, 4½"	30.00		Stem, #6106, 10 oz., water, 7⅝"	30.00	45.00
Comport, #2496, 4¾"	30.00		Stem, #6106, 15 oz., brandy inhaler, 5½"	40.00	
Cracker, #2496, 11" plate	42.50		Stem, #6106, 16 oz., magnum, 7¼"	75.00	85.00
Creamer, #2440, 4¼", ftd.	20.00		Sugar, #2440, 3⅝", ftd.	18.00	
Creamer, #2496, individual	17.50		Sugar, #2496, individual	16.00	
Cup, #2440	19.00		Syrup, #2586, Sani-cut, 5½"	350.00	
Ice bucket, #2496, 4⅜" high	110.00		Tid bit, #2496, 8¼", 3 ftd., turned up edge	22.00	
Ice bucket, #2375, 6" high	150.00		Tray, #2496½, for ind. sugar/creamer	22.00	
Mayonnaise, #2375, 3 piece	67.50		Tumbler, #6106, 5 oz., ftd., juice, 4⅝"	25.00	
Mayonnaise, #2496½, 3 piece	67.50		Tumbler, #6106, 10 oz., ftd., water, 5⅜"	25.00	
Pickle, #2496, 8"	27.50		Tumbler, #6106, 12 oz., flat, highball, 4⅞"	42.50	
Pickle, #2440, 8½"	30.00		Tumbler, #6106, 13 oz., flat,		
Pitcher, #5000, 48 oz., ftd.	335.00		double old fashioned, 3⅝"	57.50	
Plate, #2440, 6", bread/butter	11.00		Tumbler, #6106, 13 oz., ftd., tea, 5⅞"	32.00	40.00
Plate, #2440, 7½", salad	15.00		Vase, #4108, 5"	90.00	
Plate, #2440, 8½", luncheon	20.00		Vase, #4121, 5"	90.00	
Plate, #2440, 9½", dinner	45.00		Vase, #4128, 5"	90.00	
Plate, #2496, 10", hndl., cake	50.00		Vase, #2470, 10", ftd.	150.00	

Please refer to Foreword for pricing information

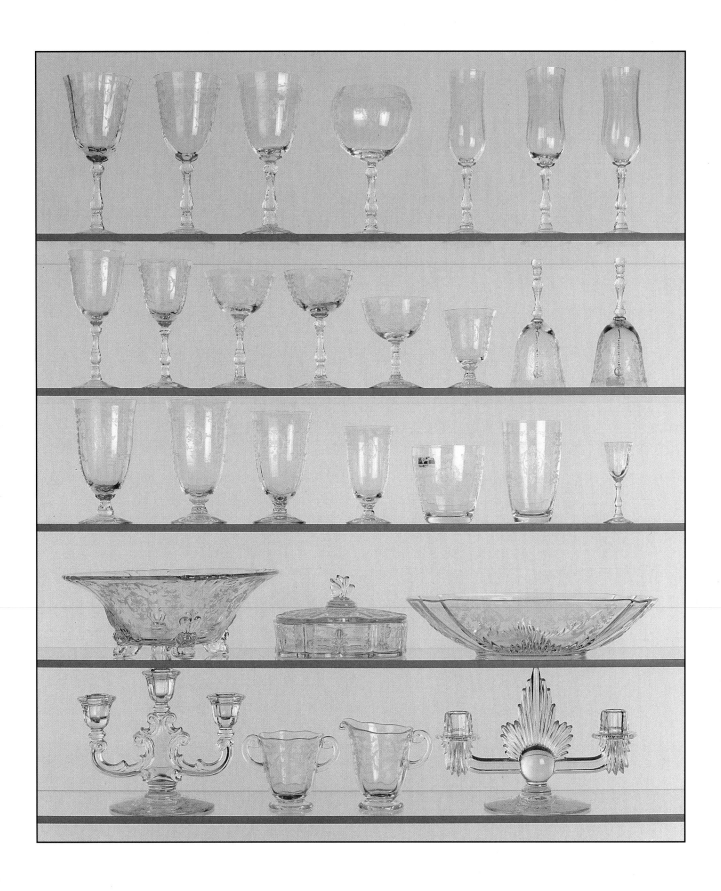

Bell | 7 in. Plate / 8 in. Plate | Double Old Fashioned | High Ball

Wilma Blue — Goblet | Wilma Crystal — Goblet | Navarre Crystal — Goblet | Low Dessert/ Champagne | High Dessert/ Champagne

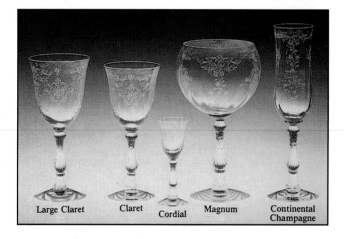

Large Claret | Claret | Cordial | Magnum | Continental Champagne

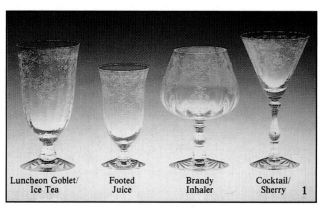

Luncheon Goblet/ Ice Tea | Footed Juice | Brandy Inhaler | Cocktail/ Sherry

1

NEW ERA #4044 A.H. HEISEY CO., 1934-1941; 1944-1957 (stems, celery tray, and candlesticks)

Colors: Crystal, frosted crystal, some cobalt with crystal stem and foot.

Production of New Era was begun in the 1930's; but the stemware so often seen now fits the era encompassed in this book. New Era is sought by "Art Deco" collectors.

Note the cobalt items on the second row. Any New Era piece with cobalt bowl will fetch $125.00 to $150.00. Keep that in mind in your journeys.

The double branched candelabra with the New Era bobeches is not hard to find, but very desirable. Dinner plates without scratches and after dinner cups and saucers will keep you searching for a long time unless you are lucky!

I might point out that luncheon plate with the unusual label shown on the right. I left the label ("flower pot saucer") on the piece that I bought in an antique mall in Evansville. I wonder who thought someone might have had monogrammed flower pot saucers? Sometimes a giggle brightens your day when you are out buying glass

	Crystal		Crystal
Ash tray or indiv. nut	30.00	Stem, 1 oz. cordial	45.00
Bottle, rye w/stopper	120.00	Stem, 3 oz. wine	35.00
Bowl, 11" floral	35.00	Stem, 3½ oz., high, cocktail	10.00
Candelabra, 2 lite w/2 #4044 bobeche & prisms	70.00	Stem, 3½ oz. oyster cocktail	10.00
Creamer	35.00	Stem, 4 oz. claret	15.00
Cup	10.00	Stem, 6 oz. sherbet, low	12.50
Cup, after dinner	60.00	Stem, 6 oz. champagne	12.50
Pilsner, 8 oz.	25.00	Stem, 10 oz. goblet	15.00
Pilsner, 12 oz.	30.00	Sugar	35.00
Plate, 5½" x 4½" bread & butter	15.00	Tray, 13" celery	30.00
Plate, 9"x 7", luncheon	25.00	Tumbler, 5 oz. ftd. soda	7.00
Plate, 10" x 8", dinner	40.00	Tumbler, 8 oz. ftd. soda	11.00
Relish, 13" 3-part	25.00	Tumbler, 10 oz., low, ftd.	11.00
Saucer	5.00	Tumbler, 12 oz. ftd. soda	13.00
Saucer, after dinner	12.50	Tumbler, 14 oz. ftd. soda	16.00

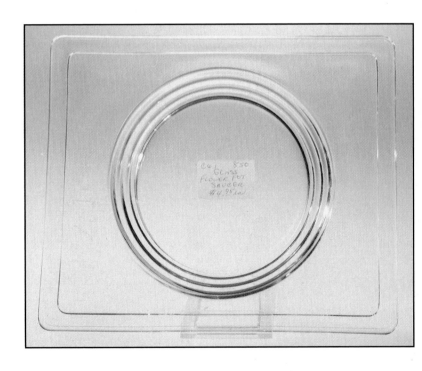

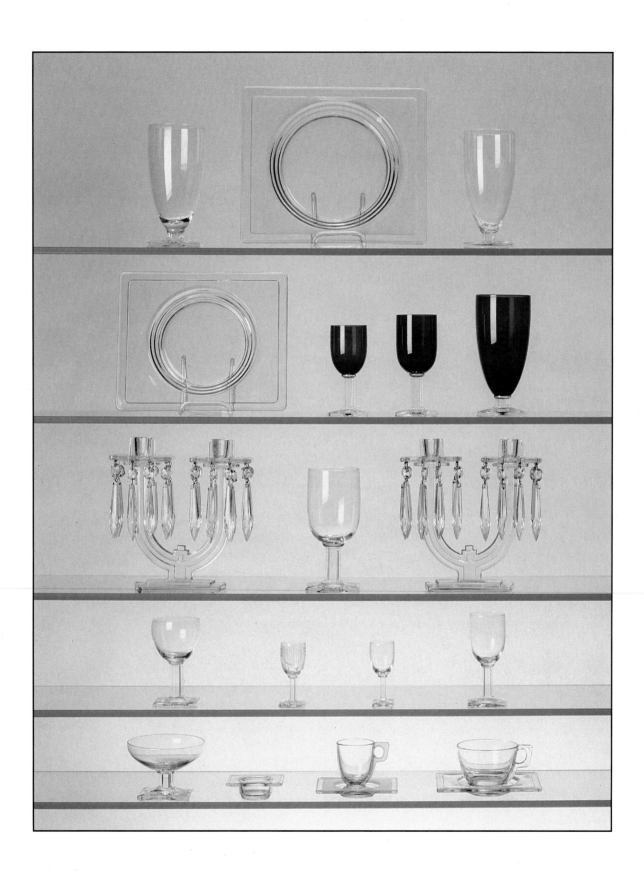

NEWPORT, "HAIRPIN" HAZEL ATLAS GLASS COMPANY, 1940-early 1950's

Colors: Platonite white and fired-on colors.

Newport is a pattern that Hazel Atlas made in the late 1930's in several transparent colors; afterward, they continued making it in Platonite until the early 1950's. This pattern splits listings into both this book and *The Collector's Encyclopedia of Depression Glass*. "Platonite" white (and white with fired on colors) was a popular line for Hazel Atlas. Notice the white edge on the fired-on pink plate in the rear. The edges and back of this plate are white. The pink (or other pastel color) decorates only the top. On the other hand, the turquoise blue bowl and dark green plate have colors completely fired-on.

Only a few hours ago I received a call from Phoenix asking me if I still needed a Platonite tumbler. Since that piece is missing in the picture, I paid "book" price so I could show you one next time. It is supposedly pink. I would entertain owning other colors! This is not a pattern that is seen very often at glass shows; so, I need help in finding additional pieces and colors.

The white color comes in two distinct shades. One is very translucent and the other is a flat white similar to what many collectors know as milk glass. The white shaker is often used by Petalware collectors for their pattern since there are no shakers in the MacBeth-Evans set. It is not unusual for collectors to be fooled into thinking these shakers really are Petalware.

If you have unlisted Platonite pieces, please let me know! Do not assume I already have information you can not find listed. I very often learn new information from collectors!

	White	Fired-on colors
Bowl, 4¾", berry	3.50	5.50
Bowl, 4¾", cream soup	5.50	8.50
Bowl, 8¼, large berry	9.50	14.00
Cup	3.50	6.00
Creamer	4.50	7.50
Plate, 6", sherbet	1.00	1.50
Plate, 8½", luncheon	3.00	5.00
Plate, 11½", sandwich	10.00	14.00
Platter, 11¾", oval	12.00	17.50
Salt and pepper, pr.	18.00	22.50
Saucer	.75	1.00
Sherbet	3.50	6.00
Sugar	4.50	7.50
Tumbler		15.00

OVIDE, incorrectly dubbed "NEW CENTURY" HAZEL ATLAS GLASS COMPANY, 1930-1950's

Colors: Green, black, white Platonite trimmed and fired-on colors in 1950's.

Ovide is another Hazel Atlas pattern that began production in the Depression era, but continued well into the 1950's. Pattern names have been uncovered for some of the pastel banded Platonite that was used in restaurants and competed with Anchor Hocking's Jade-ite Restaurant Ware line. A full page ad is shown on page 167 introducing Sierra Sunrise. The charcoal and pink combination shown below was named Informal as can be seen in the 1955 ad on page 168. This ad boldly states that pink and charcoal were popular color combinations in 1955.

There is only a little collector interest in this Platonite with pastel banded edges. This inexpensively priced glassware is being utilized as everyday dishes. Platonite works well in both the microwave and the dishwasher according to collectors who are handling it that way. Those two facts alone should attract more patrons.

The colors shown on the bottom of page 166 have been intriguing to find. I have never found a platter in any color than the one shown which I like to refer to as "Butterscotch." I am sure you can find each of the basic pieces in all colors, but serving pieces may be another matter. Let me known what you find!

One of the difficulties in ordering glass through the mail is miscommunication between buyer and seller. I ordered an eighteen piece set of dark "Moderntone" colors through the mail several years ago expecting to receive Moderntone pattern. I got Moderntone Ovide. The box is pictured at the bottom of 169 and the contents are shown at the top of the page. (The ash tray set was acquired separately.) If I had phoned the lady again and mailed the box back, I would have lost several dollars in the transaction; so I kept the box of dishes never realizing that someday it would come in handy as reference material. Evidently, **MODERNTONE** referred to the **colors and not the pattern**. In any case, the box says that it includes an eighteen piece breakfast set in burgundy, chartreuse, green and gray. Notice that "green" is the actual color designation by Hazel Atlas for what collectors have always called forest or dark green. The colors in this particular set are similar to those found in the pattern that we call Moderntone. Note how well these colors go with the popular 50's colors of Fiesta dinnerware.

Prices can be found on the top of page 166.

OVIDE, incorrectly dubbed "NEW CENTURY" (Cont.)

	White w/trims	Decorated White	Fired-on Colors	Art Deco
Ash tray, square			4.00	
Bowl, 4¾", berry	3.50	6.50	5.50	
Bowl, 5½", cereal, deep		15.00		
Bowl, 8", large berry			18.00	
Creamer	4.50	18.00	5.50	80.00
Cup	3.50	12.50	4.50	50.00
Plate, 6", sherbet	1.50	2.50		
Plate, 8", luncheon	2.50	13.00	4.00	45.00
Plate, 9", dinner	3.50			
Platter, 11"	7.50	25.00		
Refrigerator stacking set, 4 pc.		47.50		
Salt and pepper, pr.	13.00			
Saucer	1.00	2.50		20.00
Sherbet	5.50	2.00		45.00
Sugar, open	4.50	18.00	5.50	80.00
Tumbler		20.00		80.00

OVIDE

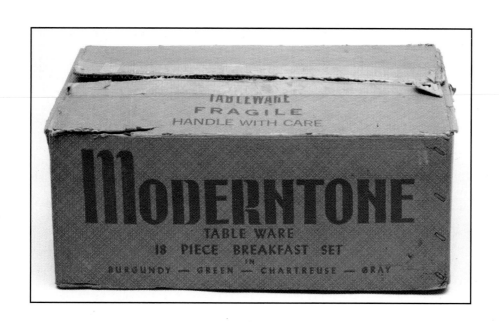

169

PANELED GRAPE, PATTERN #1881 WESTMORELAND GLASS COMPANY, 1950-1970's

Colors: White and white w/decorations.

Paneled Grape is the Westmoreland pattern most readily recognized after English Hobnail. From its introduction in 1950, Pattern #1881 soon became a line that encompassed over a hundred pieces. Westmoreland listed this pattern with both names as you can see from the catalogue pages that follow. (Please note that any pieces shown on these catalogue sheets as #1884 are part of the line known as Beaded Grape and are not priced in the Paneled Grape listing below).

Observe the differences in the epergnes shown on page 171. The one pictured on the bottom left by itself has the rarely found vase with the decoration around the top. The more commonly found epergne vase (without a pattern around the top) is shown in the top photo in the 14" flared bowl and again in the 9" lipped bowl on the bottom of page 173. The tall vases on 171 and again at the top of 173 are various sizes of swung vases. These sizes vary since they are literally swung to extend their shape!

Prices on some of the rarely found items have recently slowed their upward trend; basic pieces are holding steady. Made for so long a time, supply of #1881 has been able to keep up with the demand for now.

The catalogue pages shown on pages 174-184 are from a 1973 catalogue. Paneled Grape is one of those patterns you either love or hate. Some people can not abide white milk glass; and others think it is the most beautiful glass on earth. If everyone liked the same thing, my book would only contain one pattern. Thankfully there are many different patterns made in this time period to suit every collecting need. Collect what gives you enjoyment!

	White, w/decorations		White, w/decorations
Appetizer or canapé set, 3 pc. (9" three-part relish/round fruit cocktail/ladle)	62.50	Candelabra, 3 lite, ea.	285.00
		Candle holder, 4", octagonal, pr.	27.50
Basket, 5½", ruffled	55.00	Candle holder, 5", w/colonial hdld.	35.00
Basket, 6½", oval	25.00	Candle holder, 8", 2 lite (4 of these	
Basket, 8"	77.50	form a circular center piece)	35.00
Basket, 8", ruffled	65.00	Candy jar, 3 ftd., w/cover	32.50
Bon bon, 8", ruffled w/metal handle	50.00	Candy jar, 6¼", w/cover	25.00
Bottle, 5 oz., toilet	62.50	Canister, 7"	130.00
Bottle, oil or vinegar, w/stopper, 2 oz.	22.00	Canister, 9½"	150.00
Bowl, pedestal base, 5" (used w/12"/12½"		Canister, 11"	175.00
lipped/10" rnd. bowls & epergne)	70.00	Celery or spooner, 6"	40.00
Bowl, 4", crimped	22.00	Cheese/old fashioned butter, 7", round w/cover	57.50
Bowl, 6", crimped, stemmed	30.00	Chocolate box, 6½", w/cover	52.50
Bowl, 6", ruffled edge, stemmed	30.00	Compote, 4½", crimped	30.00
Bowl, 6½" x 12½", 3⅛" high	110.00	Compote, 7" covered, ftd.	47.50
Bowl, 6½", oval	23.00	Compote, 9" ftd., crimped	77.50
Bowl, 8", cupped	38.00	Condiment set, 5 pc. (oil and vinegar, salt	
Bowl, 8½", shallow	55.00	and pepper on 9" oval tray)	110.00
Bowl, 9", ftd., 6" high, skirted base	47.50	Creamer, 6½ oz.	16.00
Bowl, 9", ftd., w/cover	67.50	Creamer, individual	11.00
Bowl, 9", lipped	100.00	Creamer, large (goes w/lacy edge sugar)	22.50
Bowl, 9", lipped, ftd.	100.00	Creamer, small	10.00
Bowl, 9", square, w/cover	35.00	Cup, coffee, flared	13.00
Bowl, 9½", bell shape	45.00	Cup, punch, cupped	12.00
Bowl, 9½", ftd., bell shaped	100.00	Decanter, wine	145.00
Bowl, 10", oval	37.50	Dresser set, 4 pc. (2)5 oz. toilet bottles, puff	
Bowl, 10½", round	77.50	box and 13½" oval tray	225.00
Bowl, 11", oval, lipped, ftd.	110.00	Egg plate, 12"	75.00
Bowl, 11½", oval, ruffled edge	80.00	Egg tray, 10", metal center handle	57.50
Bowl, 12", lipped	115.00	Epergne vase, 8½", bell	60.00
Bowl, 12" ftd., banana	130.00	Epergne vase, pattern at top	195.00
Bowl, 12½", bell shape	130.00	Epergne set, 2 pc. (9" lipped bowl/8½" epergne vase)	110.00
Bowl, 13", punch, bell or flared	300.00	Epergne set, 2 pc. (11½" epergne flared	
Bowl, 14", shallow, round	140.00	bowl/8½" epergne vase)	110.00
Bowl, ftd., ripple top	75.00	Epergne set, 2 pc. (12" epergne lipped	
Butter w/cover, ¼ pound	22.50	bowl/8½" epergne vase)	195.00
Cake salver, 10½"	65.00	Epergne set, 2 pc. (14" flared bowl/8½"	
Cake salver, 11", round ftd., w/skirt	70.00	epergne vase)	225.00
Canapé or set, 3 pc. (12½" canapé		Epergne set, 3 pc. (12" epergne lipped	
tray/3½" cocktail/ladle)	120.00	bowl/5" bowl base/8½" epergne vase)	310.00

Please refer to Foreword for pricing information

PANELED GRAPE

	White, w/decorations		White, w/decorations
Epergne set, 3 pc. (14" flared bowl/5" bowl base/8½" epergne vase)	295.00	Salt and pepper, 4¼", small, ftd., pr.	22.50
Flower pot	47.50	*Salt and pepper, 4¼", small, ftd., pr.,	27.50
Fruit cocktail, 3½" w/6" sauce plate, bell shape	22.50	Salt and pepper, 4½", large, flat, pr.	52.50
Fruit cocktail, 4½" w/6" sauce plate, round	25.00	Sauce boat	30.00
Ivy ball	47.50	Sauce boat tray, 9"	30.00
Jardiniere, 5", cupped and ftd.	25.00	Saucer	8.50
Jardiniere, 5", straight sided	25.00	Sherbet, 3¾", low foot	16.00
Jardiniere, 6½", cupped and ftd.	35.00	Sherbet, 4¾", high foot	17.50
Jardiniere, 6½", straight sided	35.00	Soap dish	80.00
Jelly, 4½", covered	27.50	Stem, 2 oz. cordial or wine goblet	22.50
Ladle, small	10.00	Stem, 3 oz.	30.00
Ladle, punch	47.50	Stem, 5 oz., wine goblet	30.00
Lighter in 2 oz. goblet	30.00	Stem, 8 oz. water goblet	18.00
Lighter in tooth pick	33.00	Sugar w/cover, lacy edge on sugar to serve as spoon holder	32.50
Marmalade, w/ladle	57.50	Sugar, 6½"	14.00
Mayonnaise set, 3 pc. (round fruit cocktail/6" sauce plate/ladle)	35.00	Sugar, small w/cover	14.00
Mayonnaise, 4", ftd.	27.50	Tid-bit or snack server, 2 tier (dinner and breakfast plates)	65.00
Napkin ring	17.50	Tid-bit tray, metal handle on 8½" breakfast plate	27.50
Nappy, 4½", round	14.00	Tid-bit tray, metal handle on 10½" dinner plate	47.50
Nappy, 5", bell shape	22.00	Toothpick	24.00
Nappy, 5", round w/handle	30.00	Tray, 9", oval	45.00
Nappy, 7", round	30.00	Tray, 13½", oval	80.00
Nappy, 8½", round	30.00	Tumbler, 5 oz. juice	24.00
Nappy, 9", round, 2" high	40.00	Tumbler, 6 oz. old fashioned cocktail	27.50
Nappy, 10", bell	45.00	Tumbler, 8 oz.	22.50
Parfait, 6"	23.00	Tumbler, 12 oz. ice tea	25.00
Pedestal, base to punch bowl, skirted	135.00	Vase, 4", rose	20.00
Pickle, oval	21.00	Vase, 4½, rose, ftd., cupped, stemmed	35.00
Pitcher, 16 oz.	47.50	Vase, 6", bell shape	20.00
Pitcher, 32 oz.	37.50	Vase, 6½" or celery	35.00
Planter, 3" x 8½"	35.00	Vase, 8½", bell shape	25.00
Planter, 4½", square	40.00	Vase, 9", bell shape	25.00
Planter, 5" x 9"	38.00	Vase, 9", crimped top	32.00
Planter, 6", small, wall	75.00	Vase, 9½", straight	35.00
Planter, 8", large, wall	125.00	Vase, 10" bud (size may vary)	20.00
Plate, 6", bread	14.00	Vase, 11", rose (similar to bud vase but bulbous at bottom)	35.00
Plate, 7" salad, w/depressed center	25.00	Vase, 11½", bell shape	47.50
Plate, 8½", breakfast	22.00	Vase, 11½", straight	35.00
Plate, 10½", dinner	47.50	Vase, 12", hand blown	150.00
Plate, 14½"	120.00	Vase, 14", swung (size varies)	19.00
Plate, 18"	165.00	Vase, 15"	30.00
Puff box or jelly, w/cover	27.50	Vase, 16", swung (size varies)	20.00
Punch set, 15 pc. (13" bowl, 12 punch cups, pedestal and ladle)	575.00	Vase, 18", swung (size varies)	20.00
Punch set, 15 pc. (same as above w/11" bowl w/o scalloped bottom)	495.00		
Relish, 9", 3 part	39.50		

*All over pattern

PANELED GRAPE

"Panel Grape"

GIFT SUGGESTIONS TO PLEASE THE DISCRIMINATING

1881
Bowl, Crimp.

1881 Bowl,
Lip. Ftd.

1881 Bowl,
Shallow

1881
Basket, Hld.

1881
Bowl, Lip.

1881
Bowl, Oval

1881/6½"
Basket

1881
Appetizer Set

1881
Bowl, Bell

1881
Bowl, Rose

1881
Butter

1881
Bon Bon

3

FAMOUS *"Panel Grape"* THE COLLECTORS FAVORITE

1881 Plates, 14½″, 10½″ & 8½″

1881
3 pc. Canister Set

1881
Jug, Qt.

1881
Salver, Skirted

1881
Salver, Ftd.

1881
Egg Tray

1881 Snack Server

1881
Ice Tea

1881
Goblet

1881
Sauce Boat/Tray

1881
Mayonnaise

1881
Condiment Set

1881
Salt/Pepper,
Lg.

1881
Oil

1881
Salt/Pepper
(Min. 3 Sets)

1881
Candy

1881
Dish, 3 Ftd.

1881
Puff Box/
Jelly

1881
Chocolate Box

1881
Candy, Crimp.

1881
Pickle

1881
Candlestick

1881
Mayo
Set

1881
Cup/Saucer

1881
Dish, Oval

1881
Starter Set

4

PANELED GRAPE

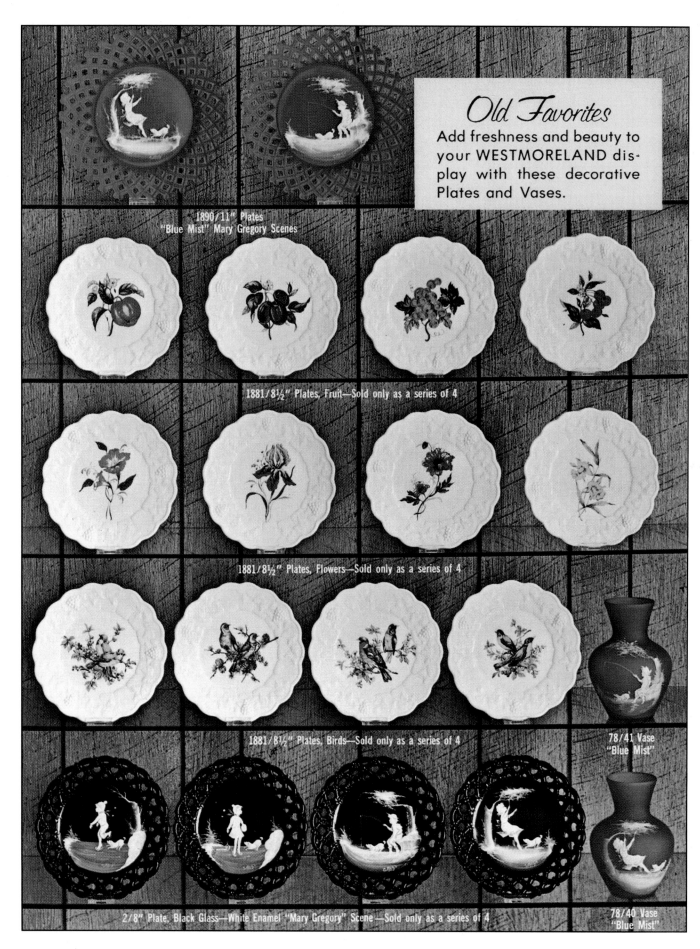

Old Favorites

Add freshness and beauty to your WESTMORELAND display with these decorative Plates and Vases.

1890/11" Plates "Blue Mist" Mary Gregory Scenes

1881/8½" Plates, Fruit—Sold only as a series of 4

1881/8½" Plates, Flowers—Sold only as a series of 4

1881/8½" Plates, Birds—Sold only as a series of 4

78/41 Vase "Blue Mist"

2/8" Plate, Black Glass—White Enamel "Mary Gregory" Scene—Sold only as a series of 4

78/40 Vase "Blue Mist"

MGT0731
Plate, 14½"

MGT0730
Plate, 10½"

MGT0734
Sauce Boat

MGT0729
Plate, 8½"

MGT0737
Sugar & Cream, Small

MGT0724
Cup & Saucer

MGT0733
Salt & Pepper
Small, Height, 4¼"

MGT0721
Appetizer Set

MGT0726
Jug, 1 Qt.

MGT0725
Goblet

MGT0736
Sugar & Cream,
Large

MGT0740
Cake

MGT0722
Butter

MGT0732
Salt & Pepper
Large, Height, 4½"

MGT0739
Wine

MGT0738
Tid Bit Tray

Milk Glass Tableware

PANELED GRAPE

1881 Sauce Boat/Tray

1881 Goblet 8 oz.

1881 Sugar/Cream, Lg.

1881 Jug, Qt.

1881 Salt/Pepper

large

small

1881 Oil, 2 oz.

small

1881 Sugar/Cream

1881 Snack Server

1881 Tid Bit Tray

1881 Appetizer Set

1881 Marmalade W/Ladle

1881 Plate, 14½"

1881 Plate, 10½"

1881 Plate, 8½"

1881 Cheese

1881 Butter

1881 Cup/Saucer

...*Kitchen & Table Accessories*

29

109 Cookie Jar

Collector's items from the vast "Paneled Grape" pattern

1881/9"
Bowl, Sq.

1881/9"
Compote, Crimped

1881
Compote, Crimped

1881/7"
Compote

1881
Candy Jar

1881
Decanter

1881
Celery/Vase

1881
Dish, 3 Ftd.

1881
Chocolate Box

1881
Candleholder

1881
Cocktail, Fruit

1881
Cheese

1881/9"
Bowl, Bell

1881/¼ #
Butter

1881
Cup/Saucer

1881
Candle

1881
Dish

1881/12"
Bowl, Lipped

1881
Bowl, Banana

1881
Bowl, Oval Lpd.

PANELED GRAPE

Excellent Gift Suggestions in a treasured pattern

1881/14½"
Plate

1881/10½"
Plate

1881/8½"
Plate

1881/6"
Plate

1881
Mayonnaise

1881/2 oz.
Oil

1881/4½"
Nappy

1881
Ice Tea

1881
Goblet

1881/1 Pt.
Jug

1881/1 Qt.
Jug

1881/6½"
Jardiniere

1881/5"
Jardiniere

1881
Pickle

1881
Mayo Set

1881
Puff Box/Jelly

1881
Flower Pot

1881
Planter, Oblong

1881
Planter, Window

1881
Planter, Sq.

1881
Ivy Ball

PAGE 8

Exquisite Reproductions from choice Originals

1881/15"
Vase

1881/2/11½"
Vase

1881/9"
Vase

1881/8½"
Vase

1881
Vase, Rose

1881
Vase, Blown

1881/18"
Vase

1881/6"
Vase

1881
Vase, Bud

1881
Sauce Boat/Tray

1881
Sugar/Cream

1881/1
Sugar/Cream

1881
Snack Server

1881/11"
Cake Salver

1881/10½"
Cake Salver

1881
Soap

1881
Salt/Pepper Set

1881
Wine

1881
Sherbet

1881
Sugar/Cream, Ind.

1881
Tumbler

1881
Toothpick

PANELED GRAPE

FAMOUS PANELED GRAPE THE MILK GLASS COLLECTOR'S FAVORITE

1881
Decanter

1881
Jug, Pt.

1881
Jug, Qt.

1881
Dish, 3 Ftd.

1881/9"
Compote, Crimp.

1881/4½"
Compote, Crimp.

1881
Goblet

1881
Ice Tea

1881
Compote

1881
Candy

1881
Celery/Vase

1881
Flower Pot

1881
Candlestick

1881
Condiment Set

1881
Candy, Crimp.

1881
Canape Server

1881
Cheese

1881
Choc. Box

1881 Dish, Oval

1881 Wine

1881 Cup/Saucer

1881 Cocktail, Fruit

13

1881
15 Pc. Punch Set
(Ind. Boxed)

1881
Pickle

1881
Snack Server

1881
Sauce Boat/Tray

1881
Oil

1881
Salt/Pepper, Lg.

1881
Cake Salver
(Ind. Boxed)

1881
Planter, Obl.

1881
Puff Box/Jelly

1881
Salt/Pepper
(Packed 3 Sets Per Box)

1881
Mayonnaise

1881
Mayo Set

1881/10½"
Plate
14½" Plate Also Available

1881/8½"
Plate

1881/6"
Plate

14

PANELED GRAPE

GIFT SUGGESTIONS TO PLEASE THE MOST DISCRIMINATING

1881/15"
Vase

1881/9"
Vase, Crimp.

1881/9"
Vase

1884/9"
Bowl, Fld.
(Ind. Boxed)

1881/6"
Vase

1881/8½"
Vase

1881
Vase, Bud

1881
Vase, Rose

1884/5"
Bowl, Fld.

1884/7"
Bowl, Sq.

1881
Sugar/Cream, Ind.

1881
Sugar/Cream

1881
Toothpick
(6 per box)

1881/1
Sugar/Cream

1884/6½"
Ash Tray

1884/5"
Ash Tray

1884/4"
Ash Tray

1884/4" Bowl, Sq.

15

PARK AVENUE FEDERAL GLASS COMPANY, 1941-early 1970's

Colors: Amber, crystal and crystal w/gold trim.

Very little Park Avenue is being found in amber; and gold trimmed pieces are difficult to find with a good gold finish. It wore off easily. I just finished a show in Sanford, Florida, where two different items from this ware were brought in for me to identify. Evidently, there was some of this line sold in the central Florida area.

The trademark F within a shield is embossed on the bottom of most of the pieces. Federal used the Star pitchers (shown on page 216) with the tumblers from this set. They made no Park Avenue pitcher, per se.

The small whisky tumbler in Park Avenue may be found with jelly labels still affixed to them. An example of this can be seen under Star on page 215. Evidently, these small tumblers were used as samples or maybe even jelly containers in restaurants (pre plastic).

All the pieces listed were made into the early 1960's except the shot glass that was in production until the early 1970's. Notice that the catalogue spells whisky without the "e" which is considered a British spelling today. This pattern is one of the smaller sized sets shown in this book and would make an ideal introductory pattern to someone wishing to keep costs down.

	Amber/Crystal
Ash tray, 3½", square	5.00
Ash tray, 4½", square	7.00
Bowl, 5", dessert	5.00
Bowl, 8½", vegetable	11.00
Tumbler, 2⅛", 1¼ oz., whisky	4.00
Tumbler, 3½", 4½ oz., juice	5.00
Tumbler, 3³⁷⁄₈", 9 oz.	6.00
Tumbler, 4¾", 10 oz.	7.00
Tumbler, 5⅛", 12 oz., iced tea	8.00

Matching lines . . . such as the famed Park Avenue on this page, or the Star Line on the next . . . new, unusual shapes, and standard staples, are shown here in Federal's selection of pressed tumblers. All are designed and engineered for eye-appeal, serviceability, and good value.

PARK AVENUE

TUMBLERS

1122 — 1¼ oz.
PARK AVENUE WHISKY
Ht. 2⅛"
Pkd. 12 doz. ctn. Wt. 16 lbs.

1122 — 4½ oz.
PARK AVENUE JUICE TUMBLER
Ht. 3½"
Pkd. 12 doz. ctn. Wt. 35 lbs.

1122 — 9 oz.
PARK AVENUE TUMBLER
Ht. 3⅞"
Pkd. 12 doz. ctn. Wt. 56 lbs.

1142—10 oz.
PARK AVENUE TUMBLER*
Ht. 4¾"
Pkd. 6 doz. ctn. Wt. 37 lbs.

1122 — 12 oz.
PARK AVENUE ICED TEA
Ht. 5⅛"
Pkd. 6 doz. ctn. Wt. 43 lbs.

*CK 1142—10 oz. PARK AVENUE TUMBLER IN CARRY-KITS
are available factory-packed: 6 tumblers to each
Carry-Kit, 12 kits to ctn. Wt. 40 lbs.

19

Own PRELUDE and be envied . . . give PRELUDE and be proud

Choose Viking's beautifully etched Prelude pattern
for your home and your important gift-giving. See your
favorite good store's exciting display.
See the stemware especially.

 Treasured American Glass

Hand made by
VIKING GLASS COMPANY
NEW MARTINSVILLE, WEST VIRGINIA

PRELUDE NEW MARTINSVILLE & VIKING GLASS COMPANY, mid 1930's- 1950's

Color: Crystal

Originally introduced under the auspices of the New Martinsville Glass Company, Prelude production was continued by the Viking Glass Company when they took over the New Martinsville Glass factory in 1943. I have included a few catalogue pages from an early 1950's Viking Glass catalogue. One thing you may notice on page 188 is that some pieces are similar, but different. My guess now is that the more ornate pieces were New Martinsville and that the identical item made at Viking was toned down to accommodate faster production! Let me know what you find that is not listed here.

Bonbon, 6", hdld.	15.00
Bonbon, 6", 3 ftd.	17.50
Bowl, 7", cupped	22.50
Bowl, 8", crimped	30.00
Bowl, 8", 3 part, shrimp	50.00
Bowl, 9", 3 ftd., crimped	40.00
Bowl, 9½", crimped, ftd.	40.00
Bowl, 10", crimped	35.00
Bowl, 10", 3 ftd.	40.00
Bowl, 10", shallow	30.00
Bowl, 10½', nut, center hdld.	35.00
Bowl, 11", 3 ftd.	45.00
Bowl, 12½", crimped	40.00
Bowl, 13", oval	35.00
Bowl, 13", shallow	40.00
Bowl, 15", 3 ftd.	55.00
Butter dish, 6½", oval w/cover	37.50
Butter dish, 8½", oval w/cover	32.50
Cake salver, 11"	45.00
Cake salver, 11" w/metal base	40.00
Candlestick, 4",	17.50
Candlestick, 4½",	20.00
Candlestick, 5", double	30.00
Candlestick, 5½",	22.50
Candlestick, 6", double	35.00
Candy box, 6", w/cover, closed knob	55.00
Candy box, 6½", w/cover, open knob	60.00
Candy box, 7", w/cover, 3 ftd.	65.00
Celery, 10½"	27.50
Cocktail shaker, w/metal lid	125.00
Compote, cheese	15.00
Compote, 6"	22.00
Compote, 7", crimped	30.00
Compote, 7½", flared	30.00
Creamer	12.50
Creamer, 4 ftd.	15.00
Creamer, individual	10.00
Cup	25.00
Ensemble set, 13" bowl w/candle holder	115.00
Ensemble set, 13" bowl w/flower epergne	125.00
Lazy susan, 18", 3 pc. set	125.00
Mayonnaise, 3 pc.	35.00
Mayonnaise, divided, 4 pc.	40.00
Oil bottle, 4 oz.	35.00
Pitcher, 78 oz.	195.00
Plate, 6", bread & butter	6.00

Plate, 6½", hdld.	12.50
Plate, 6½", lemon, 3 ftd.	12.50
Plate, 7"	8.00
Plate, 7", lemon, 3 ftd.	13.50
Plate, 8", salad	10.00
Plate, 9"	22.50
Plate, 10", dinner	35.00
Plate, 10", 3 ftd.	17.50
Plate, 11"	25.00
Plate, 11", 3 ftd., cake	35.00
Plate, 11", cracker	22.50
Plate, 13", hdld.	30.00
Plate, 14", torte	30.00
Plate, 16"	65.00
Plate, 16", 3 ftd.	55.00
Platter, 14½"	45.00
Relish, 6", 2 part	15.00
Relish, 6", 2 part, hdld.	15.00
Relish, 7", 2 part, hdld.	15.00
Relish, 7", 3 part, hdld.	15.00
Relish, 10", 3 part, hdld.	30.00
Relish, 13", 5 part	35.00
Salt and pepper, 3½" pr., 2 styles	40.00
Saucer	5.00
Stem, 1 oz., cordial	40.00

Stem, 1 oz., cordial, ball stem	42.50
Stem, 3 oz., wine	20.00
Stem, 3 oz., wine, ball stem	22.00
Stem, 3½ oz., cocktail	12.00
Stem, 4 oz., cocktail, ball stem	12.00
Stem, 6 oz., low sherbet	9.00
Stem, 6 oz., sherbet, ball stem	10.00
Stem, 6 oz., tall sherbet	12.00
Stem, 9 oz., water	22.50
Sugar	12.50
Sugar, 4 ftd.	15.00
Sugar, individual	10.00
Tid bit, 2 tier, chrome hdld.	40.00
Tray, 11", center handled	35.00
Tray, ind. cr./sug	10.00
Treasure jar, 8", w/cover	65.00
Tumbler, 5 oz., ftd. juice	15.00
Tumbler, 5 oz., juice, ball stem	17.50
Tumbler, 10 oz., water, ball stem	20.00
Tumbler, 12 oz., ftd. tea	20.00
Tumbler, 13 oz., tea, ball stem	22.50
Vase, 8"	30.00
Vase, 10", crimped	60.00
Vase, 11", crimped	65.00
Vase, 11", ftd.	65.00

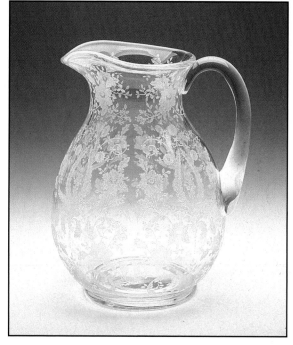

Prelude Etching

Magnificent expression of the designer's art in glass that is timeless and "right", with more than a touch of class.

5217
14" Plate

5201
13" Bowl

7539
8" Vase

5226
11" Cake Salver

5287
13" 5-pt. Relish

5223
13" 2-hdl. Plate

5238
10" 3-pt. Relish

13
Salt & Pepper

5247
Cream & Sugar

5217
14" RE. PLATE

5249
CELERY TRAY

5247
SUGAR & CREAM

5226
11" CAKE SALVER

13
3½" SALT & PEPPER
W/CHROME TOP

5201
SHALLOW BOWL

7539
8" VASE

1010
LEMON PLATE

1009
BONBON

1091
3 TOED PLATE

1003
10" CRIMPED BOWL

5287
OVAL RELISH

"PRETZEL," NO. 622 INDIANA GLASS COMPANY, late 1930's-1980's

Colors: Crystal, teal and avocado with recent issues in amber and blue.

Pretzel is one more of Indiana's numbered patterns (No. 622) which is better known by its collectors' name. I have finally found juice and ice tea tumblers that can be seen in the top photograph on page 193. In fact, I even bought a water tumbler (after the photography was completed); so now, all I have to find is a pitcher to eliminate that wretched picture on the bottom of page 193. I may never find another teal cup, but I would sacrifice that to retire this photograph. Have any of you found more teal Pretzel? If so, I would like to know what you have in your collections. The cup shown here is still the only piece that I have seen! Have you seen a saucer?

Color decorated, fruit centered pieces (shown in the photograph) have been shy, appearing to only a few collectors. These fruit pieces of Pretzel are selling for 25%–50% more than plain centered pieces. Only a few collectors are buying the non decorated Pretzel.

The 4½" fruit cup is found on a 6" plate that has a 1¼" tab handle. Astrological plates are selling in the $4.00 to 5.00 range according to readers, although some have been purchased for as little as a quarter! Sets of twelve have been seen for as little as $25.00 and as high as $75.00. The latter did not sell at that price. Evidently, these were a special order or promotional gimmick. One reader also reported finding a calendar plate with Pretzel around the sides. No picture was enclosed; so, I don't know more. Other dated pieces are being found which seem to indicate that Indiana promoted this line for special events. Let me hear if you find more pieces.

	Crystal
Bowl, 4½", fruit cup	4.50
Bowl, 7½", soup	10.00
Bowl, 9⅜", berry	18.00
Celery, 10¼", tray	1.50
Creamer	4.50
*Cup	6.00
Olive, 7", leaf shape	5.00
Pickle, 8½", two hndl.	5.50
Pitcher, 39 oz.	195.00
Plate, 6"	2.50
Plate, 6", tab hndl.	3.00
Plate, 7¼", square, indent	9.00
Plate, 7¼", square, indent 3-part	9.00
Plate, 8⅜", salad	6.00
Plate, 9⅜", dinner	10.00
Plate, 11½", sandwich	11.00
**Saucer	1.00
Sugar	4.50
Tumbler, 5 oz., 3½"	25.00
Tumbler, 9 oz., 4½"	25.00
Tumbler, 12 oz., 5½"	35.00

* Teal - $45.00
** Teal - $15.00

ROMANCE ETCHING #341, FOSTORIA GLASS COMPANY, 1942–1986

Color: Crystal.

Romance is confused with Fostoria's June because of the "bow" in the design; be sure to compare the shapes of Romance to June. Since Romance is only found in crystal, the only chaos occurs with crystal.

Therefore, by default, all colored pieces of Fostoria having a "bow" are June. My only problem comes in pricing Romance. There are distinct regional pricing differences. A couple of dealers told me they couldn't give it away, while others considered it as good as June. With several dealers contributing their pricing information, Romance has as diverse a range of "appraisals" as any pattern in this book. Remember, this pricing is to be considered only a guide. You, ultimately, decide what any piece is worth!

	Crystal		Crystal
Ash tray, 2⅝", indiv., #2364	12.50	Plate, 11", sandwich, #2364	37.50
Bowl, 6", baked apple #2364	15.00	Plate, 11¼", cracker, #2364	25.00
Bowl, 8", soup, rimmed, #2364	30.00	Plate, 14", torte, #2364	45.00
Bowl, 9", salad, #2364	37.50	Plate, 16", torte, #2364	75.00
Bowl, 9¼", ftd. blown, #6023	85.00	Plate, crescent salad, #2364	42.50
Bowl, 10", 2 hdld, #2594	45.00	Relish, 8", pickle, #2364	22.50
Bowl, 10½", salad, #2364	42.50	Relish, 10", 3 pt., #2364	25.00
Bowl, 11", shallow, oblong, #2596	47.50	Relish, 11", celery, #2364	27.50
Bowl, 12", ftd. #2364	55.00	Salt & pepper, 2⅝", pr., #2364	50.00
Bowl, 12", lily pond, #2364	45.00	Saucer, #2350	5.00
Bowl, 13", fruit, #2364	50.00	Stem, 3⅞", ¾ oz., cordial, #6017	42.50
Bowl, 13½", hdld., oval, #2594	55.00	Stem, 4½", 6 oz., low sherbet, #6017	14.00
Candlestick, 4", #2324	17.50	Stem, 4⅞", 3½ oz., cocktail, #6017	21.50
Candlestick, 5", #2596	22.50	Stem, 5½", 3 oz., wine, #6017	30.00
Candlestick, 5½", #2594	25.00	Stem, 5½", 6 oz., champagne, #6017	17.50
Candlestick, 5½", 2 lite, #6023	30.00	Stem, 5⅞", 4 oz., claret, #6017	35.00
Candlestick, 8", 3 lite, #2594	42.50	Stem, 7⅜", 9 oz., goblet, #6017	25.00
Candy w/lid, rnd., blown, #2364	85.00	Sugar, 3⅛", ftd., #2350½	16.50
Cigarette holder, 2", blown, #2364	37.50	Tray, 11⅛", ctr. hdld., #2364	32.50
Comport, 3¼", cheese, #2364	22.50	Tumbler, 3⅝", 4 oz., ftd., oyster cocktail, #6017	17.50
Comport, 5", #6030	22.50	Tumbler, 4¾", 5 oz., ftd., #6017	17.50
Comport, 8", #2364	40.00	Tumbler, 5½", 9 oz., ftd., #6017	21.00
Creamer, 3¼", ftd., #2350½	17.50	Tumbler, 6", 12 oz., ftd., #6017	27.50
Cup, ftd., #2350½	20.00	Vase, 5", #4121	40.00
Ice tub, 4¾", #4132	67.50	Vase, 6", ftd. bud, #6021	40.00
Ladle, mayonnaise, #2364	5.00	Vase, 6", ftd., #4143	50.00
Mayonnaise, 5", #2364	22.50	Vase, 6", grnd. bottom, #2619½	50.00
Pitcher, 8⅞", 53 oz., ftd., #6011	250.00	Vase, 7½", ftd., #4143	60.00
Plate, 6", #2337	8.00	Vase, 7½", grnd. bottom, #2619½	65.00
Plate, 6¾", mayonnaise liner, #2364	10.00	Vase, 9½", grnd. bottom, #2619½	90.00
Plate, 7", #2337	10.00	Vase, 10", #2614	75.00
Plate, 8", #2337	15.00	Vase, 10", ftd., #2470	105.00
Plate, 9", #2337	47.50		

ROYAL RUBY ANCHOR HOCKING GLASS COMPANY, 1938-1960's; 1977

Color: Ruby red.

Royal Ruby is the Anchor Hocking name for their red color. Only red glassware produced by Hocking or Anchor Hocking can be called by the patented name Royal Ruby. A sticker was placed on each red piece designating it as Royal Ruby no matter what pattern it was. Red Bubble or Sandwich did not mean anything but Royal Ruby to the factory. So, if you find a red piece that seems to belong to some other Hocking pattern, do not be surprised by the Royal Ruby sticker.

Actual production of Royal Ruby was begun in 1938, but most of what collectors identify as Royal Ruby was made after 1940. A Royal Ruby section in my twelfth edition of *Collector's Encyclopedia of Depression Glass* covers the pieces made in the late 1930's. I found an Anchor Hocking advertising page that shows the 6⅛"x4" "card holder" was also catalogued as a cigarette box and sold with four Royal Ruby ash trays. It remains the most difficult piece to find in this pattern. Royal Ruby will continue to be shown in both books since it can be divided into pre 1940 and post 1940 eras.

There are two styles of sherbets which seem to confuse new collectors. The non stemmed version is shown in the right foreground of the top photo on page 197. The stemmed one is in the foreground of the bottom photograph. Oval vegetable bowls remain elusive. Other items in short supply (besides the alias "card holder"/cigarette box) are the punch bowl base and the salad bowl with 13¾" underliner.

The upright, 3 quart pitcher and the 5, 9 and 13 ounce flat tumblers were listed as the Roly-Poly Line in a 1951 catalogue. That page also shows the Royal Ruby Charm which became just Royal Ruby in future catalogues. That upright pitcher has been turning up more frequently than in the past. I have been seeing reduced prices on it in many markets. At $45.00 you could not keep them in stock a year ago, but at $40.00 they are sitting with no buyers now. A year from now, you may wish you had snapped them up! As I mentioned under Charm pattern on page 70, Forest Green and Royal Ruby square were not considered to be Charm in subsequent catalogues after their introduction under that name.

I have also listed the crystal stems with Royal Ruby tops called "Boopie" by collectors as well as the stems that go with Royal Ruby Bubble. See a complete explanation under Bubble on page 16.

There were six or seven sizes of beer bottles made for Schlitz Beer company in '49, '50 or '63. That date of manufacture is embossed on the bottom of each bottle. I saw a 7 ounce bottle with the original label for $75.00 recently. It may have been worth that to someone, but not to me. Pictured is one 7 ounce bottle (no $75.00 label), but millions of these bottles were made. They were evidently more costly than amber and were discontinued. Bottle collectors find these more attractive than Royal Ruby collectors and prices are usually higher at bottle shows than at glass shows. The quart size is the most commonly seen. I have never considered them dinnerware items, although some collectors disagree!

	Red		Red
Ash tray, 4½", leaf	4.00	Plate, 13¾"	25.00
Beer bottle, 7 oz.	17.50	Punch bowl	40.00
Beer bottle, 12 oz.	22.50	Punch bowl base	37.50
Beer bottle, 16 oz.	35.00	Punch cup, 5 oz.	3.00
Beer bottle, 32 oz.	37.50	Saucer, round	2.50
Bowl, 4¼", round, fruit	5.50	Saucer, 5⅝", square	2.50
Bowl, 4¾", square, dessert	7.50	Sherbet, ftd.	8.00
Bowl, 5¼", popcorn	12.00	Sherbet, stemmed, 6½ oz.	8.00
Bowl, 7½", round, soup	12.50	*Stem, 3½ oz., cocktail	10.00
Bowl, 7⅜", square	14.00	*Stem, 4 oz., juice	10.00
Bowl, 8", oval, vegetable	37.50	Stem, 4½ oz., cocktail	10.00
Bowl, 8½", round, large berry	17.50	Stem, 5½ oz., juice	12.50
Bowl, 10", deep, popcorn (same as punch)	40.00	Stem, 6 oz., sherbet	8.00
Bowl, 11½", salad	32.50	*Stem, 6 oz., sherbet	8.00
Cigarette box/"card holder," 6⅛" x 4"	60.00	*Stem, 9 oz., goblet	14.00
Creamer, flat	8.00	Stem, 9½ oz., goblet	13.00
Creamer, ftd.	9.00	*Stem, 14 oz., iced tea	20.00
Cup, round	6.00	Sugar, flat	8.00
Cup, square	6.00	Sugar, ftd.	7.50
Goblet, ball stem	10.00	Sugar, lid	10.00
Ice bucket	35.00	Tumbler, 2½ oz., ftd. wine	13.00
Lamp	35.00	Tumbler, 3½ oz., cocktail	12.50
Pitcher, 3 qt., tilted	35.00	Tumbler, 5 oz., juice, ftd. or flat	7.50
Pitcher, 3 qt., upright	45.00	Tumbler, 9 oz., water	6.50
Pitcher, 42 oz., tilted or straight	30.00	Tumbler, 10 oz., 5", water, ftd.	6.50
Plate, 6¼", sherbet, round	4.00	Tumbler, 12 oz., 6" ftd., tea	15.00
Plate, 7", salad	5.00	Tumbler, 13 oz., iced tea	13.00
Plate, 7¾", salad, round	6.00	Vase, 4", ivy, ball-shaped	5.00
Plate, 8⅜", square	9.00	Vase, 6⅜", two styles	8.00
Plate, 9⅛", dinner, round	11.00	Vase, 9", two styles	17.50

* "Boopie"

Please refer to Foreword for pricing information

SANDWICH COLORS ANCHOR HOCKING GLASS COMPANY, 1939-1964

Colors: Desert Gold 1961-1964   Forest Green 1956-1960's   Pink 1939-1940
      Royal Ruby 1938-1939   White/Ivory (opaque) 1957-1960's

Forest Green Sandwich sustains its pricing increases except for those five little pieces that were packed in Crystal Wedding Oats. Everyone ate hot oats; so there are realistically thousands of those five pieces (4⁵⁄₁₆" bowl, custard cup, custard liner, water and juice tumblers) available today. Prices for other Forest Green pieces have risen due to scarcity and demand! Demand is the key word! All known pieces of Forest Green are shown in the photograph. The rolled edge custard cup shown in the front has never been reported in any quantity. It may be more rare than the pitchers!

Pitchers in Forest Green are scarce because of poor marketing strategy. Everyone obtained the juice and water tumblers free in oats as explained above. Juice and water sets were offered for sale with a pitcher and six tumblers. Everyone already had more than enough tumblers, so they would not buy the complete sets. Most of these sets were returned to Anchor Hocking unsold.

Even new collectors seem to gravitate to the green. Perhaps Forest Green Sandwich appears more desirable than plain Forest Green, although that has numerous fans. Dinner plates in Forest Green Sandwich are selling in the $90.00 range and this price does not seem to discourage collectors. I sell all I can find!

There are more Forest Green cups available than saucers, so prices for saucers are gradually increasing.

No Forest Green Sandwich sugar or cookie jar lids have ever been found. Employees remember those topless cookie jars being sold as vases. They must have done a convincing marketing promotion with them because so many are seen today!

I have priced Royal Ruby Sandwich here, but it is also found in *The Collector's Encyclopedia of Depression Glass* in the Royal Ruby section of that book.

I had thought only bowls were made in pink. A very light pink pitcher was found last year. It is not a vivid pink, but none of the pink is!

Amber Sandwich is beginning to attract some new collectors. However, no one is finding footed amber tumblers. The rest of the set can be obtained with some work and a lot of patience. That flashed-on blue cup and saucer may have been a special order and there could be additional colors. I have not seen other Anchor Hocking objects with this treatment. Let me know what you find!

In my area in 1964 you could buy the Ivory (with gold trim) punch bowl set for only $2.89 along with an oil change and lubrication at Marathon gas stations. Other pieces were available free with a $3.00 purchase. Ivory punch sets were first made in 1957 in plain Ivory and Ivory trimmed in 22K gold. There is little price distinction today; but that set trimmed in gold seems to be less in demand because the gold has a tendency to wear when used!

	Desert Gold	Royal Ruby	Forest Green	Pink	Ivory/White
Bowl, 4⁵⁄₁₆", smooth			3.50		
Bowl, 4⅞", smooth	3.00	16.00		4.00	
Bowl, 5¼", scalloped	6.00	20.00			
Bowl, 5¼", smooth				7.00	
Bowl, 6½", smooth	6.00				
Bowl, 6½", scalloped		27.50	40.00		
Bowl, 6¾", cereal	12.00				
Bowl, 7⅝", salad			57.50		
Bowl, 8¼", scalloped		40.00	67.50	17.50	
Bowl, 9", salad	27.50				
Cookie jar and cover	35.00		*17.50		
Creamer			27.50		
Cup, tea or coffee	3.50		20.00		
Custard cup			1.50		
Custard cup liner			1.50		
Pitcher, 6", juice			130.00		
Pitcher, ½ gal., ice lip			365.00		
Plate, 9", dinner	9.00		90.00		
Plate, 12", sandwich	14.00				
Punch bowl, 9¾"					15.00
Punch bowl stand					15.00
Punch cup					2.00
Saucer	3.00		15.00		
Sugar, no cover			27.50		
Tumbler, 3⁹⁄₁₆", 5 oz., juice			4.00		
Tumbler, 9 oz., water			5.00		
Tumbler, 9 oz., footed	125.00				

* no cover

Please refer to Foreword for pricing information

SANDWICH CRYSTAL ANCHOR HOCKING GLASS COMPANY, 1939-1964; 1977
Color: Crystal 1940-1960's.

I have split the **crystal** Anchor Hocking Sandwich from the **colors** to facilitate writing about each.

The top photograph shows all four sizes of tumblers. The footed tumbler has always been hard to find, but the 3 ounce juice has all but disappeared. I have been informed by several advanced collectors that this juice is not being offered for sale in any of the antique publications. Another new edition is the 7½" bowl shown behind the cup and saucer in that picture. Observe the smaller scallops on this as compared to those normally found. There seem to be twice the number of scallops on this newly discovered bowl.

Another recently discovered piece is the scalloped top, 6½" cereal bowl shown next to the regular cereal in the bottom photograph. A group of four was found in the Columbus, Ohio, area. Apparently, these scalloped edge pieces were a special order or a trial issue. This goes along with the scalloped rimmed plate shown as a pattern shot below! The scalloped cereals have sold for $100.00.

I should point out that the salad bowl that was listed at 9" in the catalogues is really the same bowl as the 9¾" punch bowl which is another reason why the punch bowl **stands** are harder to find than the punch bowls.

Other crystal pieces that are seldom found are the regular cereal, 5" crimped dessert bowl and unblemished dinner plates. That 5" crimped dessert listed by Anchor Hocking only measures 4⅞" in some cases. Mould variation makes size listings a major problem! Both this and the crimped sherbets are listed as occasional Sandwich pieces in the 1956 catalogue. "Crimped" is their word used to describe these occasional pieces.

Collecting Anchor Hocking's Sandwich continues to prosper while Indiana's Sandwich does not do as well. Hocking went to some trouble to preserve the collectability of their older glassware; however, Indiana did not. Prices continue to increase in this popular pattern. In fact, this may be the most collected crystal pattern in this book with the exception of Iris.

Remember that Anchor Hocking reintroduced a crystal cookie jar in the late 1970's that was much larger than the old. For a comparison of these cookie jars I am enclosing measurements. The newer one is currently selling in the $15.00 range.

	NEW	OLD
Height	10¼"	9¼"
Opening width	5½"	4⅞"
Circumference/largest part	22"	19"

Pieces in short supply continue to be found, but demand keeps absorbing these. Cups, saucers and 8" plates were premiums for buying $3.00 (about ten gallons) of gas at Marathon stations in 1964. The promotion took four weeks for cups and saucers and the next four weeks for the plates. You could have gotten the crystal punch bowl set for only $2.89 with an oil change and lube! Ah, the "good old days"! Most of these crystal punch sets were gold trimmed as were the Ivory ones.

	Crystal
Bowl, 4⁵⁄₁₆", smooth	5.00
Bowl, 4⅞"/5", crimped dessert	15.00
Bowl, 4⅞", smooth	6.00
Bowl, 5¼", scalloped	7.50
Bowl, 6½", smooth	7.50
Bowl, 6½", scalloped, deep	7.50
Bowl, 6¾", cereal	32.00
Bowl, 7", salad	7.00
Bowl, 7⅝", scalloped	8.00
Bowl, 8¼", scalloped	8.00
Bowl, 8¼", oval	7.00
Bowl, 9", salad	23.00
Butter dish, low	45.00
Butter dish bottom	25.00
Butter dish top	20.00
Cookie jar and cover	36.00
Creamer	6.00
Cup, tea or coffee	2.50
Custard cup	3.50
Custard cup, crimped, 5 oz.	12.50
Custard cup liner	17.50
Pitcher, 6", juice	60.00
Pitcher, ½ gal., ice lip	75.00
Plate, 7", dessert	10.00
Plate, 8"	4.00
Plate, 9", dinner	18.00
Plate, 9", indent for punch cup	5.00
Plate, 12", sandwich	12.50
Punch bowl, 9¾"	20.00
Punch bowl stand	30.00
Punch cup	2.25
Saucer	1.50
Sherbet, footed	8.00

	Crystal
Sugar	8.50
Sugar cover	15.00
Tumbler, 3⅜", 3 oz., juice	14.00
Tumbler, 3⁹⁄₁₆", 5 oz., juice	6.50
Tumbler, 9 oz., water	8.00
Tumbler, 9 oz., footed	27.50

Please refer to Foreword for pricing information

SANDWICH INDIANA GLASS COMPANY, 1920's-1980's

Colors: Crystal late 1920's-Today   Teal Blue 1950's-1980's   Milk White- mid 1950's
        Amber late 1920's-1980's   Red 1933/1969-early 1970's   Smokey Blue 1976-1977

Indiana's Sandwich pattern is dearly loved by some collectors. Still, many dealers and others avoid it due to the company's propensity for reissuing the glass. This procedure never allows their older glassware to attain the age status that other companies' glassware has. Pink and green Sandwich is priced in the twelfth edition of *Collector's Encyclopedia of Depression Glass* since they were made in the 1930's; and although green (now called Chantilly) has been made again, it is a different shade than the original. The older green will glow under an ultraviolet (black) light if you have one available!

Tiara Exclusives took over Sandwich from Indiana with an issue of red in 1969, amber in 1970 and crystal in 1978. Amber, Chantilly green and crystal were made into the late 1980's.

Basically, the list below incorporates the original Sandwich line from the 1920's and the original Tiara listings from the late 1960's and early 1970's. Eventually, I may add all the Tiara listings throughout the 1970's and 1980's, but only if they become desirable. So far, I've seen little evidence of this. Some ex-Tiara dealers would have you believe it is collectible.

The mould for the old wine broke and a new one was designed. All the wines made in the last few years are fatter (like Iris cocktails) than the earlier ones that were shaped like Iris wines. These older wines are 4½" tall and hold 3 oz. The newer wines are shown in Tiara catalogues but no measurements or capacities are given. If you have one, drop me a post card with the height and capacity.

Teal blue and milk glass (white) are colors issued in the 1950's; but Tiara remade a teal butter dish as an "exclusive" hostess gift that ravaged the $200.00 price tag on the old butter dish. This new Tiara one originally sold for approximately $15.00. "New" Sandwich has been touted to prospective customers as glass that's going to be valuable based on its past performance— and the company is destroying the collectability of the older glassware by selling new glass copies!

Six items in red Sandwich date from 1933, i.e., cups, saucers, luncheon plates, water goblets, creamers and sugars. Many of these pieces are inscribed 1933 Chicago World's Fair. In 1969, Tiara Home Products produced red pitchers, 9 oz. goblets, cups, saucers, wines, wine decanters, 13" serving trays, creamers, sugars, salad and dinner plates. There is little difference in pricing unless you have some red Sandwich marked 1933 Chicago World's Fair. This older, marked glass will bring more due to its being a World's Fair collectible.

Amber and crystal prices are shown, but you must realize that most of the crystal and all the amber have been made since 1970. Prices below reflect the small amounts of these colors that I see at flea markets and malls. Usually the seller is a former Tiara "Party Plan" hostess who is disposing of leftover wares.

	Amber Crystal	Teal Blue	Red		Amber Crystal	Teal Blue	Red
Ash trays (club, spade, heart, dmd. shapes, ea.)	3.50			Goblet, 9 oz.	13.00		45.00
				Mayonnaise, ftd.	13.00		
Basket, 10", high	32.50			Pitcher, 68 oz.	22.50		165.00
Bowl, 4¼", berry	3.50			Plate, 6", sherbet	3.00	7.00	
Bowl, 6"	4.00			Plate, 7", bread and butter	4.00		
Bowl, 6", hexagonal	5.00	14.00		Plate, 8", oval, indent for sherbet		6.00	12.00
Bowl, 8½"	11.00			Plate, 8⅜", luncheon	5.00		20.00
Bowl, 9", console	16.00			Plate, 10½", dinner	8.00		
Bowl, 11½", console	19.00			Plate, 13", sandwich	13.00	25.00	35.00
Butter dish and cover, domed	22.50	*155.00		Puff box	16.50		
Butter dish bottom	6.00	42.50		Salt and pepper, pr.	16.50		
Butter dish top	16.50	112.50		Sandwich server, center handle	18.00		47.50
Candlesticks, 3½", pr.	17.50			Saucer	2.25	6.00	7.00
Candlesticks 7", pr.	25.00			Sherbet, 3¼"	5.50	12.00	
Creamer	9.00		45.00	Sugar, large	9.00		45.00
Celery, 10½"	16.00			Sugar lid for large size	13.00		
Creamer and sugar on diamond shaped tray	16.00	32.00		Tumbler, 3 oz., footed cocktail	7.50		
				Tumbler, 8 oz., footed water	9.00		
Cruet, 6½ oz. and stopper		135.00		Tumbler, 12 oz., footed tea	10.00		
Cup	3.50	8.00	27.50	Wine, 3", 4 oz.	6.00		12.50
Decanter and stopper	22.50		85.00				

*Beware recent vintage sells for $25.00

Please refer to Foreword for pricing information

SHELL PINK MILK GLASS JEANNETTE GLASS CO., 1957-1959

Color: Opaque pink.

Those dramatic increases in prices for Shell Pink have finally slowed from the last edition. Yet, all pieces that were expensive have gotten even more so with all the new collectors searching for the pattern. The lazy susan and heavy bottomed vase are continuing to outdistance other pieces in price. This popular Jeannette pattern was made for only a short period in the late 1950's. It was called Shell Pink and included pieces from several popular Jeannette lines. It was marketed as "a delicate coloring that blends perfectly with all kinds of flowers. Its smooth satiny finish goes all the way through the glass — is not a spray or surface coating."

The quotes above are from a four page catalogue from Jeannette. These pages also state "Shell Pink Milk Glass' lovely color and design make women admire it — and buy it!" Today, there may be as many male collectors searching for this colored glassware as women.

The photograph at the top of page 205 shows a variety of pieces. The 9" heavy bottomed vase is shown in the back next to the oval footed, Lombardi bowl which was to be used with a pair of double candle holders like the one shown in front of it. These bowls are found plain or with a design inside. The plain centered one is found most often as you can tell by the price! Also pictured on the left are the covered wedding bowls. The honey jar is easy to spot with its beehive shape. No one could mistake the butterfly ash tray and cigarette box or the eagle candle, pheasant footed bowl or the cookie jar. That cigarette box with the butterfly finial is rather hard to find in mint condition. The price below is for mint condition butterfly boxes. The compote in the back is Windsor and the open candy in front of it is Floragold. The only item not covered is the Venetian tray, which is 16½" and can't be missed.

On the bottom of page 205 are some of the larger pieces of Shell Pink. That Harp tray and cake stand are seen more often in crystal. The large three-footed bowl is Holiday pattern, but the footed oval bowl on the left was called Florentine even though it has a similar pattern to Holiday. The Gondola fruit bowl by Jeannette is the long, handled bowl in front. The powder jar, sugar, creamer and 7" vase round out that photograph.

The Vineyard 12" relish is pictured in front of the top photo on page 206. The three-part celery and relish tray is in the rear of that photo. All other pieces should be self explanatory.

The punch set is shown on the bottom of page 206. Speaking of the punch bowl reminds me that the original ladle was pink plastic and not crystal. Cups for the punch set were the same as those used for the snack sets shown at the top of the page. "Hostess" snack sets were rather expensive at the time. A set of four was $1.75. These were a new fad for the TV trays in vogue at the time.

The elusive lazy susan is shown in the top photo on page 207; the base is the part that is almost non-existent, but original ball bearings to turn the trays are not easily found either. Some collectors have bought Dewdrop lazy susans just to get the ball bearings for their Shell Pink set. The lazy susan was packed one to a pink gift box similar to the blue one shown under Dewdrop on page 56. That photograph also shows the pieces made for "Napco Ceramics, Cleveland, Ohio." Each piece is marked thus with numbers (quoted in the price list) except for the piece with a sawtooth edge in the back that only has "Napco, Cleveland." The piece at left front is the candy bottom of a pattern Jeannette called National which was made only in crystal in the late 1940's. This Shell Pink candy bottom was promoted as a vase. The cake plate in the back is a new listing. It is Anniversary. The reverse side is shown at the bottom of the page so you can see the pattern.

I will point out a few original prices for your information: cookie jar and cover, $1.10; lazy susan, $2.00; butterfly cigarette set (box and two trays) $1.00; heavy bottom vase, $0.75 and finally the 12-piece punch set, $4.00 with extra cups at $1.25 dozen. There are reports of an ash tray and another style bird candlestick. Keep looking and report your findings.

	Opaque Pink		Opaque Pink
Ash tray, butterfly shape	17.50	"Napco" #2255, ftd. bowl w/saw tooth top	25.00
Base, for lazy susan, w/ball bearings	120.00	"Napco" #2256, square comport	12.50
Bowl, 6½", wedding, w/cover	22.50	"National" candy bottom	10.00
Bowl, 8", Pheasant, ftd.	37.50	Pitcher, 24 oz., ftd., Thumbprint	27.50
Bowl, 8", wedding, w/cover	27.50	Powder jar, 4¾", w/cover	32.00
Bowl, 9", ftd., fruit stand, Floragold	25.00	Punch base, 3½", tall	25.00
Bowl, 10", Florentine, ftd.	27.50	Punch bowl, 7½ qt.	50.00
Bowl, 10½", ftd., Holiday	42.50	Punch cup, 5 oz. (also fits snack tray)	6.00
Bowl, 10⅞", 4 ftd., Lombardi, designed center	42.00	Punch ladle, pink plastic	20.00
Bowl, 10⅞", 4 ftd., Lombardi, plain center	27.00	Punch set, 15 pc. (bowl, base, 12 cups, ladle)	165.00
Bowl, 17½", Gondola fruit	27.50	Relish, 12", 4 part, octagonal, Vineyard design	40.00
Cake plate, Anniversary	150.00	Stem, 5 oz., sherbet, Thumbprint	10.00
Cake stand, 10", Harp	32.00	Stem, 8 oz., water goblet, Thumbprint	12.50
Candle holder, 2 light, pr.	37.50	Sugar cover	14.00
Candle holder, Eagle, 3 ftd., pr.	70.00	Sugar, ftd., Baltimore Pear design	11.00
Candy dish w/cover, 6½" high, square	30.00	Tray, 7¾" x 10", snack w/cup indent	9.00
Candy dish, 4 ftd., 5¼", Floragold	20.00	Tray, 12½" x 9¾", 2 hndl., Harp	52.50
Candy jar, 5½", 4 ftd., w/cover, grapes	20.00	Tray, 13½", lazy susan, 5 part	40.00
Celery and relish, 12½", 3 part	45.00	Tray, 15¾", 5 part, 2 hndl.	40.00
Cigarette box, butterfly finial	97.50	Tray, 16½", 6 part, Venetian	35.00
Compote, 6", Windsor	20.00	Tray, lazy susan complete w/base	160.00
Cookie jar w/cover, 6½" high	80.00	Tumbler, 5 oz., juice, ftd., Thumbprint	8.00
Creamer, Baltimore Pear design	15.00	Vase, 5", cornucopia	15.00
Honey jar, beehive shape, notched cover	37.50	Vase, 7"	35.00
"Napco" #2249, cross hatch design pot	15.00	Vase, 9", heavy bottom	70.00
"Napco" #2250, ftd. bowl w/berries	15.00		

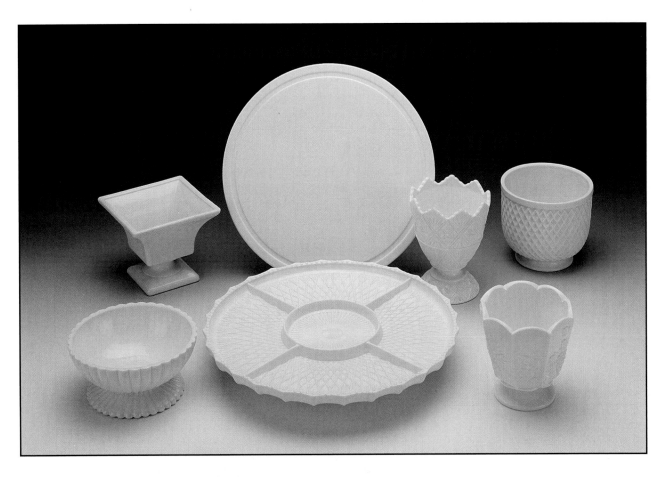

Color: White with crystal edge.

Silver Crest continues to be one of Fenton's longest production patterns. Every time they have discontinued its manufacture, requests force them to reissue it. There are ways to help date your pieces. Before 1958, the white was called opal and had an opalescence to it when held up to the light. In 1958, a formula change to milk glass made the glass look very white without "fire" in the white. Any pieces reintroduced after 1973 will be signed Fenton. Fenton began signing Carnival pieces in 1971 and in 1973 they continued this practice with all pieces. If you run into items that have white edging outside the crystal, this was called Crystal Crest and dates from 1942.

The pitcher, punch bowl set and the hurricane lamps continue to be very difficult to acquire, but high in demand. Tumbler prices are creeping upward; so latch on to a few before they are unreasonable. Observe two different styles of shakers in row 4 on page 209. The bowling pin shaker next to the normally found shaker has no crest; but the line number on this shaker in a 1954 catalogue indicates that it was sold as Silver Crest. In the bottom row are two tumblers shown side by side. I hope you will be able to see that there are distinct differences in the crest on these pieces. I assume these are from two different issues; but this could cause some confusion if you are not aware of that problem. As with Emerald Crest, you will find several styles of tid-bits using bowls and plates or a combination of both.

There are pieces of Silver Crest with two different line numbers. Originally, this line was #36 and all pieces carried that designation. In July 1952, Fenton began issuing a Ware Number for each piece. That is why you see two different numbers for some of the items below.

See page 58 for prices on Emerald Crest. Aqua Crest has a blue edge and prices run between those of Silver Crest and Emerald Crest.

	White		White
Basket, 5" hndl., (top hat) #1924	37.50	Candle holder, low, ruffled, pr. #7271	20.00
Basket, 5", hndl. #680	37.50	Candle holder, ruffled comport style, pr. #7272	52.50
Basket, 6½", hndl. #7336	37.50	Candy box #7280	67.50
Basket, 7" #7237	27.50	Candy box, ftd., tall stem #7274	118.00
Basket, 12" #7234	45.00	Chip and dip (low bowl w/mayo in center) #7303	65.00
Basket, 13" #7233	75.00	Comport, ftd. #7228	11.00
Basket, hndl. #7339	60.00	Comport, ftd., low #7329	18.00
Bon bon, 5½" #7225	11.00	Creamer, reeded hndl. #680	16.00
Bon bon, 8" #7428	11.00	Creamer, reeded hndl. (same as #680) #7201	16.00
Bonbon, 5½" #36	11.00	Creamer, ruffled top	45.00
Bowl, 5½", soup #680	32.50	Creamer, straight side #1924	32.50
Bowl, 5", finger or deep dessert #680	26.00	Creamer, threaded hndl. #680	17.50
Bowl, 7" #7227	18.00	Cup, reeded hndl. #680, 7209	22.50
Bowl, 8½" #7338	32.50	Cup, threaded look hndl. #680	22.50
Bowl, 8½" flared #680	32.50	Epergne set, 2 pc. (vase in ftd. bowl) #7202	55.00
Bowl, 9½" #682	46.00	Epergne set, 3 pc. #7200	115.00
Bowl, 10" #7224	46.00	Epergne set, 6 pc. #1522/951	115.00
Bowl, 10" salad #680	46.00	Epergne, 2 pc. set #7301	77.50
Bowl, 11" #5823	46.00	Epergne, 4 pc. bowl w/3 horn epergnes #7308	110.00
Bowl, 13" #7223	46.00	Epergne, 5 pc. bowl w/4 horn epergnes #7305	110.00
Bowl, 14" #7323	46.00	Lamp, hurricane #7398	160.00
Bowl, banana, high ft. w/upturned sides #7324	65.00	Mayonnaise bowl #7203	11.00
Bowl, banana, low ftd. #5824	50.00	Mayonnaise ladle #7203	5.00
Bowl, deep dessert #7221	32.50	Mayonnaise liner #7203	27.50
Bowl, dessert, shallow #680	32.50	Mayonnaise set, 3 pc. #7203	45.00
Bowl, finger or dessert #202	18.00	Nut, ftd. #7229	10.00
Bowl, ftd., (like large, tall comport) #7427	67.50	Nut, ftd. (flattened sherbet) #680	10.00
Bowl, ftd., tall, square #7330	67.50	Oil bottle #680	80.00
Bowl, low dessert #7222	26.00	Pitcher, 70 oz. jug #7467	175.00
Bowl, shallow #7316	46.00	Plate, 5½" #680	6.00
Cake plate, 13" high, ftd. #7213	47.50	Plate, 5½", finger bowl liner #7218	6.00
Cake plate, low ftd. #5813	37.50	Plate, 6" #680	6.50
Candle holder, 6" tall w/crest on bottom, pr. #7474	70.00	Plate, 6½" #680, 7219	14.00
Candle holder, bulbous base, pr. #1523	27.50	Plate, 8½" #680, 7217	27.50
Candle holder, cornucopia, pr. #951	60.00	Plate, 10" #680	37.50
Candle holder, cornucopia (same as #951), pr. #7274	57.50	Plate, 10½" #7210	37.50
		Plate, 11½" #7212	37.50
Candle holder, flat saucer base, pr. #680	22.00	Plate, 12" #680	47.50
		Plate, 12" #682	47.50

Please refer to Foreword for pricing information

SILVER CREST (Cont.)

	White		White
Plate, 12½" #7211	47.50	Tid-bit, 3 tier plates #680	47.50
Plate, 16", torte 7216	55.00	Tid-bit, 3 tier, ruffled bowl #7397	85.00
Punch bowl #7306	250.00	Top hat, 5" #1924	47.50
Punch bowl base #7306	70.00	Tray, sandwich #7291	27.50
Punch cup #7306	12.50	Tumbler, ftd. #7342	57.50
Punch ladle (clear) #7306	22.50	Vase, 4½" #203	11.00
Punch set, 15 pc. #7306	500.00	Vase, 4½" #7254	11.00
Relish, divided #7334	32.50	Vase, 4½", double crimped #36, #7354	11.00
Relish, heart, hndl. #7333	22.50	Vase, 4½", fan #36	11.00
Saucer #680, #7209	5.00	Vase, 5" (top hat) #1924	46.00
Shaker, pr. #7206	100.00	Vase, 6" #7451	16.00
Shaker, pr (bowling pin shape)	125.00	Vase, 6", doubled crimped #7156	19.00
Sherbert #680	10.00	Vase, 6¼", double crimped #36, #7356	17.50
Sherbet #7226	10.00	Vase, 6¼", fan #36	17.50
Sugar, reeded hndl. #680	17.50	Vase, 7" #7455	17.50
Sugar, reeded hndl. (same as #680) #7201	17.50	Vase, 8" #7453	17.50
Sugar, ruffled top	45.00	Vase, 8", bulbous base #186	46.00
Sugar, sans hndls. #680	32.50	Vase, 8", doubled crimped #7258	22.00
Tid-bit, 2 tier (luncheon/dessert plates) #7296	47.50	Vase, 8", wheat #5859	42.50
Tid-bit, 2 tier (luncheon/dinner plates) #7294	47.50	Vase, 8½" #7458	47.50
Tid-bit, 2 tier plates #680	47.50	Vase, 9" #7454	47.50
Tid-bit, 2 tier, ruffled bowl #7394	75.00	Vase, 9" #7459	47.50
Tid-bit, 3 tier (luncheon/dinner/dessert plates) #7295	47.50	Vase, 10" #7450	110.00
		Vase, 12" (fan topped) #7262	100.00

SQUARE, NO. 3797 CAMBRIDGE GLASS COMPANY, 1952-mid 1950's

Colors: Crystal, some red and black.

Cambridge Square is shown in the 1949 Cambridge catalogue as patent pending. I recently bought a dozen cordials that not only had Cambridge labels attached, but also had labels that stated "patent pending." It was the first time I had run into this, but I suppose it may be common in this later pattern. This is one of the few patterns made by Cambridge that absolutely falls into the time span of this book.

A few pieces of Square were made in color; however, some Ruby pieces were also made by Imperial in the late 1960's. Carmen pieces by Cambridge are rarely seen, but the red (Ruby) from Imperial can be found with some work. Four Carmen pieces are pictured on the bottom of 213. The "crackle" tumbler shown in the back right of the top photograph on page 214 sells for $55.00. There were several sizes of Square stemware made in Crackle.

On the bottom of page 214 is a Cambridge square cordial which has a Cambridge sticker as well as a patent pending sticker.

	Crystal		Crystal
Ash tray, 3½" #3797/151	8.00	Plate, 9½", tidbit #3797/24	20.00
Ash tray, 6½" #3797/150	11.00	Plate, 11½" #3797/26	25.00
Bon bon, 7" #3797/164	13.50	Plate, 13½" #3797/28	30.00
Bon bon, 8" #3797/47	24.00	Relish, 6½", 2 part #3797/120	17.50
Bowl, 4½", dessert #3797/16	11.00	Relish, 8", 3 part #3797/125	22.50
Bowl, 6½", individual salad #3797/27	13.50	Relish, 10", 3 part #3797/126	25.00
Bowl, 9", salad #3797/49	22.00	Salt and pepper, pr. #3797/76	22.50
Bowl, 10", oval #3797/48	23.00	Saucer, coffee #3797/17	5.00
Bowl, 10", shallow #3797/81	27.50	Saucer, tea #3797/15	5.00
Bowl, 11", salad #3797/57	37.50	Stem, #3798, 5 oz., juice	10.00
Bowl, 12", oval #3797/65	30.00	Stem, #3798, 12 oz., iced tea	12.00
Bowl, 12", shallow #3797/82	35.00	Stem, #3798, cocktail	17.50
Buffet set, 4 pc. (plate, div. bowl, 2 ladles)		Stem, #3798, cordial	25.00
#3797/29	47.50	Stem, #3798, sherbet	11.00
Candle holder, 1¾", block #3797/492, pr.	25.00	Stem, #3798, water goblet	12.00
Candle holder, 2¾", block #3797/493, pr.	27.50	Stem, #3798, wine	20.00
Candle holder, 3¾", block #3797/495, pr.	27.50	Sugar #3797/41	10.00
Candle holder, cupped #3797/67, pr.	27.50	Sugar, individual #3797/40	10.00
Candy box and cover #3797/165	30.00	Tray, 8", oval, for individual sug/cr #3797/37	17.50
Celery, 11" #3797/103	23.00	Tumbler, #3797, 5 oz., juice	12.50
Comport, 6" #3797/54	25.00	Tumbler, #3797, 14 oz., iced tea	17.50
Creamer #3797/41	10.00	Tumbler, #3797, low cocktail	12.00
Creamer, individual #3797/40	10.00	Tumbler, #3797, low cordial	27.50
Cup, coffee, open handle #3797/17	10.00	Tumbler, #3797, low sherbet	10.00
Cup, tea, open handle #3797/15	10.00	Tumbler, #3797, low wine	15.00
Decanter, 32 oz. #3797/85	85.00	Tumbler, #3797, water goblet	13.50
Ice tub, 7½" #3797/34	35.00	Vase, 5", belled #3797/92	22.50
Icer, cocktail w/liner #3797/18	35.00	Vase, 5½", belled #3797/91	25.00
Lamp, hurricane, 2 pc. #3797/68	42.00	Vase, 6" #3797/90	22.50
Mayonnaise set, 3 pc. (bowl, plate, ladle)		Vase, 7½", ftd. #3797/77	22.50
#3797/129	30.00	Vase, 7½", rose bowl #3797/35	33.00
Oil bottle, 4½ oz. #3797/100	20.00	Vase, 8", ftd. #3797/80	20.00
Plate, 6", bread and butter #3797/20	8.00	Vase, 9½", ftd. #3797/78	27.50
Plate, 7", dessert or salad #3797/23	12.00	Vase, 9½", rose bowl #3797/36	42.50
Plate, 7", salad #3797/27	11.00	Vase, 11", ftd. #3797/79	37.50
Plate, 9½", dinner or luncheon #3797/25	27.50		

Please refer to Foreword for pricing information

SQUARE

STAR FEDERAL GLASS COMPANY, 1950's

Colors: Amber, crystal and crystal w/gold trim.

Federal's Star pattern is beginning to attract the attention of collectors. I recently attended a show in Minnesota where a dealer thanked me for putting this pattern in my book. He had brought a large, amber set to the show and every piece sold the first day!

Although there were not many pieces made, you can put together a set for reasonable prices. Notice the "star" shaped design on each piece. I now have two of the pitchers, but have been unable to find a reasonably priced 85 ounce jug. Cathy remembers seeing these pitchers marketed with small colored soaps. Pitchers were also sold with Park Avenue tumblers.

Note the individual shot of a decorated juice pitcher. These pitchers are found with matching tumblers. Several designs can be found. Watch for a similar pitcher matching the red trimmed floral Petalware in my Depression Glass book. The one I saw was frosted, but not for sale. I'd like to find one for that book!

Note that the word whisky is spelled without the "e" in the original catalogue listing. That whisky tumbler in the picture is shown with two different labels indicating jelly was contained in them. Does anyone remember if these were samples or individual servings?

	Amber/Crystal
Bowl, 4⅝", dessert	4.00
Bowl, 8⅜", vegetable	9.00
Pitcher, 5¾", 36 oz., juice	8.00
Pitcher, 7", 60 oz.	12.00
Pitcher, 9¼", 85 oz., ice lip	15.00
Plate, 6³⁄₁₆" salad	3.00
Plate, 9⅜", dinner	5.00
Tumbler, 2¼", 1½ oz., whisky	3.00
Tumbler, 3⅜" 4½ oz., juice	4.00
Tumbler, 3⅞", 9 oz., water	5.50
Tumbler, 5⅛", 12 oz., iced tea	8.00

STAR

PRESSED TUMBLERS

1123 — 1½ oz.
STAR WHISKY
Ht. 2¼"
Pkd. 12 doz. ctn. Wt. 17 lbs.

1123 — 4½ oz.
STAR JUICE TUMBLER
Ht. 3⅜"
Pkd. 12 doz. ctn. Wt. 37 lbs.

1123 — 9 oz.
STAR TUMBLER
Ht. 3⅞"
Pkd. 12 doz. ctn. Wt. 56 lbs.

1123 — 12 oz.
STAR ICED TEA
Ht. 5⅛"
Pkd. 6 doz. ctn. Wt. 42 lbs.

2844 —36 oz.
STAR JUICE JUG
Ht. 5¾"
Pkd. 2 doz. ctn. Wt. 37 lbs.

(Also available — 2845-60 oz. **JUG**
Ht. 7" Pkd. 1 doz. ctn. Wt. 26 lbs.)

2846 — 85 oz.
STAR ICE LIP JUG
Ht. 9¼"
Pkd. 1 doz. ctn. Wt. 38 lbs.

1116 — 5 oz.
PANEL JUICE TUMBLER
Ht. 3⅜"
Pkd. 12 doz. ctn. Wt. 38 lbs.

1116 — 9 oz.
PANEL TUMBLER
Ht. 4"
Pkd. 12 doz. ctn. Wt. 59 lbs.

1116 — 12 oz.
PANEL ICED TEA
Ht. 5⅜"
Pkd. 6 doz. ctn. Wt. 43 lbs.

1131 — 9 oz.
CATHEDRAL TUMBLER
Ht. 4"
Pkd. 12 doz. ctn. Wt. 58 lbs.

STARS and STRIPES ANCHOR HOCKING GLASS GLASS COMPANY, 1942

Color: Crystal.

I considered retiring this little pattern, but there are some avid fans who would say interesting words to me. In the first edition of this book, we were in the middle of Desert Storm and so this pattern seemed to fit the patriotic fervor of the time. When writing the second, we were dropping bombs on Iraq again. Russia is doing the bomb dropping for this third book. Dare we hope no one will be bombing anyone at the next writing?

I have been asked questions about this little pattern for years. Most collectors seemed to think that these pieces were Queen Mary, but this catalogue page proves conclusively that it is a completely different pattern appropriately named "Stars and Stripes." Tumblers seem to be almost non-existent while sherbets are fairly common. Plates cost twice as much as other pieces originally, but that has certainly changed in today's market.

	Crystal
Plate, 8"	12.50
Sherbet	14.00
Tumbler, 5", 10 oz.	30.00

217

SWANKY SWIGS 1930's-1950's

Swanky Swigs were originally packed with a Kraft cheese product in them. Illustrated here are the Swigs produced from the late 1930's into the 1950's with a collectible 1976 Bicentennial also shown. Smaller size glasses and the larger 10 oz. seem to have been issued in Canada. The limited availability of these sizes in the states makes their prices soar. Tulip No. 2 only turns up on the West Coast and prices are a little less there. Earlier Swanky Swigs can be found in *The Collector's Encyclopedia of Depression Glass* if you get hooked on collecting these. Some original lids from these tumblers are shown on page 222. The two jars on row 2 of page 219 are store display Swankys (painted to look full of cheese). Lids fetch $5.00 up depending upon condition and the advertisement! Those with Kraft caramels, Miracle Whip and TV show ads run $10 up.

Page 219:

Row 1: Tulip No. 1
black, blue, red, green	3½"	3.00-4.00
black w/label	3½"	10.00-12.00
Blue, red, green	4½"	12.50-15.00
green	3¼"	12.50-15.00

Row 2: Tulip No. 3
lt. blue, yellow display jars	3¾"	25.00-30.00
lt. blue, red, yellow	3¾"	2.50-3.50
lt. blue, yellow	3¼"	12.50-15.00
red	4½"	12.50-15.00

Cornflower No. 1
lt. blue	4½"	12.50-15.00
lt. blue	3½"	4.00-5.00
lt. blue	3¼"	12.50-15.00

Row 3: Tulip No. 2
black, green, red	3½"	22.50-27.50
Carnival blue, green, red, yellow	3½"	4.00-6.00

Tulip No. 3
dk. blue	4½"	12.50-15.00
dk. blue	3¾"	2.50-3.50
Dk. blue	3¼"	12.50-15.00

Row 4: Posy Jonquil
yellow	4½"	15.00-17.50
yellow	3½"	5.00-6.00
yellow	3¼"	15.00-17.50

Posy: Tulip
red	4½"	12.50-15.00
red	3½"	4.00-5.00
red	3¼"	12.50-15.00

Posy: Violet
purple	4½"	15.00-17.50
purple	3½"	5.00-6.00
purple	3¼"	12.50-15.00

Row 5: Cornflower No. 2
dk. blue, lt. blue, red, yellow	3½"	2.50-3.50
dk. blue, lt. blue, yellow	3¼"	12.50-15.00

Forget-Me-Not
dk. blue,	3½"	2.50-3.50
dk. blue or yellow w/label (yel p 220)	3½"	10.00-12.50
dk. blue	3¼"	12.50-15.00

Page 220:

Row 1: Forget-Me-Not
lt. blue, red, yellow	3½"	2.50-3.50
lt. blue, red, yellow	3¼"	12.50-15.00

Daisy
red & white	3¾"	20.00-25.00
red & white	3¼"	30.00-35.00

Rows 2-5: Daisy
red, white & green	4½"	12.50-15.00
red, white & green	3¾"	2.00-3.00
red, white & green	3¼"	12.50-15.00

Bustling Betsy:
all colors	3¾"	12.50-15.00
all colors	3¾"	4.00-5.00

Antique Pattern:
all designs	3¼"	12.50-15.00
all designs	3¾"	4.00-500

clock & coal scuttle brown;
lamp & kettle blue;
coffee grinder & plate green;
spinning wheel & bellows red;
coffee pot & trivet black;
churn & cradle orange

Kiddie Cup:
all designs	4½"	17.50-20.00
	3¾"	4.00-5.00
	3¼"	12.50-15.00

bird & elephant red;
bear & pig blue;
squirrel & deer brown;
duck & horse black;
dog & rooster orange,
cat and rabbit green
bird & elephant w/label	3¾"	10.00-12.50
dog & rooster **w/cheese**	3¾"	25.00-30.00

Bicentennial issued in 1975;
yellow, red, green	3¾"	3.00-5.00

Please refer to Foreword for pricing information

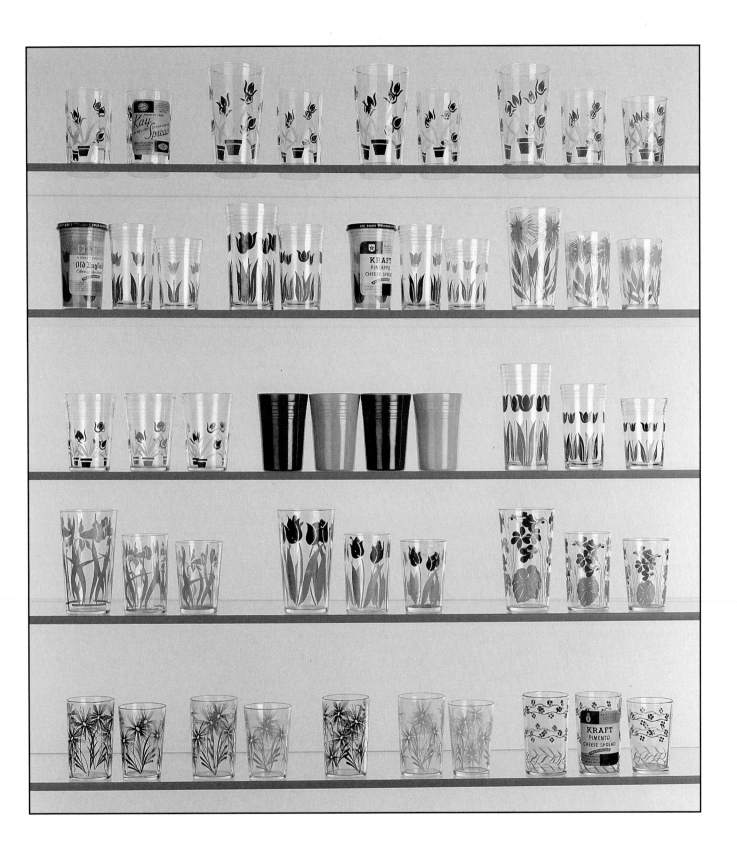

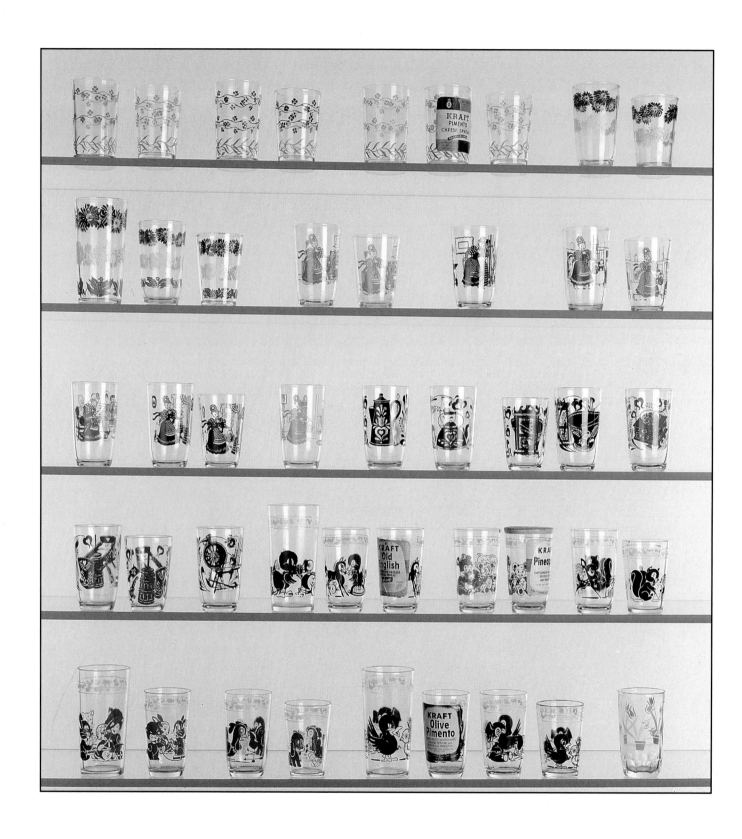

A Publication I recommend:

DEPRESSION GLASS **DAZE**

THE ORIGINAL NATIONAL DEPRESSION GLASS NEWSPAPER

Depression Glass Daze, the original, national monthly newspaper dedicated to the buying, selling and collecting of colored glassware of the 20's and 30's. We average 60 pages each month, filled with feature articles by top-notch columnists, readers' "finds," club happenings, show news, a china corner, a current listing of new glass issues to be aware of and a multitude of ads! You can find it in the **DAZE**! Keep up with what's happening in the dee gee world with a subscription to the **DAZE**. Buy, sell or trade from the convenience of your easy chair.

Name _____ Street _____

City _____ State _____ Zip _____

☐1 Year - $21.00   ☐Check Enclosed   ☐Please bill me

☐Mastercard   ☐Visa   (Foreign subscribers - Please add $1.00 per year)

Card No. _____ Exp. Date _____

Signature _____

Send to: D.G.D., Box 57GF, Otisville, MI 48463-0008 - Please allow 30 days

---

Heisey Collectors of America
P.O. Box 27GF
Newark, OH 43055

Dues: $18.50 Individual Membership
$2.50 each Associate Membership

National Cambridge Collectors Inc.
P.O. Box 416GF
Cambridge, OH 43725

Dues: $15.00 Individual Membership
$3.00 each Associate Membership

Other Books By Gene Florence

Kitchen Glassware of the Depression Years, 5th Edition $19.95
Pocket Guide to Depression Glass, 9th Edition $9.95
Collector's Encyclopedia of Akro Agate $14.95
Collector's Encyclopedia of Depression Glass, 12th Edition $19.95
Collector's Encyclopedia of Occupied Japan I $14.95
Collector's Encyclopedia of Occupied Japan II $14.95
Collector's Encyclopedia of Occupied Japan III $14.95
Collector's Encyclopedia of Occupied Japan IV $14.95
Collector's Encyclopedia of Occupied Japan V $14.95
Elegant Glassware of the Depression Era, VI $19.95
Very Rare Glassware of the Depression Years I $24.95
Very Rare Glassware of the Depression Years II $24.95
Very Rare Glassware of the Depression Years III $24.95
Very Rare Glassware of the Depression Years IV $24.95

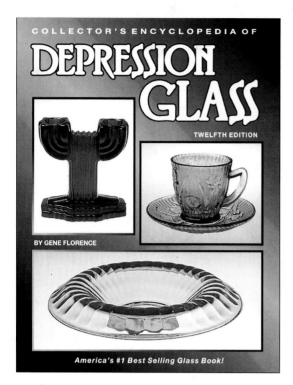